Crafting Turbo C Software
Components and Utilities

Richard S. Wiener

John Wiley & Sons

New York • Chichester • Brisbane • Tronto • Singapore

Trademarks

Library of Congress Cataloging in Publication Data:

Wiener, Richard, 1941–
   Crafting Turbo C software components and utilities.
   Bibliography: p.
   ISBN 0-471-63477-8 (pbk.)
   1. C (Computer program language) 2. Turbo C (Computer program)
I. Title.
QA76.73.C15W53   1988
005.26 88-20465

Printed in the United States of America

10 9 8 7 6 5 4 3 2 1

Computer art on cover created and photographed by Helen Iranyi.
Cover design by Suzanne Bennett & Associates.

This book is dedicated with love to

Sheila, Erik, Marc, Mary, Irving, Esther, and to
the memory of Murray.

Preface

This book does what the title implies. It presents and describes Turbo C software components and utilities. It is assumed that the reader has learned Turbo C by reading the companion book, *Turbo C at Any Speed* by Richard Wiener or another book on Turbo C. This book is aimed at intermediate and advanced C programmers.

The first part of this book, "Crafting Components," discusses reusable software components in general and Turbo C Software components specifically. Topics in the first part of the book include the physical decomposition of a Turbo C software system, the MAKE utility, writing generic software components, Turbo C input and output library functions, memory models, global variables, and Turbo C DOS and BIOS functions.

The principles of creating reusable Turbo C software components are illustrated with the following components: generic heap sorting, generic search table implemented using AVL trees, keyboard handling components, screen output components, cursor manipulation, timing functions, random number generation, user prompts and messages, and fast file input and output functions.

The second part of the book presents and discusses useful utilities written in Turbo C. Many advanced techniques of Turbo C programming are illustrated. the source listings and discussions of code allow the reader to see the power of Turbo C in action. Included are utilities for stuffing the keyboard look-ahead buffer with characters, superfast spelling checking, efficient file compression and decompression, rollbook data-base management system, screen dump to file, and a disk update program.

I am most grateful to my son, Erik Wiener for assisting in the construction of some of the utility programs and for helping with the proofreading of the book. His keen interest and support for this project have been significant.

Devin Ben Hur helped tremendously with his technical editing. I am greatly appreciative of his useful suggestions.

I heartily thank Diane Cerra, Editor at John Wiley and Sons, for her cheerful encouragement and help at every stage of this project.

I wish to thank Gene Haltiwanger for contributing the assembly language programs that are presented in Part 1 of the book and for helping with the testing of some of the utilities in Part 2 of the book.

I greatly appreciate the patience, love, and support of the other members of my family, my wife Sheila, and my son Marc. Without their support, this book would not exist.

Richard S. Wiener
Colorado Springs, Colorado

Contents

Listings and Figures

Listings

Figures

Part 1

Crafting Components

1

Reusable Software Components

Software engineering is concerned with the economical development of software that is robust, efficient, reliable, and easy to maintain. Reusable software components contribute to software reliability, efficiency, and ease of maintenance. They also lower the cost of software development.

In the C programming language, a reusable software component is an object file that, when linked to various applications, provides support for these applications. Frequently such a reusable software component is obtained by compiling a C source file that defines a key data structure and a set of functions that perform a set of logically related operations on the data structure. These functions are designed to assist programmers in the development of software systems. A header file (.h file) that contains function prototypes often accompanies the source file (.c file) that contains the function definitions. This header file may be included in any C file that uses one or more functions from the reusable software component.

As an illustration, Listings 1.1 and 1.2 present the source code for a simple integer stack. The object file obtained by compiling Listing 1.2 represents the reusable stack component. Listing 1.3 is a short test program that uses the integer stack software component.

The integer stack abstracts the operations of push, pop, and examine. The calling program can perform these operations without having access to the implementation details of each of the operations, but the integer stack falls short of qualifying as a general purpose reusable software component, because the code is dependent on the base type, int, stored in the stack.

The operations of push, pop, and examine are intrinsically independent of any particular base type of data. It would be desirable to construct a generic stack component that would allow a set of any homogeneous elements of arbitrary base type to be stored in the structure. Such a generic stack would be robust because it could serve across a wide range of applications. The integer stack given in Listings 1.1 and 1.2 is much more limited in its scope of application and thus much less useful.

1

In Section 1.3, generics are discussed. A robust generic version of the stack component is presented in that section.

Listing 1.1 Prototypes for the integer stack software component

```
/* intstack.h */

typedef struct stack STACK;

struct stack
{
  int info;
  STACK *next;
};

/* Push data onto the stack
**
** ARGUMENTS
**   s        pointer to stack address
**   item     integer to be pushed
**   error    pointer to error value
**     0   no error
**     1   not enough memory
**
** RETURNS
**   none
*/
extern void push( STACK **s, int item, int *error );


/* Pop data from the stack
**
** ARGUMENTS
**   s        pointer to stack address
**   error    pointer to error value
**     0  no error
**     1  no data to pop from stack
**
** RETURNS
**   integer value returned from stack
*/
extern int pop( STACK **s, int *error );


/* Examine the top of the stack
**
** ARGUMENTS
**   s        pointer to stack
```

```
**    error    pointer to error value
**       0   no error
**       1   no value on the top of the stack
**
** RETURNS
**    integer value on the top of the stack
*/
extern int examine( STACK *s, int *error );
```

Listing 1.2 Definitions for an integer stack software component

```c
/* File: intstack.c */

#include <alloc.h>
#include <stdlib.h>
#include "intstack.h"

/* Push data onto the stack
**
** ARGUMENTS
**    s          pointer to stack address
**    item       integer to be pushed
**    error      pointer to error value
**       0    no error
**       1    not enough memory
**
** RETURNS
**    none
*/
void push( STACK **s, int item, int *error )
{
  STACK *new_item;

  /* Allocate space for new stack node */
  if ( !( new_item = ( STACK * ) malloc( sizeof( STACK ) ) ) )
  {
    *error = 1;
  }

  /* transfer data to stack node */
  new_item -> info = item;

  /* add new stack node to the beginning of list */
  new_item -> next = *s;
  *s = new_item;
  *error = 0;
}
```

(continued)

```
/* Pop data from the stack
**
** ARGUMENTS
**    s         pointer to stack address
**    error     pointer to error value
**      0  no error
**      1  no data to pop from stack
**
** RETURNS
**    integer value returned from stack
*/
int pop( STACK **s, int *error )
{
  STACK *old_item = *s;
  int old_info = 0;

  if ( *s )
  {
    /* get info from the first node in the list */
    old_info = old_item -> info;

    /* set a new first node in the list */
    ( *s ) = ( *s ) -> next;

    /* remove old first node from list */
    free( old_item );

    *error = 0;
  }
  else
    *error = 1;
  return ( old_info );
}


/* Examine the top of the stack
**
** ARGUMENTS
**    s         pointer to stack
**    error     pointer to error value
**      0  no error
**      1  no value on the top of the stack
**
** RETURNS
**    integer value on the top of the stack
*/
int examine( STACK *s, int *error )
{
  if ( s )
```

```
{
    *error = 0;
    return s -> info;
}
else
{
    *error = 1;
    return 0;
}
}
```

Listing 1.3   Test program that uses integer stack component

```
/* Test program that uses integer stack component */

#include <stdio.h>
#include "intstack.h"

STACK *s1, *s2;

main()
{
    int error, error2;

    /* Push and examine four values onto the stack s1 */
    push( &s1, 12, &error );
    printf( "examine( s1 ) = %d\n", examine( s1, &error ) );
    push( &s1, 13, &error );
    printf( "examine( s1 ) = %d\n", examine( s1, &error ) );
    push( &s1, 14, &error );
    printf( "examine( s1 ) = %d\n", examine( s1, &error ) );
    push( &s1, 15, &error );
    printf( "examine( s1 ) = %d\n", examine( s1, &error ) );

    /* Push the four values popped from s1 onto s2 */
    push( &s2, pop( &s1, &error ), &error2 );
    push( &s2, pop( &s1, &error ), &error2 );
    push( &s2, pop( &s1, &error ), &error2 );
    push( &s2, pop( &s1, &error ), &error2 );

    /* Pop and print the values on stack s2 */
    printf( "pop( &s2 ) = %d\n", pop( &s2, &error ) );
    printf( "pop( &s2 ) = %d\n", pop( &s2, &error ) );
    printf( "pop( &s2 ) = %d\n", pop( &s2, &error ) );
    printf( "pop( &s2 ) = %d\n", pop( &s2, &error ) );
}
```

The output of the test program of Listing 1.3 is as follows:

```
examine( s1 ) = 12
examine( s1 ) = 13
examine\( s1 ) = 14
examine( s1 ) = 15
pop( &s2 ) = 12
pop( &s2 ) = 13
pop( &s2 ) = 14
pop( &s2 ) = 15
```

Software Component Ideals

Reusable software components allow a programmer to work at a higher level of abstraction without having to be concerned about the implementation details of the underlying software components. For example, in Listing 1.3, the programmer needs only to understand the purpose of a stack and the prototypes to functions push, pop, and examine. In fact, the source code given in Listing 1.2 may not be available to the programmer who needs to use the stack.

In order for a reusable software component to be useful, it must be efficiently designed, robust (that is, useful across a wide range of application areas), easy to use, and extensively tested in order to ensure the highest level of reliability. A programmer must be able to use such a component with complete trust. If a problem arises in the user's application, the user should be able to rule out a problem with the reusable software component.

These are, of course, ideals that are difficult to achieve. Software libraries have been known to contain defects. Because of this reality, it is most desirable if reusable software components are delivered to the user with source code. The user may then customize or repair the components to suit his or her needs.

History of Software Components

In reference [1], the history of scientific subroutine libraries is discussed. This discussion is summarized here.

An early collection of reusable scientific software components was described by Wilkes, et.al. [2], in 1951. This library was developed in machine language. During 1960-1961, the Communications of the Association for Computing Machinery published 73 algorithms that qualify as reusable software components. In 1961, IBM distributed a collection of reusable FORTRAN-based software components called the SSP (Scientific Subroutine Package) library. In the 1960s other FORTRAN-based scientific software libraries were developed and include the Boeing library, the Sandia Mathematical Library Project, and the Harwell Atomic Energy Research Establishment subroutine library.

In the 1970s some important scientific and engineering commercial libraries with wide distribution were developed. These include the International Mathematical and Statistical Libraries (IMSL) reference [3] and the Numerical Algorithms Group (NAG) library, reference [4]. The IMSL library and NAG library each contain over 500 mathematical functions that have been thoroughly tested and are robust in their application.

More recently, the C Language Scientific Subroutine Library, reference [5], has been distributed. It implements many of the important functions previously available in the FORTRAN libraries.

There has been an explosion of general purpose reusable software components that support many languages and many application areas. One of the most highly developed set of reusable components was developed in connection with the UNIX™ operating system and the C language by AT&T, Bell Labs.

The Smalltalk ™ language and programming environment, developed at Xerox PARC in the late 1970s and early 1980s, see reference [6], has led to a base of Smalltalk reusable software components involving several thousand functions from several hundred modules.

One of the most dramatic and recent developments in reusable software technology is the emergence of the icon-based desktop programming metaphor developed by Apple Computer in the Lisa and Macintosh Computers and inspired by the Smalltalk environment developed by Xerox. Macintosh application programmers may purchase an Applications Toolkit that provides the interfaces to the powerful ROM-based desk manager that consists of hundreds of reusable functions.

More recently, the Stepstone Corporation (formally Productivity Products International), see reference [7], has developed an extensive base of reusable software components for the Objective-C programming language. These components are modeled after the Smalltalk libraries and provide an applications framework for object-based programming. Stepstone refers to their reusable components as software ICs.

The Turbo C programmer has access to over two hundred useful functions from the runtime library. Some of these functions are described in Chapter 2. The reader should also consult the *Turbo C Reference Guide*.

In developing a large or complex Turbo C application, the programmer must frequently develop new software components that may be reusable in other applications. As an example, the basic input-output functions prototyped in the standard C header file stdio.h, produce relatively slow screen displays on IBM PC compatible computers. A programmer developing an application that requires fast screen displays, such as a text editor application, must write new output functions that directly access the memory-mapped area of the video card. Such output functions may be desirable in many applications. Similarly, some of the file stream input-output functions prototyped in stdio.h perform relatively slowly. If an application demands faster file input and output, the user may wish to write a file input/output reusable software component that may serve across many applications. Such software components will typically not be portable to non-80x86 environments but they will execute much faster within the IBM-PC compatible family.

Part 1 of this book presents concepts and techniques related to the successful development of reusable software components in Turbo C for IBM-PC compatible computers. Several important reusable software components are presented and discussed in detail.

1.1 *Physical Decomposition of a Turbo C Software System*

The C programming language allows a programmer many options in the physical decomposition of a software system. One extreme case involves placing all functions and data into one gigantic program file. Such a monolithic program would generally be difficult to read and maintain. If any small change were made to even a single line of code, the entire file would have to be recompiled. Even allowing for the blinding speed of the Turbo C compiler, this situation is undesirable. At the other extreme, a programmer may package each function into a separate file. After compiling each of the many files, the Turbo C linker would then create an executable EXE file by linking all the individual function files. This approach is undesirable because it involves too much complexity.

A middle ground between the two extreme cases given above is usually the most desirable. Logically related functions should be grouped together into separate files or compilation units. Each grouping of functions in a function definition file (.c file) should have an associated header file (.h file).

It is necessary to include a header file in a function definition file if there are forward references to functions that return values other than integers, or the header file contains constants or external variables or defined types that are required in the function definition file.

A header file can be used to document the usage of the functions whose prototypes are specified. This usage information may be provided in the form of extended comments next to each function prototype. The header file then serves as a mini user's guide that assists programmers in using the functions that are defined in the function definition file (.c file).

Figure 1.1 depicts the physical decomposition of a C software system into header files and associated function definition files. Here, each function definition file (that is, file_1.c, file_2.c, and file_3.c, includes the associated header file. The main program file includes file_1.h, file_2.h, and file_3.h.

The physical decomposition of a small - sized software system using the approach suggested in Figure 1.1 is illustrated by taking, with permission, an example from Chapter 8 from the companion book, *Turbo C at Any Speed*, Richard Wiener, John Wiley and Sons, 1988.

We wish to write a Turbo C software system that tabulates the frequency of occurrence of every word in an input text file. The software system is partitioned into the following modules:

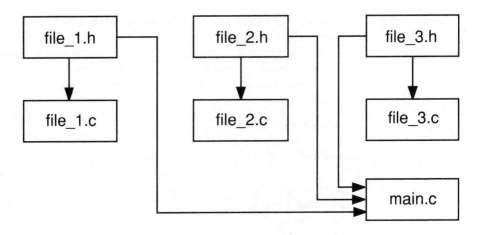

Figure 1.1 Physical decomposition of C software

word_fq.c   Main driver module that reads an input file and sends a table of word frequencies to an output file.

word_ut.h   The header file for word_ut.c. This file provides the prototypes to two important functions: string_save, and get_word.

The first function, string_save, allocates memory sufficient to hold the input string, s, and stores the string s at the memory location that is returned.

The second function, get_word, returns the next word in the file, if any exists. The value 1 is returned if a word is found. Otherwise, the value 0 is returned. Words, in this application are assumed to be delimited by nonalphabetical characters.

word_ut.c   The definitions of the functions string_save and get_word.

tree.h   A binary tree structure is declared in this header file. Each node of the tree contains the members: word (a string), freq (the number of times the word appears in the file), left, and right (pointers to the left and right children of the given node).

The prototypes to the functions create_tree and display, are presented in file tree.h.

The function create_tree builds a search tree from the words in the file. Its implementation requires the function, get_word, from file word_ut.c.

The function display generates a table of word frequencies from the word tree.

tree.c   The definitions of the functions create_tree and display.

Figure 1.2 depicts the interelationships among the modules in the system.

The object code associated with tree.c does not qualify as a robust and reusable software component because the tree is defined in terms of a specific base struct type. This specific struct type is given by:

```
typedef struct node NODE;

struct node
{
  char *word;
  unsigned freq;
  NODE *left;
  NODE *right;
};
```

and contains a string as the first field, a freq counter as the second field and pointers to the left and right child as the third and fourth fields.

A robust tree component should be generic and more efficient. There is no provision in function create_tree for ensuring that the binary tree is near balanced. If the words of the input text are ordered, even partially, the resulting binary tree will be unbalanced leading to excessive search times.

The source code for a generic AVL tree reusable software component is presented in Section 4.2. This reusable software component is independent

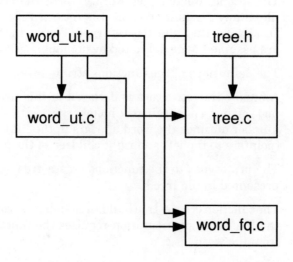

Figure 1.2   Word frequency system

of the base type stored in the tree and uses the most efficient tree-balancing algorithms to ensure minimum search times.

Listing 1.4 is the header file to word_ut.

Listing 1.4 The header file to word_ut

```
/* File word_ut.h */

#define MAXSIZE 50

/* Allocate space and save string that is input
**
** ARGUMENTS
**    s            string to be saved
**
** RETURNS
**    address of saved string
*/
extern char *string_save( char *s );



/* Get a word from stdin
**
** ARGUMENTS
**    w            string that is obtained from text file
**
** RETURNS
**    0            if at end of file
**    1            if a word is returned
*/
extern int get_word( char *w );
```

Listing 1.5 presents the source listing of word_ut.c.

The function string_save allocates strlen(s) + 1 bytes and returns the address p, a pointer to type char, to the call function.

The function get_word uses the standard Turbo C macro, isalpha as follows:

```
while ( !isalpha( ch = getchar() ) && ch != EOF )
    ;
```

This while loop gets nonalphabetical characters from the input stream stdin. If the EOF character is encountered before getting a word, the function terminates and returns the value 0.

The next while loop gets alphabetical characters from the input stream. Each character is converted to lower case and loaded into a string, w. At the end of the loop, the word, w, is terminated with a null character. The value 1 is returned indicating the successful acquisition of a word.

Listing 1.5 Function definitions in word_ut

```c
/* File word_ut.c */

#include <stdio.h>
#include <string.h>
#include <ctype.h>
#include <alloc.h>
#include "word_ut.h"

/* Allocate space and save string that is input
**
** ARGUMENTS
**    s           string to be saved
**
** RETURNS
**    address of saved string
*/
char *string_save( char *s )
{
  char *p;

  if ( ( p = malloc( strlen( s ) + 1 ) ) != NULL )
    strcpy( p, s );
  return ( p );
}


/* Get a word from stdin
**
** ARGUMENTS
**    w           string that is obtained from text file
**
** RETURNS
**    0           if at end of file
**    1           if a word is returned
*/
int get_word( char *w )
{
  int ch,
      count = 0;

  /* Advance to the first character of a word */
  while ( !isalpha( ch = getchar() ) && ch != EOF )
    ;
  if ( ch == EOF )
    return 0;
  else
  {
```

```
/* Build a word at address w */
*w++ = tolower( ch );
count++;
while ( isalpha( ch = getchar() ) && ch != EOF )
  if ( ++count < MAXSIZE )
    *w++ = tolower( ch );
*w = '\0'; /* Terminate the word with the null
              character */
return 1;
  }
}
```

Listing 1.6 defines a NODE structure and the prototypes for functions create_tree and display.

Listing 1.6 Header file tree.h

```
/* File tree.h  */

typedef struct node NODE;

struct node
{
  char *word;
  unsigned freq;
  NODE *left;
  NODE *right;
};

/* Build a binary tree of words
**
** ARGUMENTS
**    None
**
** RETURNS
**    A pointer to the root node of the tree
*/
NODE *create_tree( void );


/*  Display an alphabetized listing of words in the tree
**
** ARGUMENTS
**    None
**
** RETURNS
**    Nothing
*/
void display( NODE *p );
```

Listing 1.7 presents the source listing of tree. The algorithm for tree insertion is discussed in *Turbo C at Any Speed* and is not discussed here.

Listing 1.7 Source listing of tree

```c
/* File tree.c  */

#include <stdio.h>
#include <alloc.h>
#include "tree.h"
#include "word_ut.h"

static NODE *alloc_node( void )
/* This function is hidden from the linker */
{
  return ( ( NODE * ) malloc( sizeof( NODE ) ) );
}


/* Build a binary tree of words
**
** ARGUMENTS
**    None
**
** RETURNS
**    A pointer to the root node of the tree
*/
NODE *create_tree( void )
{
  extern char *string_save();
  extern NODE *alloc_node();

  NODE *current, *previous;
  NODE *root = 0;
  char w[ MAXSIZE + 1 ];
  int distinct;

  while( get_word( w )  )
  {
    if ( root == 0 )
    {
      root = alloc_node();
      root -> word = string_save( w );
      root -> left = root -> right = 0;
      root -> freq = 1;
      distinct = 0;
    }
    else
    {
      previous = 0;
      current = root;
```

```
        distinct = 1;
        while ( current != 0 )
        {
          previous = current;
          if ( strcmp( w, current -> word ) < 0 )
            current = current -> left;
          else if ( strcmp( w, current -> word ) > 0 )
            current = current -> right;
          else /* w already in the tree */
          {
            current -> freq++;
            distinct = 0;
            break;
          }
        }
        if ( distinct )
        {
          current = alloc_node();
          current -> word = string_save( w );
          current -> left = current -> right = 0;
          current -> freq = 1;
          if ( strcmp( w, previous -> word ) < 0 )
            previous -> left = current;
          else
            previous -> right = current;
        }
      }
    }
  return root;
}


/*  Display an alphabetized listing of words in the tree
**
** ARGUMENTS
**    p - Pointer to the root node of the tree
**
** RETURNS
**    Nothing
*/
void display( NODE *p )
{
  /* Performs an in-order traversal of the tree */
  if ( p != 0 )
  {
    display( p -> left );
    printf( "%-40s  %-6d\n", p -> word, p -> freq );
    display( p -> right );
  }
}
```

Listing 1.8 presents the main driver program, word_fq.c. Because of the abstraction created in files word_ut.c and tree.c, the main program is only a few lines of code.

Listing 1.8 Main driver program for tabulating word frequencies

```
/*
   Correct usage:  word_fq   <infile   >outfile
   File word_fq.c
*/

#include <stdio.h>
#include "tree.h"

main()
{
  NODE *root;

  root = create_tree();
  display( root );
}
```

If the software system given by Listings 1.4, 1.5, 1.6, 1.7, and 1.8 is run using an early draft of the first paragraph of this chapter as it is input, the output is given in Table 1.1.

Table 1.1 *Word Frequencies from First Paragraph of Chapter 1*

also	1	lower	1
and	2	maintain	1
components	1	maintenance	1
concerned	1	of	3
contribute	1	reliability	1
cost	1	reliable	1
development	2	reusable	1
ease	1	robust	1
easy	1	software	5
economical	1	that	1
efficiency	1	the	2
efficient	1	they	1
engineering	1	to	2
is	2	with	1

1.2 Turbo C MAKE Utility and PROJECT MAKE

The Turbo C system provides two utilities for managing version control in a multifile software system: the stand-alone MAKE utility, based on the UNIX MAKE utility, and the PROJECT MAKE that is part of the integrated environment.

The goal of each MAKE utility is to automate the recompilation of a Turbo C software system after one or more changes are made to the constituent files.

Each MAKE utility evaluates the file dependencies that are input by the user and determines which subset of the software system must be recompiled based on the date and time stamps of each file. In order for this to work, it is imperative that the system maintain an accurate date and time stamp for each file as it is created.

1.2.1 Stand-Alone MAKE Utility

We will illustrate the typical use of the MAKE utility by considering an example. The reader should consult the *Turbo C Reference Guide*, Appendix D, for a complete discussion of the MAKE utility.

Suppose the following files have been created in a Turbo C software system:

```
file1.h
file2.h
file3.h
file4.h
file5.h
file1.c
file2.c
file3.c
file4.c
file5.c
main.c
```

The dependencies of these files is shown below (—> means "is dependent on"):

```
file1.c -> file1.h
file2.c -> file2.h
file3.c -> file1.h file2.h file3.h
file4.c -> file2.h file4.h
file5.c -> file3.h file4.h file5.h
main.c -> file1.h file2.h file3.h file4.h file5.h
```

The interdependencies are depicted in Figure 1.3.

The programmer must create and name a file that contains the interdependencies. The default file name that MAKE looks for is called MAKEFILE. For the system defined above, the MAKEFILE given in Table 1.2 would be created (assume that the system must be compiled with the large memory model):

Table 1.2   *Makefile for a Sample System*

```
# MAKEFILE for main.exe
main.exe: main.obj file1.obj file2.obj file3.obj file4.obj \
          file5.obj
   tlink @myfile
# Table 1.3 contains a listing of the response file myfile
file1.obj: file1.c file1.h
   tcc -ml -c file1.c
file2.obj: file2.c file2.h
   tcc -ml -c file2.c
file3.obj: file3.c file1.h file2.h file3.h
   tcc -ml -c file3.c
file4.obj: file4.c file2.h file4.h
   tcc -ml -c file4.c
file5.obj: file5.c file3.h file4.h file5.h
main.obj: main.c file1.h file2.h file3.h file4.h file5.obj
   tcc -ml -c main.c
```

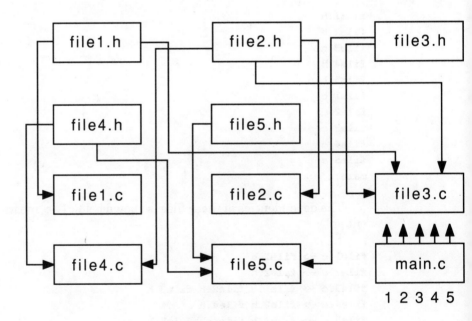

Figure 1.3   Dependencies in a C software system

The MAKEFILE in Table 1.2 may be interpreted as follows:

The symbol # is used for comments.

The symbol \ is used to extend one line to another.

The response file, myfile, given in Table 1.3, contains all the link information.

1. The file main.exe depends on the files file1.obj, file2.obj file3.obj, file4.obj, and file5.obj.

2. If any of the five files that main.exe depends on have a later date and time stamp than main.exe, the command, tlink @myfile, is invoked. This example assumes that the user has configured his or her system so that the library files are located on drive d: in subdirectory \tlib. It is noted that these libraries may more commonly be found in c:\turboc\lib.

3. The file file1.obj depends on the files file1.c and file1.h.

4. If either of these files has a later time and date stamp than file1.obj, the command tcc -ml -c file1.c is invoked.

5.   The file file2.obj depends on the files file2.c and file2.h.

6. If either of these files has a later time and date stamp than file2.obj, the command tcc -ml -c file2.c is invoked.

7. The file file3.obj depends on the files file3.c, file1.h, file2.h, and file3.h.

8. If any of these files has a later time and date stamp than file file3.obj, the command, tcc -ml -c file3.c is invoked.

9. The file file4.obj depends on the files file4.c, file2.h, and file4.h.

10. If any of these files has a later time and date stamp than file file4.obj, the command, tcc -ml -c file4.c is invoked.

11. The file file5.obj depends on the files file5.c, file3.h, file4.h, and file5.h.

12. If any of these files has a later time and date stamp than file file5.obj, the command, tcc -ml -c file5.c is invoked.

13. The file main.obj depends on the files main.c file1.h, file2.h, file3.h, file4.h, and file5.h.

14. If any of these files has a later time and date stamp than file main.obj, the command, tcc -ml -c main.c is invoked.

Table 1.3   *The Response File, myfile, for Linking*

```
d:\tlib\c0l main.obj file1.obj file2.obj file3.obj file4.obj+
file5.obj, main.exe, , d:\tlib\emu d:\tlib\mathl d:\tlib\cl
```

An implicit rule could be added to the MAKEFILE in Table 1.2 as follows:

```
.c.obj:
  tcc -ml -c $<
```

This implicit rule means that any file ending with .OBJ depends on the file with the same name that ends in .C. If such .C file has a later date than the corresponding .OBJ file, take the action given by the command tcc. The macro $< represents the file name with the .C extension.

Table 1.4 shows the MAKEFILE for the sample software system if the implicit rule is used. The command,

```
tlink @myfile
```

means link the response file, myfile, given in Table 1.3.

Table 1.4 *Revised Makefile for a Sample System*

```
# MAKEFILE for main.exe
.c.obj:
  tcc -ml -c $<
main.exe: main.obj file1.obj file2.obj file3.obj file4.obj \
          file5.obj
  tlink @myfile
main.obj: file1.h file2.h file3.h file4.h file5.obj
file1.obj: file1.h
file2.obj: file2.h
file3.obj: file1.h file2.h file3.h
file4.obj: file2.h file4.h
file5.obj: file3.h file4.h file5.h
```

If the file file2.h were modified, the invocation of MAKE would require that the files main.c, file2.c, file3.c, and file4.c be recompiled, and the system linked. This follows because these are the files that are dependent on file2.h.

If the file file4.h were modified, the invocation of MAKE would require that the files main.c, file4.c, and file5.c be recompiled and the system linked.

If the file file1.h were modified, the invocation of MAKE would require that the files main.c, file1.c, and file3.c be recompiled and the system linked.

If the file file3.c were recompiled (thus changing the file file3.obj), the system would have to be relinked.

Finally, if the file file3.c were modified, it would have to be recompiled, and the system relinked.

1.2.2 PROJECT MAKE

The PROJECT MAKE utility available in the integrated environment requires the programmer to create a .PRJ file. This file consists of a list of all the .c files that comprise the software system.

If the MAKE option is selected from the integrated menu, the programmer can select the .PRJ file that is applicable. Under the Compile option, the user may select MAKE. The compiler will then compile and link all the files that are specified in the .PRJ file.

1.3 Generic Software Components

Generic software components encapsulate a set of logically related operations that may be performed on arbitrary data. A generic component is more robust than a data specific component, because it may be reused in many applications that require different base types.

The data type that supports the development of generic components is void*. When used as a formal parameter type in C functions, void* is assignment compatible with any address that may be sent into the function.

We illustrate the notion of a generic reusable software component by building one. We wish to construct a generic stack with the operations of push and pop.

The header file to the generic stack component is given in Listing 1.9.

Listing 1.9 Prototypes for a generic stack component

```
/* gstack.h */

/* Stack operation errors */
#define STACK_OK 0
#define STACK_SIZE_ERROR 1
#define STACK_MEM_ERROR 2
#define STACK_EMPTY 3
#define STACK_NOT_DEFINED 4

/* Allocate a stack
**
** ARGUMENTS
**    none
**
** RETURNS
**    pointer to a stack
**    NULL if insufficient memory
*/
extern void *define( void );
```

(continued)

```
/* Push data onto the stack
**
** ARGUMENTS
**   s        pointer to the stack
**   item     pointer to data to be pushed
**   size     number of bytes in item
**
** RETURNS
**   STACK_OK   successful push
**   STACK_SIZE_ERROR     illegal size for item
**   STACK_MEM_ERROR      not enough memory
**   STACK_NOT_DEFINED    function define not invoked
*/
extern int push( void *s, void *item, unsigned size );


/* Pop data from the stack
**
** ARGUMENTS
**   s   pointer to stack
**   itempointer to location to put data
**
** RETURNS
**   STACK_OK        successful pop of stack
**   STACK_EMPTY     no data to pop from stack
**   STACK_NOT_DEFINED    function define not invoked
*/
extern int pop( void *s, void *item );
```

A function, define, is specified with the prototype:

```
void *define( void );
```

This function must be invoked before push or pop. It is used to establish a user defined stack. For example, in the user's main program, the code,

```
void *my_stack;

my_stack = define();
```

creates a stack called my_stack. If a user declares a stack globally, so that its initial address is NULL, functions push and pop can detect the failure on the user's part to invoke function define before invoking either push or pop.

The function push has the prototype:

```
int push( void *s, void *item, unsigned size );
```

The first parameter takes a user specified stack such as my_stack, given above. The second parameter takes the address of the arbitrary data structure to be put into the stack. The third parameter takes the size, in bytes, of the arbitrary data structure to be put into the stack. The function returns one of the error values given in Listing 1.9.

Suppose the data, my_data, a structure, has been defined and filled with information. A typical call to function push might be as follows:

```
result = push( stack1, &my_data, sizeof( my_data ) );
```

The function pop has the prototype:

```
extern int pop( void *s, void *item );
```

The first parameter takes a user specified stack such as my_stack, given above. The second parameter takes the address of the arbitrary data structure to be returned. The function returns one of the error values given in Listing 1.9.

Using the user defined data, my_data, a typical call to function pop might be

```
result = pop( stack1, &my_data );
```

Listing 1.10 presents the function definitions for the generic stack component. The code is heavily commented to indicate the purpose of each segment.

The first line of code in functions push and pop is

```
st = ( STACK * ) s;
```

This line converts the untyped parameter s, a pointer to void, to the typed variable st, a pointer to a STACK.

We look at function push in some detail. The reader is urged to inspect function pop and compare its code to function push.

The first segment of code determines whether the structure field, size, has been set. If not, this field is assigned the value of parameter size. If size has been previously assigned, a test is performed to determine whether the size of the element being pushed is equal to this value. If not, an error value is returned.

The next segment of code allocates memory in the heap for a new node. If no memory is available, an error value is returned.

The next segment of code allocates memory in the heap for the contents field of NODE n. If no memory is available, an error value is returned.

The next segment of code inserts the new node, n, into the front of the linked list.

The last segment of code uses the function memcpy which is prototyped in header file mem.h. This memory transfer function assigns size bytes from the memory address of item to the memory address given by the contents field of node n.

It must be noted that the generic stack may be misused. An unwary or careless user might push two items of different types onto the stack. If the base types of the two items were the same size, in bytes, the push function would not detect this error. When the user popped the stack, the results would be unpredictable! The correct usage of the generic stack is to build stacks of homogeneous but arbitrary elements.

Listing 1.10 Source listing of a generic stack component

```
/* gstack.c */

#include <stdio.h>
#include <alloc.h>
#include <mem.h>
#include "gstack.h"

typedef struct stack STACK;
typedef struct node NODE;

struct stack
{
  unsigned size;    /* size of a stack datum */
  NODE *top;        /* pointer to top of the stack */
};

struct node
{
  NODE *next;       /* Pointer to the next node in list */
  void *contents;   /* Information stored in stack node */
};


/* Allocate a stack
**
** ARGUMENTS
**    none
**
** RETURNS
**    pointer to a stack
**    NULL if insufficient memory
*/
void *define( void )
{
  STACK *s;

  /* Allocate space for the stack header node */
  if ( ! ( s = ( STACK * ) malloc( sizeof( STACK ) ) ) )
    return ( NULL );

    /* set size and next pointer */
    s -> size = 0;
    s -> top = NULL;

    return ( s );
}
```

```c
/* Push data onto the stack
**
** ARGUMENTS
**    s         pointer to the stack
**    item      pointer to data to be pushed
**    size      number of bytes in item
**
** RETURNS
**    STACK_OK              successful push
**    STACK_SIZE_ERROR      illegal size for item
**    STACK_MEM_ERROR       not enough memory
**    STACK_NOT_DEFINED     function define not invoked
*/
int push( void *s, void *item, unsigned size )
{

  NODE *n;
  STACK *st;

  st = ( STACK * ) s;

  if ( ! st )
    return ( STACK_NOT_DEFINED );

  /* set size if it hasn't been set */
  if ( !( st ) -> size )
    ( st ) -> size  = size;
  else if ( st -> size != size )
    return ( STACK_SIZE_ERROR );

  /* get space for the new node */
  if ( !( n = ( NODE * ) malloc( sizeof( NODE ) ) ) )
    return STACK_MEM_ERROR;

  /* get space for contents */
  if ( !( n -> contents = malloc( size ) ) )
    return STACK_MEM_ERROR;

  /* insert new node at the top of the stack */
  n -> next = st -> top;
  st -> top = n;

  /* move data to new node */
  memcpy( n -> contents, item, size );

  return ( STACK_OK );
}
```

(continued)

```
/* Pop data from the stack
**
** ARGUMENTS
**    s               pointer to stack
**    item            pointer to location to put data
**
** RETURNS
**    STACK_OK             successful pop of stack
**    STACK_EMPTY          no data to pop from stack
**    STACK_NOT_DEFINED  function define not used
*/
int pop( void *s, void *item )
{
  NODE *oldnode;
  STACK *st;

  st = ( STACK * ) s;

  if ( ! st )
    return ( STACK_NOT_DEFINED );

  /* test to see if the stack is empty */
  if ( !( oldnode = st -> top ) )
    return ( STACK_EMPTY );

  /* move data from stack to oldnode */
  memcpy( item, oldnode -> contents, st -> size );

  /* remove the old node from the top of the stack */
  st -> top = oldnode -> next;

  /* free the memory taken by the oldnode */
  free( oldnode -> contents );
  free( oldnode );

  return( STACK_OK );
}
```

Listing 1.11 presents a test program that illustrates the use of the generic stack component. Two stacks are constructed. The first stack contains elements of struct type MY_RECORD (see Listing 1.11). The second stack contains elements of type float.

Listing 1.11 Test program for generic stack

```
/* Generic stack test program */

#include "gstack.h"
#include <string.h>
```

```c
#include <stdio.h>
#include <stdlib.h>

typedef struct my_record MY_RECORD;

struct my_record
{
  char name[ 30 ];
  unsigned int age;
};

void stack_error( int result )
{
  if ( result == STACK_SIZE_ERROR )
  {
    printf( "\nIllegal push operation:  Stack size error\n" );
    exit( 1 );
  }
  else if ( result == STACK_MEM_ERROR )
  {
    printf( "\nIllegal push operation:  Stack mem error\n" );
    exit( 1 );
  }
  else if ( result == STACK_NOT_DEFINED )
  {
    printf( "\nIllegal push operation:  Stack not defined\n" );
    exit( 1 );
  }
}

void *stack1, *stack2;

main()
{
  MY_RECORD my_data;
  int result;
  int i;
  float r;

  /* Define stack1 */
  stack1 = define();

  /* assign to my_data, push onto stack, test stack */
  strcpy( my_data.name, "John Smith" );
  my_data.age = 26;
  result = push( stack1, &my_data, sizeof( my_data ) );
  stack_error( result );
  strcpy( my_data.name, "Mary Jones" );
  my_data.age = 24;
```
(continued)

```c
result = push( stack1, &my_data, sizeof( my_data ) );
stack_error( result );

strcpy( my_data.name, "Barnaby Zachary" );
my_data.age = 20;
result = push( stack1, &my_data, sizeof( my_data ) );
stack_error( result );

strcpy( my_data.name, "Confounded Confusion" );
my_data.age = 16;
result = push( stack1, &my_data, sizeof( my_data ) );
stack_error( result );

/* Pop the stack repetitively until it is empty. Print the
   results
*/
result = pop( stack1, &my_data );
while ( result == STACK_OK )
{

  printf( "\nName:   %s", my_data.name );
  printf( "\nAge :   %d\n", my_data.age );
  result = pop( stack1, &my_data );
}
while ( result == STACK_OK );

/* Define stack2 */
stack2 = define();

/* Push the numbers 1 to 10 onto the stack */
for ( i = 1; i <= 10; i++ )
{
  r = ( float ) i;
  push( stack2, &r, sizeof( r ) );
}

/* Pop and print the numbers in stack2 */
printf( "\n" );
result = pop( stack2, &r );
while ( result == STACK_OK )
{
  printf( "%f\n", r );
  result = pop( stack2, &r );
}
}
```

The output of the test program is

```
Name:   Confounded Confusion
Age :   16
```

```
Name:   Barnaby Zachary
Age :   20

Name:   Mary Jones
Age :   24

Name:   John Smith
Age :   26

10.000000
9.000000
8.000000
7.000000
6.000000
5.000000
4.000000
3.000000
2.000000
1.000000
```

1.4   References

[1] Sincovec, R. and R. Wiener. 1987. *Modula-2 Software Components*. New York: John Wiley and Sons, Inc.

[2] Wilkes, M.V., J.D. Wheeler, and S. Gill. 1951. *The Preparation of Programs for an Electronic Digital Computer*. Reading: Addison-Wesley.

[3] IMSL, Inc. Sixth Floor—NBC Building, 7500 Bellaire Boulevard, Houston, Texas 77036-5085.

[4] Numerical Algorithms Group, Inc. 1101 31 Street, Suite 100, Downers Grove, Illinois 60515.

[5] *C Language Scientific Subroutine Library*. New York: John Wiley and Sons, Inc. 1985.

[6] Goldberg, A., and D. Robson. 1985. *Smalltalk-80—The Language and Its Implementation*. Reading: Addison-Wesley.

[7] Stepstone Inc., 75 Glen Road, Sandy Hook, Connecticut 06482.

2

Turbo C Library
Software Components

Before developing our own reusable software components, we should carefully examine the rich array of functions that are supplied with the Turbo
C system.

It is not the intent of this chapter to rewrite the excellent *Turbo C Reference Guide*. The reader is urged to study this manual carefully. Instead,
this chapter presents short summaries of some of Turbo C's important
library functions, particularly those that deal with input and output and
specialized DOS capabilities.

Many of the functions and macros provided in the Turbo C libraries are
UNIX compatible and are portable across many C systems. Other more
specialized functions such as those prototyped in dos.h provide outstanding
support for C programming in the PC environment but are not portable to
other operating systems or other C systems.

As C has evolved over the years, the functions that support input and
output have become fairly standardized.This has contributed greatly to C's
relatively high level of portability.

Parts of this chapter are taken with permission from parts of Chapters
10 and 12 of *Turbo C at Any Speed*, Richard Wiener, John Wiley and Sons,
1988.

2.1 *Turbo C Input and Output Functions and Macros*

A list of many of Turbo C's functions that support standard input and output
as well as MS-DOS specific low-level input and output is given in Table 2.1.

Table 2.1 *Some Turbo C Input / Output Functions*

Function Name	Prototype In	Function Name	Prototype In
access	io.h	fseek	stdio.h
cgets	conio.h	fwrite	stdio.h
close	io.h	getc	stdio.h
cprintf	conio.h	getch	conio.h
cputs	conio.h	getchar	stdio.h
creat	io.h	gets	stdio.h
creatnew	io.h	getw	stdio.h
creattemp	io.h	kbhit	conio.h
eof	io.h	lock	io.h
fclose	stdio.h	lseek	io.h
fcloseall	stdio.h	open	io.h
fdopen	stdio.h	perror	stdio.h
feof	stdio.h	printf	stdio.h
ferror	stdio.h	puts	stdio.h
fflush	stdio.h	read	io.h
fgetc	stdio.h	remove	stdio.h
fgetchar	stdio.h	rename	stdio.h
fgets	stdio.h	rewind	stdio.h
filelength	io.h	scanf	stdio.h
fileno	stdio.h	setbuf	stdio.h
fputc	stdio.h	setmode	io.h
fputchar	stdio.h	sopen	io.h
fputs	stdio.h	sprintf	stdio.h
fread	stdio.h	sscanf	stdio.h
freopen	stdio.h	ungetc	stdio.h
fscanf		ungetch	io.h

2.1.1 Stream Input and Output

The term stream is derived from the notion of a sequential structure of information records. This "stream" of information is stored on disk. The basic operations related to a stream are

- Read a block of data from stream to RAM (one or more records).
- Write a block of data from RAM to the stream.
- Update a block of data in the stream.
- Read a specific record of data from the stream.
- Write a specific record of data to the stream.

The structure FILE, given in stdio.h, holds information about a file stream. This structure, copied directly from the Turbo C file stdio.h is given as:

```
typedef struct
{
    short level;              /* fill/empty level of buffer */
    unsigned flags;           /* File status flags */
    char fd;                  /* File descriptor */
    char hold;                /* Ungetc char if no buffer */
    short bsize;              /* Buffer size */
    unsigned char *buffer;    /* Data transfer buffer */
    unsigned char *curp;      /* Current active pointer */
    short token;              /* Used for validity checking */
} FILE;
```

The global file variables, stdin, stdout, stdprn, stdaux, and stderr are initialized by the system prior to the execution of any application program.

The file stdin is initialized to the keyboard but maybe redirected using MS-DOS's redirection command. These redirection commands are, of course, derived from the older and more established UNIX file redirection commands. To redirect stdin to a file, infile, the user must issue the following command to execute his or her program:

```
program_name < infile
```

All file input functions that accept input from the file stdin, will obtain their input from infile.

The file stdout is initialized to the output terminal but may also be redirected to a user's file (or printer). To redirect stdout to a file, outfile, the user must issue the following command to execute his or her program:

```
program_name > outfile
```

All file output functions that write to stdout will write their output to outfile.

The file stderr is initialized to the user's output terminal and cannot be redirected to another file at the DOS command line. Thus whenever the user wishes to write a message to the user's terminal, the output stream, stderr, should be used.

Header file stdio.h provides support for Turbo C's file stream functions. All of these functions are UNIX compatible.

2.1.2 Text and Binary Streams

A text stream consists of a sequence of characters partitioned into lines. The newline character, '\n', is used to separate lines. Text streams (files) are portable from one environment to another if the characters contained within the text stream come from the standard character set(no extended characters such as IBM's graphic characters, etc.).

Turbo C, like most C implementations for the 80x86 machines, uses the ASCII codes to map integers to characters. The entire set of 256 characters, including the IBM graphics characters are available for use in building Turbo C text files.

The draft ANSI C standard, which Turbo C supports, requires implementations to support text streams with at least 254 characters.

Binary streams are sequences of values of type char. There is no portability from one C environment to another using binary streams. Any data set can be mapped to a sequence of characters. The mapping varies from one C system to another.

2.1.3 EOF Character

EOF is defined as follows:

```
#define EOF -1
```

This value may be used to test for the end of a file if signed characters or short are being used. It is noted that the important standard library functions fgetc and others return type int and not type char.

2.1.4 fopen

The function fopen is used to open a stream. The prototype for this function is

```
FILE *fopen( char *filename, char *mode );
```

A legal DOS file name must be sent into the function as the first parameter.

The second parameter determines the mode in which the file will be opened. The following choices exist:

"r"   Open an existing file for input.

"w"   Create a new file or truncate an existing file for output.

"a"   Create a new file or append to an existing file for output.

"r+" Open an existing file for update starting at the beginning of the file.

"w+" Create a new file or open an existing file for update.

"a+" Create a new file or append to an existing file for update.

In addition, the character, 'b', may be appended to any of the above type strings to indicate that a binary file should be opened.

The function fopen returns a pointer to a file structure, FILE. If any error is encountered in opening a file, fopen transmits an error code (number) to errno and returns a null (0) pointer.

2.1.5 fflush

The function fflush is used to empty any internal buffers to the destination stream. Its prototype is

```
int fflush( FILE *stream );
```

The stream remains open after this function is invoked. If an error is detected during the execution of fflush, the value EOF is returned. Otherwise, the value 0 is returned.

2.1.6 fclose

The function fclose has the following prototype:

```
int fclose( FILE *stream );
```

It empties the appropriate buffer to the destination file, and performs an orderly shutting down of the specified stream. The value 0 is returned if a normal shut-down occurs, otherwise the value EOF is returned.

2.1.7 fgetc, getc

The function fgetc has the following prototype:

```
int fgetc( FILE *stream );
```

This function reads the next character from the specified stream and returns it as a type int. If an error occurs or the end of file is reached, the function returns the value EOF.

The macro getc performs exactly as the function fgetc.

2.1.8 getchar

The macro getchar is defined as getc(stdin).

```
int getchar();
```

If the standard input stream has not been redirected,input is expected from the keyboard. Otherwise, input is expected from the redirected input file that is specified on the command line when the program is invoked.

2.1.9 ungetc

The prototype to function ungetc is the following:

```
int ungetc( char ch, FILE *stream );
```

The character ch is pushed back onto the specified stream.This character will be the next to be returned by an immediate call to fgetc, getc, or getchar. The value of the character is returned when the function encounters no error, otherwise the value EOF is returned.

The ungetc function is useful whenever it is desirable to look ahead one character without disturbing the input stream.

2.1.10 fseek

The prototype for fseek is the following:

```
int fseek( FILE *stream, long offset, int wherefrom );
```

This function is used for random access usually within a binary stream.

The first argument specifies the particular stream for which direct access to a particular byte offset is requested.

The second argument, offset, is a signed long integer that specifies the number of bytes of offset from the wherefrom parameter given as parameter three.

The third parameter, wherefrom, specifies whether the offset given by the second parameter is to be taken from:

```
value 0 - beginning of file
value 1 - current file position
value 2 - the end of the file
```

The following constants are defined to control fseek:

```
#define SEEK_SET 0
#define SEEK_CUR 1
#define SEEK_END 2
```

The following call could be used to position the file pointer to the end of the file:

```
fseek( stream_name, 0L, SEEK_END );
```

2.1.11 rewind

The function rewind has the following prototype:

```
void rewind( FILE *stream );
```

This function positions the file pointer to the beginning of the file. This could also be accomplished by calling,

```
fseek( stream_name, 0L, SEEK_SET );
```

The function rewind also clears any error indicators. Both functions clear EOF.

2.1.12 fgets

The function fgets has the following prototype:

```
char *fgets( char *s, int n, FILE *stream );
```

Characters are read into the string, s, until:

1. A new line is encountered.

2. End of file is encountered.

3. n - 1 characters have been read without encountering condition 1 or 2.

A terminating null character is appended to string s after the characters are read from the input stream. If a newline character is encountered (condition 1), this character is included in s before the null character. The address of s is returned if the operation is successful, otherwise the value NULL is returned.

2.1.13   gets

The prototype for function gets is the following:

```
char *gets( char *s );
```

The function gets reads characters from the standard input stream, stdin. When the input is terminated by a newline character, '\n', the function gets discards this character and does not put it into the string s.

Since gets does not contain a numerical limit parameter, as fgets does, this function is potentially dangerous. It is possible for the number of characters input from stdin to exceed the storage of string s.

2.1.14   fputc, putc

The prototype for function fputc is the following:

```
int fputc( char ch, FILE *stream );
```

This function writes the character ch to the specified stream. If the operation is successful, the value of ch as type int is returned, otherwise the EOF value is returned.

The function putc is identical to fputc but is usually implemented as a macro.

2.1.15   putchar

The macro putchar is defined to be the following:

```
putc( ch, stdout );
```

2.1.16 fputs

The prototype for function fputs is the following:

```
int fputs( char *s, FILE *stream );
```

The null terminated string, s, is written to the stream without the null terminating character. If an error is encountered, the value EOF is returned otherwise a nonzero value.

2.1.17 puts

The prototype for function puts is the following:

```
int puts( char *s );
```

This function works just as fputs except the characters are written to stdout and an additional newline character, '\n', is written to the stream regardless of whether the string s contains this character.

2.1.18 fread

The function fread has the following prototype:

```
int fread( void *ptr, unsigned elem_size, int count, FILE *stream );
```

This function reads up to count elements of size elem_size (in bytes), into the address, ptr. The actual number of elements that are read is returned.

2.1.19 fwrite

The prototype for function fwrite is the following:

```
int fwrite( void *ptr, unsigned elem_size, int count, FILE *stream );
```

This function writes up to count elements of size elem_size (in bytes) from the address, ptr. The actual number of elements that are written is returned.

2.1.20 feof

The macro feof is defined to be:

```
#define feof( stream ) ( ( f ) -> flags & _F_EOF )
```

If the end of file has been reached while reading input from the specified stream, the value zero is returned, otherwise a nonzero value.

The macro feof does not signal that the end of the file has been reached unless an attempt is made to read past the last character in the file.

2.1.21 ferror

The macro ferror is defined as:

```
#define ferror( stream ) ( ( stream ) -> flags & _F_ERR )
```

This macro returns the error status of the specified stream after reading or writing to the stream. A value of zero indicates that no error has occurred, whereas a nonzero value indicates that an error has occurred.

The function clearerr must be used to reset the error status.

2.1.22 clearerr

The function clearerr has the following prototype:

```
void clearerr( FILE *stream );
```

This function resets the error status for the specified stream to 0. Closing the stream also resets the error status to 0 for the stream.

2.1.23 rename

The function rename has the following prototype:

```
int rename( char *oldname, char *newname );
```

This function changes the name of the file from oldname to newname. The value 0 is returned if the operation is successful, otherwise a nonzero value is returned.

2.1.24 fprintf, printf, sprintf, cprintf

The description in this section is taken in part from the Borland International *Turbo C Reference Manual*.

The functions fprintf, printf, and sprintf perform formatted output to a specified stream, the stdout stream, and to a specified string respectively. The function cprintf in Version 1.5 writes to either video RAM or BIOS depending on how DIRECTVIDEO is set. See the *Turbo C Reference Manual* for details.

The prototypes for these function are given as follows:

```
int fprintf( FILE *stream, char *format, additional arguments );

int printf( char *format, additional arguments );

int sprintf( char *s, char *format, additional arguments );

int cprintf( char *format, additional arguments );
```

Each of these functions returns EOF if an error occurs otherwise returns the number of characters sent to the destination.

The format string contains text to be copied verbatim to the destination except for specific format conversion specifications. These format conversion specifications may call for additional arguments not contained in the format string.

The format conversion specifications have the form,

```
% [ flags ] [ width ] [ .prec ] [ F | N | h | l ] type
```

where:

```
[ flags ] are an optional sequence of flag characters

[ width ] is an optional width specifier

[ .prec ] is an optional precision specifier

[ F | N | h | l ] is an optional input size modifier
```

type is the conversion type character.

More specifically, the optional flags determine the output justification, numeric signs, decimal points, trailing zeros, octal or hexidecimal prefixes.

The width determines the minimum number of characters to output, padding with blanks or zeros.

The precision determines the maximum number of characters to output. For integers, the precision determines the minimum number of digits to output.

The size determines the size of the argument as follows:

```
N = near pointer,
F = far pointer,
h = short int,
l = long int.
```

Table 2.2 lists the format conversion characters and their meaning.

Table 2.2 *Format Conversion Characters for printf Family*

Conversion character Numbers	Input Argument	Format of Output
d	integer	Signed decimal int
i	integer	Signed decimal int
o	integer	Unsigned octal int
u	integer	Unsigned decimal int

x, X	integer	Unsigned hex int For x: a, b, c, d, e, f
		For X: A, B, C, D, E, F
f	floating pt	Signed value of the form [-]dddd.dddd
e	floating pt	Signed value of the form [-1]d.dddd e [+/-]ddd
g	floating pt	Signed value in either e or f form, based on given value and precision. Trailing zeros and decimal points are output only if necessary
E	floating pt	Same as E but uses E for exponent
G	floating pt	Same as g but uses E for exponent if e format is used

Characters

c	character	Single character
s	string ptr	Outputs string until null-terminator is encountered or precision is reached
%	none	The % character is output

Pointers

| n | pointer to int | Stores in the location pointed to by the input argument a count of the characters written so far |
| p | pointer | Outputs the pointer address. Far pointers are output as SSSS:OOOO. Near pointers are output as OOOO (offset only) |

Notes

For e or E

- One digit precedes the decimal point.

- The number of digits after the decimal point equals the precision.

- The exponent always contains three digits.

For f

- The argument is converted to decimal notation in the style [-] ddd.ddd... where the number of digits after the decimal point equals the precision.

For g or G

- The argument is printed in style e, E, or f, with the precision determining the number of significant digits. Trailing zeros are removed from the result. A decimal point appears only if necessary.

- Style e is used only if the exponent that results from the conversion is either greater than the precision or less than -4.

Table 2.3 lists the flag characters and their meaning.

Table 2.3 *Flag Characters and Their Meaning*

-	Left justifies the result, pads on the right with blanks. If not present, right-justifies the result, and pads on the left with zeros or blanks.
+	Output always begins with a plus (+) or minus (-) sign.
blank	If value is non-negative, the output begins with a blank, not a plus sign. Negative values begin with a minus sign.
#	Specifies that argument is to be converted using an "alternate form".

Format Conversion Character	Alternate Forms
c, s, d, i, u	No effect.
o	O will be prepended to a nonzero argument.
x or X	0x or 0X will be prepended to argument.
e, E, or f	The result will always contain a decimal point even if no digits follow the decimal point.
g or G	Same as e, or E except that trailing zeros are not removed.

Table 2.4 lists the width specifiers and their meaning.

Table 2.4 *Width Specifiers and Their Meaning*

Width Specifier	Action
n	At least n characters are printed. If the output value has less than n characters, the output is padded with blanks (right-padded if "-" is given, otherwise left-padded).
On	At least n characters are printed. If the output value has less than n characters, it is filled on the left with zeros.
*	The argument list supplies the width specifier, which must precede the actual argument being formatted.

Table 2.5 lists the precision specifiers and their meaning.

Table 2.5 *Precision Specifiers and Their Meaning*

Precision Specifier	Action
none	Default: 1 for d, i, o, u, x, X; 6 for e, E, f; All significant digits for g or G; Print to null for s
.0	For d, i, o u, x, precision set to default. For e, E, f, no decimal point is printed
.n	n characters or n decimal places are printed. If the output value has more than n characters, the output might be truncated or rounded.
*	The argument list supplies the precision specifier which mus precede the actual argument being formatted.

How Precision Affects Conversion

d, i	.n specifies that at least n digits will be output.
o, u,	If the input argument is less than n digits, the x output value is left-padded with zeros. If the input X argument has more than n digits, the output value is not truncated.
e, E	.n specifies that n characters will be printed after the decimal point.
f	The last digit is rounded.
g, G	.n specifies that at most n significant digits are output.
c	.n has no effect on the output.
s	.n specifies that no more than n characters will be output.

An example of the use of the .* precision specifier and * width specifier is shown in Listing 2.1.

The output of Listing 2.1 is

```
r = 1.235
With width 20 and precision 1 r =    1.2
```

Listing 2.1 The use of the .* precision specifier

```c
#include <stdio.h>

main()
{
  double r = 1.2345678;
  int precision = 3;
  int width = 20;

  printf( "\nr = %.*lf", precision, r );
  precision = 1;
  printf( "\nWith width %d and precision %d r = %*.*f\n",
          width, precision, width, precision, r );
}
```

The input size modifiers (F, N, h, and l) affect how the family of printf functions interpret the input argument. F and N apply only to input arguments that are pointers (%p, %s, %n). h and l apply to input arguments that are numeric.

Table 2.6 lists the size specifiers and their meanings.

Table 2.6 Size Specifiers and Their Meanings

Size Specifier	Action
F	Argument is read as a far pointer
N	Argument is read as a near pointer. Cannot be used in huge model
h	Argument is interpreted as a short int for d, i, o, u, x, or X
l	Argument is interpreted as a long int for d, i, o, u, x, or X
	Argument is interpreted as a double for e, E, f, g or G

2.1.25   scanf, fscanf, sscanf, cscanf

The prototypes to functions fscanf, scanf, sscanf, and cscanf are

```
int scanf( char *format, additional arguments );
int fscanf( FILE *stream, char *format, additional arguments );
int int sscanf( char *string, char *format, additional arguments );
int cscanf( char * format, additional arguments );
```

The function scanf inputs from stdin. The function fscanf inputs from the user specified stream. The function sscanf inputs from the specified string. The function cscanf inputs from the console.

Every function in the scanf family scans input fields, one character at a time, converting them according to a specified format.

The first input field is converted according to the first format conversion specification and stores the result in the first address argument. The next input field is converted according to the second format conversion specification, and so forth.

The format for the scanf family of functions is

```
% [ * ] [ width ] [ F | N ] [ h | l } type_character
```

Because of the great similarity to the functions described in section 2.1.24, no further details are presented here. The reader is urged to consult the *Turbo C Reference Manual*.

2.2   Low-Level File Input and Output

In addition to the stream input and output functions described in Section 2.1, Turbo C provides other UNIX compatible low-level file functions. The prototypes for these functions and macros are in the file io.h. These include the following:

```
access
close
creat
dup
dup2
eof
filelength
getftime
isatty
lseek
open
read
setftime
setmode
tell
write
```

Each of the above low-level file functions are briefly described in the next sections.

2.2.1 access

The prototype to function access is

```
int access( char *filename, int amode );
```

Function access may be used to check whether the specified file exists, whether it can be read, whether it can be written to or whether it can be executed.

The bit pattern in amode is created by "ORing" the following values:

```
06 Check for read and write permission
04 Check for read permission
02 Check for write permission
01 Execute (Ignored in DOS)
00 Check for existence of file
```

Under MS-DOS, all existing files have read access so amode 00 and amode 04 return the same result. Also, under MS-DOS, amode values of 06 and 02 return the same result.

If filename is a (sub)directory, access determines whether the (sub)directory exists or not.

Function access returns 0 if the requested access is allowed, otherwise the value -1 is returned. Errno is set to:

```
ENOENT Path name or file name not found
EACCES Permission denied
```

2.2.2 close

The prototype to function close is the following:

```
int close( int fd );
```

The file handle, fd, is returned from one of the functions: creat, creatnew, creattemp, dup, dup2, or open described in later subsections.

Function close shuts down the file associated with the specified file handle.

Function close returns a value of 0 if successful, otherwise it returns a value of -1.

2.2.3 creat

The prototype for function creat is the following:

```
int creat( char* filename, int permiss );
```

Function creat creates a new file or prepares to rewrite an existing file with the specified file name. The parameter permiss applies only to new files.

The values of permiss, defined in sys\stat.h, are the following:

```
S_IWRITE              Permission to write
S_IREAD               Permission to read
S_IREAD|S_IWRITE      Permission to read and write
```

In MS-DOS, write permission implies read permission.

If a file exists and the permiss parameter is set to write, creat truncates the file to 0 bytes leaving the file attribute unchanged. If the existing file has the read-only attribute set, function creat fails and the file remains unchanged.

2.2.4   dup, dup2

Function dup is available on all UNIX systems whereas function dup2 is not available on UNIX system III.

The prototypes for these functions are

```
int dup( int handle );
int dup2( int oldhandle, int newhandle );
```

Functions dup and dup2 return a new file handle that:

- Has same open file as the original file handle
- Has the same file pointer as the original file handle
- Has the same access mode as the original file handle

Function dup2 returns the next file handle that is available.

If successful, function dup returns the new file handle, a non-negative integer, otherwise returns -1.

If successful, function dup2 returns 0, otherwise returns -1. If an error occurs, errno is set to:

```
EMFILE  Too many open files
EBADF   Bad file number
```

2.2.5   eof

The prototype for function eof is the following:

```
int eof( int handle );
```

This function determines whether the file associated with handle has reached end-of-file.

If the current position is end-of-file, eof returns 1, otherwise it returns 0. A return value of -1 indicates an error. In this case, errno is set to: EBADF, bad file number.

2.2.6 filelength

The prototype for filelength is the following:

```
long filelength( int handle );
```

The function returns the length of the file with the specified handle, in bytes. If there is an error, the function returns -1L and errno is set to EBADF, bad file number.

2.2.7 getftime, setftime

These functions are available only under MS-DOS and are not UNIX compatible. The prototypes are

```
int getftime( int handle, struct ftime *ftime_date );
int setftime( int handle, struct ftime *ftime_date );
```

These functions get/set the file time and date for the specified handle. The ftime structure gets contains the file's time and date.

This structure is defined as:

```
struct ftime
{
    unsigned ft_tsec  : 5;
    unsigned ft_min   : 6;
    unsigned ft_hour  : 5;
    unsigned ft_day   : 5;
    unsigned ft_month : 4;
    unsigned ft_year  : 7;
}
```

A value of 0 is returned by these functions if successful otherwise they return -1. The variable errno is set to one of the following if the return value is -1:

```
EINVFNC    Invalid function number
EBADF      Bad file number
```

2.2.8 isatty

The prototype for function isatty is

```
int isatty( int handle );
```

Function isatty checks to see whether the file associated with the specified file handle is a terminal, a console, a printer, or a serial port. If the file is a character device, isatty returns a nonzero integer, otherwise it returns 0.

2.2.9 lseek

The prototype for function lseek is the following:

```
long lseek( int handle, long offset, int fromwhere );
```

Function lseek sets the file pointer of the file with the specified handle to a position that is offset bytes from the value fromwhere. The parameter fromwhere must be 0, 1, or 2 associated with the constants:

```
SEEK_SET (0)   file beginning
SEEK_CUR (1)   current file pointer
SEEK_END (2)   end-of-file
```

The function returns the offset of the new position measured in bytes from the beginning of the file. If there is an error, the function returns -1 and errno is set to:

```
EBADF  Bad file number
EINVAL Invalid argument
```

2.2.10 open

The user should include <fcntl.h> and <sys\stat.h>.
The function open has the following prototype:

```
int open( char *filename, int access [, int permiss ] );
```

Function open opens the file with the specified file name and prepares it for reading or writing as determined by the value of access. The values of access that may be "ORed" together are provided in two lists. Only one value from the first list may be used but any combination of values may be used from the second list.

List 1—Access values

O_RDONLY   Open for reading only
O_WRONLY   Open for writing only
O_RDWR   Open for reading and writing

List 2—Access values

O_APPEND   The file pointer is set to the end of the file prior to each write
O_CREAT   If the file exists the flag has no effect. Otherwise the file is created and the bits of permiss are used to set the file attribute bits.
O_TRUNC   If the file exists, its length is truncated to 0.
O_BINARY   The file is opened in binary mode.
O_TEXT   The file is opened in text mode.

If O_CREAT is set, then the optional argument permiss may be set to one of the following:

S_IWRITE	Permission to write
S_IREAD	Permission to read
S_IREAD ⎮ S_IWRITE	Permission to read and write

On a successful completion, function open returns the file handle and the file pointer is set to the beginning of the file. On error the value returned is -1 and errno is set to one of the following:

ENOENT	Path or file name not found
EMFILE	Too many files open
EACCES	Permission denied
EINVACC	Invalid access code

2.2.11   read

The prototype for function read is the following:

```
int read( int handle, void *buffer, int nbytes );
```

The function read attempts to read nbytes from the file with the specified file handle to the buffer that is specified.

For a file opened in text mode, read removes carriage returns and reports end-of-file when a CTRL-Z character is read.

The file handle is obtained from one of the functions creat, open, dup, or dup2. These functions are described in other subsections under Section 2.2.

After a read operation is completed, the file pointer is advanced by the number of bytes read.

After a successful completion, the number of bytes read into the buffer is returned. In text mode, read does not count carriage returns or Ctrl-Z characters in the number of bytes read.

If the end-of-file is encountered, the value 0 is returned. If an error occurs, the value -1 is returned and errno is set to one of the following:

```
EACCES  Permission denied
EBADF   Bad file number
```

2.2.12   setmode

The prototype for function setmode is the following:

```
int setmode( int handle, unsigned mode );
```

The function setmode sets the mode of the open file with the specified handle to one of the following, from <fcntl.h>:

```
O_BINARY        Binary mode
O_TEXT  Text mode
```

If the function is successful it returns 0, otherwise it returns -1 and errno is set to EINVAL, invalid argument.

2.2.13 tell

The function tell has the following prototype:

```
long tell( int handle );
```

This function returns the current position of the file pointer.

2.2.14 write

The prototype for function write is

```
int write( int handle, void *buffer, int nbytes );
```

Function write attempts to write nbytes to buffer from the specified file handle. For text files a linefeed character is replaced by the CR-LF combination.

The value returned is the actual number of bytes written. If this is less than nbtyes, a disk full error has occurred.

For files opened with O_APPEND, the file pointer is positioned to EOF before writing the data.

In the event of an error, function write returns -1 and errno is set to one of the following:

```
EACCES  Permission denied
EBADF   Bad file number
```

2.3 Important Nonstandard Library Functions

In addition to the Berkeley UNIX V.3 standard library supported by Turbo C, there are MS-DOS specific functions and macros that offer the Turbo C programmer enormous power specific to the DOS environment.

The use of many DOS specific functions and macros are illustrated in the software utilities presented in Part 2 of this book.

The MS-DOS specific function prototypes given in dos.h, bios.h, and dir.h are listed.

2.3.1 Header file dir.h

Table 2.7 lists the functions prototyped in the header file dir.h. A few of the functions are UNIX compatible, while most are MS-DOS specific. The compatibility of each function is indicated in Table 2.7. The reader is urged to consult the Borland *Turbo C Reference Guide* for details concerning each function.

Table 2.7   *Functions Prototyped in dir.h*

Function	UNIX Compatible	Meaning
chdir	Yes	Change directory
findfirst	No	Find first file
findnext	No	Find next file
fnmerge	No	Make new file name
fnsplit	No	Split file name
getcurdir	No	Get current dir.
getcwd	No	Get working dir.
getdisk	No	Get current drive
mkdir	Yes	Make directory
mktemp	Yes	Make unique file name
rmdir	Yes	Remove directory
searchpath	No	Search for file
setdisk	No	Set current drive

2.3.2   Header file dos.h

Table 2.8 lists the functions prototyped in header file dos.h. All of these functions are MS-DOS specific. The reader is urged to consult the Borland *Turbo C Reference Guide* for details concerning each function.

Table 2.8   *Functions Prototyped in dos.h*

Function	Purpose
absread	Read specific disk sector
abswrite	Write specific disk sector
bdos	MS-DOS system calls
bdosptr	MS-DOS system calls
country	Formatting for country dependent data
ctrlbrk	Sets a new control break handler
disable	Disables interrupts
dosexterr	Fills in DOS error structure after failure
enable	Enable interrupts
FP_OFF	Returns offset of far pointer
FP_SEG	Returns segment of far pointer

Table 2.8 *(continued)*

freemem	Frees previously allocated block
getinterrupt	Gets interrupt
getcbrk	Gets control break interrupt
getdfree	Gets free disk space
getdta	Gets disk transfer area
getfat	Gets file allocation table
getfatd	Gets file allocation table
getpsp	Gets program segment prefix
getvect	Gets interrupt vector entry
getverify	Returns current state of verify flag
harderr	Sets hardware error handler
hardresume	Hardware error handler function
hardretn	Hardware error handler function
inport	Inputs from hardware port
inportb	Inputs from hardware port
int86	Software interrupt
int86x	Software interrupt
intr	Software interrupt
keep	Exit and remain resident
MK_FP	Make far pointer from seg and off
outport	Outputs to hardware
outportb	Outputs to hardware
parsfnm	Parses a string
peek	Examine specific memory location
peekb	Examine specific memory location
poke	Put data at specific memory location
pokeb	Put data at specific memory location
randbrd	Random block read
randbwr	Random block write
segread	Reads segment registers
setdta	Sets disk transfer area
setvect	Sets interrupt vector
setverify	Sets verify flag
sleep	Suspends execution for interval
unlink	Deletes a file

2.3.3 Header file bios.h

Table 2.9 lists the functions prototyped in the header file bios.h. All of these functions are MS-DOS specific. The reader is urged to consult the Borland *Turbo C Reference Guide* for details concerning each function.

Table 2.9 *Functions Prototyped in bios.h*

Function	Purpose
bioscom	RS232 communications
biosdisk	Disk operations directly from BIOS
biosequip	Checks equipment
bioskey	Keyboard operations
biomemory	Returns memory size
biosprint	Printer functions
biostime	Returns time of day

3

Coding Considerations

3.1 Memory Models

The size of a pointer in Turbo C is dependent on the memory model that is used when compiling a program. Programs may be compiled with six memory models: tiny, small (the default mode), medium, compact, large, and huge. Code that uses special Turbo C extensions to exploit a particular memory model will not be portable.

A program has storage requirements from four sources: program code, program data, memory allocated by the programmer dynamically (in the heap), and transitory memory allocated by the compiler while the program is running (in the stack).

The memory area for program code remains constant throughout a program. Likewise, the memory area provided for static data remains constant throughout a program. The memory required in the heap area changes as a program runs depending on how much memory the programmer allocates using the functions calloc and malloc. Likewise, the memory required in the stack area is constantly changing as automatic variables are activated within functions, and parameters are stored on the stack because of function calls.

Table 3.1 presents the memory models supported by Turbo C, with explanations of each model.

Table 3.1 *Memory Models Supported by Turbo C*

Tiny:	All four segment registers (CS, DS, SS, ES) are set to the same address. There is 64K of memory available for program code, static data, dynamically allocated data, and the stack. This memory model is quite constraining and should be used only when memory is scarce.
	Pointer variables are only two bytes (near pointers) in this memory model. Only the offset within the fixed memory segment is represented by a pointer variable.
Small:	The memory segment for program code is 64K. The stack and near heap and static data share a 64K segment of memory. This memory model is the default model that serves many small to medium applications.
	Pointer variables are only two bytes (near pointers) in this memory model. Only the offset within the fixed memory segment is represented by a pointer variable.
Medium:	The memory area for program code is limited by 1MB. That is, far pointers are used for code. The stack and the near heap and static data share a memory segment of 64K as with the small model. This memory model should be used for very large programs that do not have large data requirements.
	All addresses (pointers) in the code portion use far pointers (segment and offset) and are 4 bytes in size. That is, all function calls are performed as far calls and all returns from functions are far. Data pointers are near pointers, which are 2 bytes.
Compact:	The memory area for program code is 64K. The memory area for data is 1MB. The static data is limited to 64K and the stack, as in all models, is limited to 64K. This memory model should be used for small to medium size programs that have large data requirements.
	Pointers in the code portion are near pointers (2 bytes). Data pointers are far pointers, which are 4 bytes.
Large:	The memory area for program code is 1MB. The memory area for static data is 64K. The data area is limited by 1MB. This memory model is required by many larger applications.
	Pointers for both program code and data are far pointers, requiring 4 bytes. Static data is limited to 64K in this model.
Huge:	The same as the large memory model only static data can total more than 64K. The huge memory model does not imply huge pointers.

Turbo C defines seven reserved words not found in the draft ANSI standard. These are near, far, huge, _cs, _ds, _es, and _ss. These can be used as modifiers to pointers.

The reserved words _cs, _ds, _es, and _ss are 16 bit pointer modifiers corresponding to the segment registers CS, DS, ES, and SS. They are not names for the segment registers. Their upper case equivalents _CS, _DS, etc. along with _AX, _BX, etc. are psuedovariables that map directly to the 80x86 registers.

The effect of the lower case _cs, _ds, _es, etc. is to declare a near pointer (16 bit offset) whose implied segment is the one named.

As an example, the declaration,

```
int _ss *p;
```

means that p contains a 16 bit offset into the stack segment.

Functions and pointers can be modified with the reserved words near, far, and huge.

As an example, the following segment of code is taken from the spelling checker utility described in Chapter 7.

The buffer variable must hold up to 100,000 bytes of text. The program is compiled with the compact memory model so in this model, no single pointer variable can hold more than 64K of data.

The dynamic array, buffer, is declared using the nonstandard huge storage specifier. The call to the nonstandard farmalloc function attempts to allocate 100,000 bytes in the heap, if it is available. If it is not available, the error message, "Not enough memory for buffer" is output.

```
/* Code segment taken from spelling checker application */ #define
buffersize 100000

char huge *buffer;

if ( ( buffer = ( char huge * )
        farmalloc( buffersize ) ) == NULL )
  error( "\aNot enough memory for buffer", "" );
```

The compiler switch that is used determines the memory model and the function and data pointers used. If no compiler switch is explicitly used to set the memory model, the small model is used by default. As seen earlier, it is sometimes desirable or necessary to override the default pointer size for specific functions or data. This can be done by using the modifiers near, far, or huge.

An example of a memory pointer modifier used in declaring a function is the following:

```
float near example( int x, char *s )
{
  . . .
}
```

If the program containing the function example is compiled using the large memory model, then because of the modifier, all calls to it are near calls saving stack and execution time overhead. The function example may only be invoked within the code segment in which it was compiled. This restriction can potentially cause problems.

3.2   DOS and BIOS Calls

Turbo C allows the user to access directly the MS-DOS operating system or the ROM BIOS by making "DOS calls" or "BIOS calls." The reader may wish to consult the outstanding reference, *Programmer's Guide to the IBM PC*, by Peter Norton, MicroSoft Press, 1985, for a wealth of information concerning the dozens of DOS and BIOS calls that are available. The file dos.h provides the function prototypes, structures, and macro definitions that support DOS and BIOS calls.

Listing 3.1 presents some important structures that are defined in the "include file", dos.h.

Listing 3.1   Important structures defined in dos.h

```
struct WORDREGS
{
  unsigned int ax, bx, cx, dx, si, di, cflag, flags;
};


struct BYTEREGS
{
  unsigned char  al, ah, bl, bh, cl, ch, dl, dh;
};


union REGS
{
  struct      WORDREGS x;
  struct      BYTEREGS h;
};


struct SREGS
{
  unsigned int es;
  unsigned int cs;
  unsigned int ss;
  unsigned int ds;
};
```

Listing 3.2 presents the prototypes for some important nonstandard functions and macros that support DOS and BIOS calls.

Listing 3.2 Prototypes for important functions from dos.h that support DOS and BIOS calls

```
int int86( int intno, union REGS *inregs,
           union REGS *outregs );

int int86x( int intno, union REGS *inregs,
            union REGS *outregs, struct SREGS *segregs );

int intdos( union REGS *inregs, union REGS *outregs );

int intdosx( union REGS *inregs, union REGS *outregs,
             struct SREGS *segregs );

#define FP_OFF(fp) ((unsigned)(fp))

#define FP_SEG(fp) ((unsigned)((unsigned long)(fp) >> 16))
```

The two macros FP_OFF and FP_SEG return the offset and segment of the argument, fp.

We illustrate the use of BIOS calls in Listing 3.3.

This code includes functions for setting and fetching the current cursor position in the text mode. The function, gotoxy, allows the user to set the horizontal and vertical coordinates of the cursor. The function, getxy, allows the user to fetch the horizontal and vertical coordinates of the cursor.

All the ROM BIOS video services are obtained using interrupt 16 (hexidecimal 0x10). The number of the service (there are 16 services—see Norton book referenced above) is specified in the ah register.

For cursor position setting (fetching), the page number is specified in the bh register. The row number is set (returned) in the dh register. The column number is set (returned) in the dl register.

Function gotoxy uses ROM BIOS video service 2 whereas function getxy uses ROM BIOS video service 3. These values are set in the ax register. Functions gotoxy and getxy set register bx to 0 for page 0. The dh and dl registers are used to assign or retrieve the horizontal and vertical coordinates of the cursor position.

It is noted that these functions are implemented in Version 1.5. They are included here to provided the reader with insight in how BIOS calls can be made from Turbo C.

Listing 3.3 Illustration of BIOS calls
Getting and setting cursor position

```
#include <dos.h>

/* Sets the horizontal and vertical cursor position
**
** ARGUMENTS
**   h  horizontal cursor position (0 .. 79)
**   v  vertical cursor position   (0 .. 24)
```
(continued)

```
**
** RETURNS
**    none
*/
void gotoxy( unsigned h, unsigned v )
{
  union REGS regs;

  if ( ( h >= 0 ) && ( h <= 79 ) && ( v >= 0 ) && ( v <= 24 ) )
    if ( ( h != 79 ) || ( v != 24 ) )
    {
      regs.h.ah = 0x02;
      regs.h.bh = 0;
      regs.h.dl = h;
      regs.h.dh = v;
      int86( 0x10, &regs, &regs );
    }
}



/* Returns the horizontal and vertical cursor position
**
** ARGUMENTS
**    h  horizontal cursor position (0 .. 79)
**    v  vertical cursor position   (0 .. 24)
**
** RETURNS
**    none
*/
void getxy( unsigned *h, unsigned *v )
{
  union REGS regs;

  regs.h.ah = 0x03;
  regs.h.bh = 0x0;
  int86( 0x10, &regs, &regs );
  *h = regs.h.dl;
  *v = regs.h.dh;
}
```

Listings 3.4 and 3.5 illustrate DOS calls.

In Listing 3.4, function gtime returns the current clock time in hours, minutes, seconds, and hundreths of a second. The number of the DOS call for this service is 0x2C. This value is assigned to register ah. The current time in hours is returned in the register ch. The current time in minutes is returned in the register cl. The current time in seconds is returned in the register dh. Finally, the current time in hundreths is returned in register dl.

Listing 3.4 Illustration of DOS call
The current clock time

```
#include <dos.h>

/* This function gets the current clock time
**
** ARGUMENTS
**    hour      The current hour       (0-23)
**    minute    The current minute     (0-59)
**    sec       The current second     (0-60)
**    hund      The current hundreth   (0-99)
**
** RETURNS
**    nothing
*/
void gtime( unsigned *hour,
            unsigned *minute,
            unsigned *sec,
            unsigned *hund )
{
  union REGS inreg, outreg;

  inreg.h.ah = 0x2C;
  intdos( &inreg, &outreg );
  *sec = outreg.h.dh;
  *hund = outreg.h.dl;
  *hour = outreg.h.ch;
  *minute = outreg.h.cl;
}
```

In Listing 3.5, a file with name filename is opened for reading and writing. The number of this DOS service is 0x3D. Setting the low-order byte of register ax to 02 specifies that the file is to be opened for both reading and writing. The offset address of the filename is assigned to the dx register. The ds register must be assigned to the segment of the filename if one of the large memory models is used. Then the DOS call function, intdosx, is used. Otherwise the intdos function is used. Conditional compilation is used to allow the appropriate block of code, based on the given memory model, to be used.

The error return value is given in the cflag register. For a normal return (error = 0), the file handle is returned in the ax register. Otherwise, the ax register contains the error return value. An error return of 2 means that the file was not found. An error return of 5 means that access is denied. Finally, an error return of 12 means an invalid access code.

Listing 3.5 Illustration of DOS call
Opening a file

```
/*  This function opens a file, filename
**
```
(continued)

```
**  ARGUMENTS
**     filename  The disk directory name of the file to open
**
**  RETURNS
**     If error not equal to 0
**     2  - File not found
**     5  - Access denied
**     12 - Invalid access code
**     If error equal to 0
**     file handle is returned
*/

int error;

#include <dos.h>

int openfile( char* filename )
{
  union REGS, inreg, outreg;

  inreg.h.ah = 0x3D;
  inreg.h.al = 0x02; /* Read and write access */
  #if defined( __COMPACT__ ) || defined( __LARGE__ ) || \
      defined( __HUGE__ )
  inreg.x.dx = FP_OFF( filename );
  segreg.ds = FP_SEG( filename );
  intdosx( &inreg, &outreg, &segreg );
  #else
  inreg.x.dx = ( unsigned ) filename;
  intdos( &inreg, &outreg );
  #endif
  error = outreg.x.cflag;
  return outreg.x.ax;
}
```

3.3   DOS Calls vs. Turbo C Library Functions

A Turbo C programmer often has a choice of accomplishing a low-level task with a DOS call, a BIOS call, or with a Turbo C library function invocation. Although these methods accomplish the same task, the library function call is often much more portable and spares the programmer the necessity of writing and testing low-level code.

As an example, suppose a programmer wishes to trap keyboard input with a function that returns 1 if one or more keys have been hit (character(s) in the type ahead buffer) and 0 if no key has been hit.

A function that accomplishes this task with a DOS call is given in Listing 3.6.

DOS call 0x0B is used for this purpose. If the value returned in the register al is equal to 255, the type ahead buffer contains one or more characters. Otherwise, this buffer is empty.

Listing 3.6   Function for trapping keyboard input

```
/* Determines whether a key has been hit
**
** ARGUMENTS
**    none
**
** RETURNS
**    0 - key not hit
**    1 - key hit
*/

#include <dos.h>

int keypressed( void )
{
  union REGS regs;

  regs.h.ah = 0x0B;
  intdos( &regs, &regs );
  return ( regs.h.al == 255 );
}
```

The equivalent Turbo C function is kbhit. The prototype for this function, from conio.h, is given as:

```
int kbhit( void );
```

3.4   Direct Memory Access

It is often necessary to access or assign values to specified memory locations. A common example of this is writing to, or reading from, the bit-mapped memory area that corresponds to the video terminal.

The functions peek and poke read and write to specific memory addresses. These functions are nonportable. Their implementation is dependent on the compiler and the underlying architecture of the computer. The Turbo C library contains both peek and poke functions. The prototypes for these functions are given in dos.h and are

```
int peek( int segment, unsigned offset );

char peekb(int segment, unsigned offset );

void poke( int segment, int offset, int value );

void pokeb( int segment, int offset, char value );
```

If these functions are invoked when dos.h has been included, they will be treated as macros that expand to inline code. If dos.h is not included, the functions rather than the macros will be invoked.

Functions peek and peekb allow either a word or byte to be accessed from a specified segment and offset address. Functions poke and pokeb allow either a word or byte to be assigned to a specified segment and offset address.

Examples of the use of peekb and pokeb are given in Listing 3.7. The address, 0xB000, corresponds to the starting address of the bit-mapped memory area of the monochrome video card or the hercules card. The address, 0xB800 corresponds to the starting address of the bit-mapped area of the color adapter card. Other cards have different starting addresses given in the user's guide accompanying the video card.

In text mode, the bit-mapped memory area begins with the top left corner of the screen. There are two bytes for each screen position. The first of these two bytes contains the character value. The second of these two bytes contains the attribute. The bytes for succeeding characters follow from left to right and from top to bottom. The offset to any screen character from the starting address is given by:

```
offset = ( row_number * 80 ) + ( column_number * 2 )
```

The odd byte offsets are the attribute bytes. The attributes include normal, reverse, underline, highlight, and blinking.

The call to pokeb(hercules, 84, 66) puts the character, 'B', (ASCII value 66) in column 42, row 0. The call to pokeb(hercules, 86, 67) puts the character, 'C', in column 43, row 0.

Listing 3.7 Example of peek and poke functions

```
#include <stdio.h>
#include <dos.h>

#define hercules 0xB000

main()
{
  unsigned char ch;

  pokeb( hercules, 84, 66 );
  pokeb( hercules, 86, 67 );

  ch = peekb( hercules, 84 );
  printf( "\nThe value of ch = %c", ch );
  ch = peekb( hercules, 86 );
  printf( "\nThe value of ch = %c", ch );
}
```

Listing 3.8 presents a function for writing characters to the bit-mapped memory area of the video terminal and a short test program. If a monochrome card is installed in your system, add the line #define MONOCHROME where shown in the comment.

Listing 3.8 Function for writing to bit-mapped memory area and test program

```c
#include <stdio.h>
#include <dos.h>
#include "util.h"
/* This library is defined later in the book */

/*
   Add the line #define MONOCHROME if such a card is
   installed.
*/

#if defined( MONOCHROME )
#define address 0xB000
#else
#define address 0xB800
#endif

/* Write message directly to bit-mapped area with given
** attributes.  A monochrome or color adapter card
** is assumed.
**
** ARGUMENTS
**    fore_attrib, back_attrib    attributes
**        for IBM Monochrome adapter
**        _____
**
**        fore_attrib/back_attrib      Meaning
**        0/0                          Do not display
**        1/0                          Underline
**        7/0                          Normal
**        0/7                          Reverse video
**        Add 8 to fore_attrib to intensify
**        Add 8 to back_attrib to blink
**
**    message                          pointer to message
**
** RETURNS
**    nothing
*/
void write_string( unsigned fore_attrib,
                   unsigned back_attrib,
                   char *message )
{
  unsigned char attribute =
    ( back_attrib << 4 ) | ( fore_attrib & 0x0F );          (continued)
```

```c
    unsigned x, y;
    unsigned offset;

    getxy( &x, &y );
    offset = y * 80 + x * 2;

    /* Transfer message to the screen */
    while ( *message )
    {
      pokeb( address, offset++, *message++ );
      pokeb( address, offset++, attribute );
    }
}

main()
{
    /* Normal display */
    printf( "\n\n" );
    write_string( 7, 0, "This is a test" );

    /* Underlined display */
    printf( "\n\n" );
    write_string( 1, 0, "This is a test" );

    /* Reverse video display */
    printf( "\n\n" );
    write_string( 0, 7, "This is a test" );

    /* Reverse video blinking display */
    printf( "\n\n" );
    write_string( 0, 15, "This is a test" );
}
```

3.5 Assembly Coding

We illustrate the process of linking an assembly language module to a C program in this section. The reader is directed to books on assembly language programming for details on how to write assembly language programs. We assume in this section that the reader has experience in writing assembly language modules.

The assembly language module that we wish to link to is given in Listing 3.9. Assembly language implementations of peekb and pokeb are provided. To avoid any name conflicts with the dos.h peek and poke functions, the prefix, asm, is used in front of each function name. An underscore character, _, is required for each public identifier that is to be referenced in the C program.

It is assumed that the name of the assembly language file is spoke.asm and the object file is spoke.obj.

Listing 3.9 Assembly language module for peek and poke
Small memory model implementation

```
_TEXT     SEGMENT BYTE PUBLIC 'CODE'
          ASSUME cs:_TEXT

          PUBLIC _asm_peek, _asm_peekb, _asm_poke, _asm_pokeb

          ;peekb returns the value stored at the
          ;memory location segment:offset.

          ;pokeb stores the byte value at the
          ;memory location segment:offset.

_asm_peekb   PROC NEAR                   ;CALL peek( seg, off )
          push    bx
          push    ds
          push    bp
          mov     bp, sp
          mov     ax, [bp] + 8     ;segment from stack
          mov     ds, ax
          mov     ax, [bp] + 10    ;offset from stack
          mov     bx, ax
          mov     ax, 0            ;clear ax
          mov     al, [bx]         ;leave function value in al
          pop     bp
          pop     ds
          pop     bx
          ret
_asm_peekb   ENDP


_asm_pokeb   PROC NEAR             ;CALL poke( seg, off, value )
          push    bx
          push    ds
          push    bp
          mov     bp, sp
          mov     ax, [bp] + 8     ;segment from stack
          mov     ds, ax
          mov     ax, [bp] + 10    ;offset from stack
          mov     bx, ax
          mov     ax, 0            ;clear ax
          mov     ax, [bp] + 12    ;value from stack
          mov     [bx], al
          pop     bp
          pop     ds
          pop     bx
          ret
_asm_pokeb   ENDP
```

(continued)

```
_TEXT     ENDS
          END
```

A test program that exercises the functions asm_pokeb and asm_peekb is given in Listing 3.10.

Listing 3.10   A C program that links to the assembly language peek and poke functions

```c
#include <stdio.h>

#define hercules 0xB000

main()
{
  extern char asm_peekb( int segment, unsigned offset );

  extern void asm_pokeb( int segment, int offset,
                         char value );

  unsigned char ch;

  asm_pokeb( hercules, 84, 66 );
  asm_pokeb( hercules, 86, 67 );

  ch = asm_peekb( hercules, 84 );
  printf( "\nThe value of ch = %c", ch );
  ch = asm_peekb( hercules, 86 );
  printf( "\nThe value of ch = %c", ch );
}
```

To compile and link the test program in Listing 3.10 in the small memory model, the user should invoke the compiler as,

```
tcc test.c spoke.asm
```

The masm.exe program will be invoked automatically by the compiler. This creates object code for the spoke assembly code. Then the two object files will be linked to obtain an executable file.

3.6   *Use of Static Storage Specifier*

The static storage specifier can be used to hide variables or functions from the linker. A global variable that is defined as static is visible only in the file in which it is defined. Similarly, a function that is defined with the static specifier can only be invoked within the given file. A function that is defined without a static specifier (that is, the normal case) may be invoked anywhere in the software system if the function is correctly prototyped by the caller using the keyword extern.

Static specifiers may therefore be used to great advantage in desiging reusable software modules. In order to hide and protect variables and functions that client modules should not access and to avoid naming conflicts with client modules, the Turbo C software developer should use static specifiers wherever appropriate.

4

Generic Software Components

The goal of this chapter is to illustrate the construction of several powerful generic software components. As indicated in Section 1.3, a generic software component encapsulates a set of logically related operations that may be performed on arbitrary data.

Whenever an algorithm is invariant with respect to the type of the underlying data that is being manipulated, the algorithm is a candidate for a generic implementation.

Sorting algorithms are a candidate for generic implementation. An algorithm for sorting an array depends only on the presence of a comparison operation that allows any two elements of the underlying data set to be compared. If such a comparison function is provided as an input parameter to the generic sorting function, this function requires no knowledge of the underlying data that is being ordered. In Section 4.1 an efficient generic sorting function is examined.

A search tree is another example of a structure in which the basic manipulations of insertion, deletion, and lookup are independent of the underlying data being stored in the structure. To facilitate a generic search, the user must supply through a function parameter a definition of comparison, that enables any two elements of the underlying data set to be compared. In Sections 4.2 and 4.3, a generic search table and a super-efficient generic search table are presented.

The reader may wish to review Section 1.3 before continuing with this chapter.

4.1   *Generic Sorting*

Many super-efficient sorting algorithms have been developed. Among the best and most widely used in this class are quicksort, mergesort, and heapsort. In this section we use the heapsort algorithm as the basis for developing a generic sorting function. This algorithm is particularly desirable because the data is sorted in-place. That is, the storage provided in the input data array is used to rearrange the data during the sorting manipulations. No auxiliary storage is required.

4.1.1 The Heapsort Algorithm

This section briefly reviews the heapsort algorithm. The reader who is unfamiliar with this algorithm may wish to consult a data structures or algorithms book for more details. The algorithm is presented in a language independent manner. Later it is modified and implemented in C.

A heap structure is a special type of binary tree. Specifically, a heap of size n is a binary tree containing n nodes that satisfies the following three conditions:

1. The key value of each node is less than or equal to the value of its parent.
2. Every leaf node in the tree is at level k or at level k + 1.
3. If any node in the tree has a right descendant at level k + 1, then all its left descendants which are leaf nodes are also at level k + 1.

The reader should recall that there is a useful one-to-one mapping between the elements in an array and the nodes in a binary tree. In Figure 4.1, the binary tree corresponding to the array x[1], x[2], ... , x[19] is shown. If i corresponds to an index location in the array x, the operation,

```
i = 2 * i
```

corresponds to moving from the node i to its left child if one exists, and the operation,

```
i = 2 * i + 1
```

corresponds to the moving from the node i to its right child, if one exists. If k > 1 corresponds to an index location in the array, the operation,

```
k = k / 2
```

corresponds to moving from the node i to its parent.

It follows from the definition of a heap structure that the root node must contain the largest key value. This feature of the heap is exploited in the heapsort algorithm. This algorithm is presented in Listing 4.1.

The formheap procedure interchanges appropriate elements of the array (that is, exchanges appropriate nodes of the tree) so that the resulting array (that is, tree structure) is a heap. The algorithm for accomplishing this is given in Listing 4.2.

Then within the for loop, the element x[1] (largest element) is exchanged with the element x[i]. As a consequence of this, the structure is no longer a heap. The procedure rebuildheap, given in Listing 4.3, exchanges appropriate elements in the array (that is, exchanges appropriate nodes of the tree) to restore the heap property.

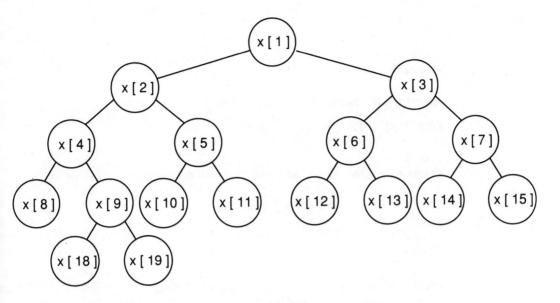

Figure 4.1 Heap data structure

By repeating this sequence of actions, each time with the value of i decremented by one, the largest value in the array is deposited in the position x[n], the second largest value in the array is deposited in the position x[n - 1], the third largest value in the array is deposited in the position x[n - 2], etc. until the entire array is sorted. Both the formheap procedure and the rebuild procedure are extremely efficient thus accounting for the overall efficiency of the heapsort algorithm.

Listing 4.1 Heapsort algorithm

```
Data : x[ i ], i = 1, ..., n.
The data consists of any array of data for which an ordering
relationship exists.

formheap( x, n )
for ( i = n; i >= 2; i- )
  interchange x[ 1 ] and x[ i ]
  rebuildheap( x, i - 1 )
end loop
```

Listing 4.2 Formheap algorithm

```
Data : x[ i ], i = 1, ..., n.

for ( node = 2; node <= k; node++ )
  i := node
  j := i div 2 (* j is parent of i *)
  while ( i != 1 ) and ( x[ j ] < x[ i ] ) loop
    interchange x[ i ] and x[ j ]
```

(continued)

```
      i := j
      j := i div 2
   end loop
end loop
```

Listing 4.3 Rebuild heap algorithm

```
Data : x[ i ], i = 1, ..., n.

i := 1
/* Compute the larger of node i's two children */
j := 2
if ( k >= 3 ) and ( x[ 3 ] > x[ 2 ] )
then
   j := 3
end if

while ( j <= k ) and ( x[ j ] > x[ i ] ) loop
   interchange x[ i ] and x[ j ]
   i := j
   j := 2 * i
   if j + 1 <= k
   then
     if x[ j + 1 ] > x [ j ]
     then
        j := j + 1
     end if
   end if
end loop
```

A nongeneric heapsort function that is based on the algorithms of Listings 4.1, 4.2, and 4.3 and sorts an array of floating point numbers is presented in Listing 4.4. The reader should note the discrepancy between the implementation details of functions formheap, rebuildheap and heapsort and the algorithms given in Listings 4.1, 4.2, and 4.3. This discrepancy is due to the index range of the array x used as parameters in these functions. In the algorithm, the range is assumed to be from 1 to n. In the C code of Listing 4.4, the range is from 0 to n - 1. The reader is urged to verify that the code of Listing 4.4 maps easily to the algorithms of Listings 4.1, 4.2, and 4.3.

Listing 4.4 A nongeneric heapsort function that sorts an array of floating point numbers

```
void interchange( float *ptr1, float *ptr2 )
{
   float temp = *ptr2;
   *ptr2 = *ptr1;
   *ptr1 = temp;
}
```

```c
void formheap( float *x, int k )
{
  int node, i, j;

  for ( node = 1; node < k; node++ )
  {
    i = node;
    j = ( ( i + 1 ) / 2 ) - 1;
    while ( i != 0 && x[ j ] <= x[ i ] )
    {
      interchange( x + i , x + j );
      i = j;
      j = ( ( i + 1 ) / 2 ) - 1;
    }
  }
}

void rebuildheap( float *x, int k )
{
  int i = 0;
  int j = 1;

  if ( k >= 2 && x[ 2 ] > x[ 1 ] )  j = 2;
  while ( j <= k && x[ j ] > x[ i ] )
  {
    interchange( x + i, x + j );
    i = j;
    j = ( 2 * ( i + 1 ) ) - 1;
    if ( j + 1 <= k )
     if ( x[ j + 1 ] > x[ j ] )
       j++;
  }
}

void heapsort( float *x, int n )
{
  int i;

  formheap( x, n );
  for ( i = n - 1; i >= 1; i-- )
  {
    interchange( x, x + i );
    rebuildheap( x, i - 1 );
  }
}
```

4.1.2 Construction of Generic Heapsort Function

The prototype for a generic heapsort function is given in Listing 4.5. The user-defined function that compares two elements of the underlying base type that is being sorted is provided as the fourth parameter of function sort. The type definition,

```
typedef int ( *compare_type ) ( void *element1,
                                 void *element2 );
```

establishes a template that the user's client program must employ. A sample compare_type function is given in Listing 4.7. The prototype for this function corresponds to the template given above in the type definition. A type cast, (int *) is used to convert the pointer to void to a pointer to integer. The result of this conversion is dereferenced to obtain an integer value. This illustrates the basic strategy for constructing any compare_type function.

Listing 4.6 presents the definition of the generic heapsort function, sort.

If parameter x, declared as, char *x, is the address of the array of data, the operation interchange(x[j], x[i]) is accomplished as follows:

```
interchange( x + j * elem_size, x + i * elem_size ).
```

The following loop, inside of function interchange, performs a byte-by-byte exchange of element1 with element2:

```
for ( k = 0; k < elem_size; k++ )
{
  temp = element1[ k ];
  element1[ k ] = element2[ k ];
  element2[ k ] = temp;
}
```

The reader should compare the code of Listing 4.6 with the code of Listing 4.4.

Listing 4.5 Prototypes for generic heapsort function

```
/* Prototype for generic heap sort function
   File gheapsrt.h
*/

typedef int ( *compare_type ) ( void *element1,
                                void *element2 );
/* Functions of compare_type return:
      -1 if element1 < element2
       0 if element1 = element2
       1 if element1 > element2
*/

/* Generic heap sort function
**
** ARGUMENTS
```

```
**    data       - Array of elements to be sorted
**    num_elem   - Number of elements to be sorted
**    elem_size  - Size of each element, in bytes
**    compare    - User defined function for comparing
**                    two elements:
**                        Returns 1 if element1 < element2
**                        Otherwise returns SA0
**
** RETURNS
**    nothing
*/
void sort( void *data, int num_elem, int elem_size,
           compare_type compare );
```

Listing 4.6 Definitions for generic heapsort function

```
/* A Generic sort function
   File gheapsrt.c
*/


typedef int ( *compare_type )( void *element1,
                               void *element2 );


/* Generic heap sort function
**
** ARGUMENTS
**    data       - Array of elements to be sorted
**    num_elem   - Number of elements to be sorted
**    elem_size  - Size of each element, in bytes
**    compare    - User defined function for comparing
**                    two elements:
**                        Returns 1 if element1 < element2
**                        Otherwise returns 0
**
** RETURNS
**    nothing
*/
void sort( void *data, int num_elem, int elem_size,
           compare_type compare )
{
  extern void interchange( char *element1, char *element2,
                           int elem_size );

  extern void formheap( char *x, int k, int elem_size,
                        compare_type compare );

  extern void rebuildheap( char *x, int k, int elem_size,
                           compare_type compare );
```

(continued)

```
    int i;
    char* dta = ( char * ) data;

    formheap( dta, num_elem, elem_size, compare );
    for ( i = num_elem - 1; i >= 1; i- )
    {
      interchange( dta, dta + i * elem_size, elem_size );
      rebuildheap( dta, i - 1, elem_size, compare );
    }
}


/* Generic interchange function
**
** ARGUMENTS
**    element1, element2 - Address of each element
**    elem_size- Size, in bytes, of each element
**
** RETURNS
**    nothing
*/
static void interchange( char *element1, char *element2,
                         int elem_size )
{
  char temp;
  int k;

  for ( k = 0; k < elem_size; k++ )
  {
    temp = element1[ k ];
    element1[ k ] = element2[ k ];
    element2[ k ] = temp;
  }
}


/* Generic formheap function
**
** ARGUMENTS
**    x        - The starting address of the array of data
**    k        - The number of nodes to form into a heap
**    elem_size - Size, in bytes, of each element
**    compare  - The function used to compare two elements
** RETURNS
**    nothing
*/
static void formheap( char *x, int k, int elem_size,
                      compare_type compare )
{
  int node, i, j;
```

```
      for ( node = 1; node < k; node++ )
      {
        i = node;
        j = ( ( i + 1 ) / 2 ) - 1;
        while ( i != 0 &&
                ( ( compare( x + j * elem_size,
                             x + i * elem_size ) < 0 ) ) )
        {
          interchange( x + i * elem_size, x + j * elem_size,
                       elem_size );
          i = j;
          j = ( ( i + 1 ) / 2 ) - 1;
        }
      }
    }


    /* Generic rebuildheap function
    **
    ** ARGUMENTS
    **    x          - The starting address of the array of data
    **    k          - The number of nodes to form into a heap
    **    elem_size  - Size, in bytes, of each element
    **    compare    - The function used to compare two elements
    ** RETURNS
    **    nothing
    */
    static void rebuildheap( char *x, int k, int elem_size,
                             compare_type compare )
    {
      int i = 0,
          j = 1;

      if ( k >= 2 &&
           compare( x + 2 * elem_size, x + elem_size ) > 0 )
        j = 2;
      while ( j <= k &&
              compare( x + j * elem_size,
                       x + i * elem_size ) > 0 )
      {
        interchange( x + i * elem_size, x + j * elem_size,
                     elem_size );
        i = j;
        j = ( 2 * ( i + 1 ) ) - 1;
        if ( j + 1 <= k )
          if ( compare( x + ( j + 1 ) * elem_size,
                        x + j * elem_size ) > 0 )
            j++;
      }
    }
```

Listing 4.7 A sample compare_type function

```
/* A user defined function to compare two integers
**
** ARGUMENTS
**    int1, int2 - The addresses of the integers to compare
**
** RETURNS
**    -1 if the first integer is smaller than the second
**     0 if the first integer is equal to the second
**     1 if the first integer is larger than the second
*/
int compare_int( void *int1, void *int2 )
{
  if ( *( ( int * ) int1 ) < *( ( int * ) int2 ) )
    return -1;
  else if ( *( ( int * ) int1 ) == ( *( int * ) int2 ) )
    return 0;
  else
    return 1;
}
```

Listing 4.8 presents a test program that illustrates the use of the generic sort function. In this program, an array of ten integers, six floats, and ten fruit are sorted. In the case of the array of ten fruit, the sorting is first done by name and then by id_number. The significant point is that in all four cases, the same sort function supported by a user-defined compare_type function is employed.

Listing 4.8 Test program that illustrates the use of the generic heapsort
function

```
/*
  This program sorts several arrays of data using
  the generic sort function
*/

#include <string.h>
#include <stdio.h>
#include "gheapsrt.h"

int data1[] = { 6, 4, 5, 0, 6, -2, 7, -1, 8, 2 };

float data2[] = { 6.12, 4.04, 5.67, -2.14, -3.15, -1.12 };

typedef struct
{
  char name[ 20 ];
  int id_number;
} RECORD;
```

```
RECORD fruit[] = { "Orange", 5,
                   "Apple", 6,
                   "Lime", 8,
                   "Apricot", 9,
                   "Pineapple", 7,
                   "Pear", 3,
                   "Grapefruit", 4,
                   "Lemon", 1,
                   "Plum", 0,
                   "Prune", 2
               };

/* A function to compare two fruit according to name
**
** ARGUMENTS
**    fruit1, fruit2 - The two elements to compare
**
** RETURNS
**    -1 if the first fruit name is smaller than the second
**     0 if the first fruit name is equal to the second
**     1 if the first fruit name is larger than the second
*/
int compare_fruit_name( void *fruit1, void *fruit2 )
{
  return strcmp( ( ( RECORD * ) fruit1 ) -> name,
                 ( ( RECORD * ) fruit2 ) -> name );
}


/* A function to compare two fruit according to id_number
**
** ARGUMENTS
**    fruit1, fruit2 - The two elements to compare
**
** RETURNS
**    -1 if the first fruit id_number is smaller than the
**        second
**     0 if the first fruit id_number is equal to the second
**     1 if the first fruit id_number is larger than the
**        second
*/
int compare_fruit_id( void *fruit1, void *fruit2 )
{
  if ( ( ( RECORD * ) fruit1 ) -> id_number <
       ( ( RECORD * ) fruit2 ) -> id_number )
    return -1;
  else if ( ( ( RECORD * ) fruit1 ) -> id_number ==
            ( ( RECORD * ) fruit2 ) -> id_number )
    return 0;
```

(continued)

```
      else
         return 1;
   }


   /* A function to compare two integers
   **
   ** ARGUMENTS
   **    int1, int2 - The two elements to compare
   **
   ** RETURNS
   **    -1 if the first integer is smaller than the second
   **     0 if the first integer is equal to the second
   **     1 if the first integer is larger than the second
   */
   int compare_int( void *int1, void *int2 )
   {
      if ( *( ( int * ) int1 ) < *( ( int * ) int2 ) )
         return -1;
      else if ( *( ( int * ) int1 ) == ( *( int * ) int2 ) )
         return 0;
      else
         return 1;
   }


   /* A function to compare two floating point numbers
   **
   ** ARGUMENTS
   **    flt1, flt2 - The two elements to compare
   **
   ** RETURNS
   **    -1 if the first number is smaller than the second
   **     0 if the first number is equal to the second
   **     1 if the first number is larger than the second
   */
   int compare_float( void *flt1, void *flt2 )
   {
      if ( *( ( float * ) flt1 ) < *( ( float * ) flt2 ) )
         return -1;
      else if ( *( ( float * ) flt1 ) == ( *( float * ) flt2 ) )
         return 0;
      else
         return 1;
   }


   main()
   {
      int i;

      /* Sort and output the array of 10 integers */
```

```
      sort( ( void * ) data1, 10, sizeof( int ), compare_int );
      for ( i = 0; i < 10; i++ )
        printf( "%d\n", data1[ i ] );
      printf( "\n\n" );

      /* Sort and output the array of 6 real numbers */
      sort( ( void * ) data2, 6, sizeof( float ),
              compare_float );
      for ( i = 0; i < 6; i++ )
        printf( "%.2f\n", data2[ i ] );
      printf( "\n" );

      /* Sort and output the array of 10 fruit by name */
      sort( ( void * ) fruit, 10, sizeof( RECORD ),
            compare_fruit_name );
      for ( i = 0; i < 10; i++ )
        printf( "%s    %d\n", fruit[ i ].name,
                fruit[ i ].id_number );
      printf( "\n" );

      /* Sort and output the array of 10 fruit by id_number */
      sort( ( void * ) fruit, 10, sizeof( RECORD ),
            compare_fruit_id );
      for ( i = 0; i < 10; i++ )
        printf( "%s    %d\n", fruit[ i ].name,
                fruit[ i ].id_number );
}
```

The output of this program is as follows:

```
-2
-1
0
2
4
5
6
6
7
8


-3.15
-2.14
-1.12
4.04
5.67
6.12

Apple    6
Apricot    9
```

(continued)

```
Grapefruit    4
Lemon    1
Lime    8
Orange    5
Pear    3
Pineapple    7
Plum    0
Prune    2


Plum    0
Lemon    1
Prune    2
Pear    3
Grapefruit    4
Orange    5
Apple    6
Pineapple    7
Lime    8
Apricot    9
```

4.2 Generic Search Table

Some of the material in this section is based on section 9.2 of the companion book, *Turbo C at Any Speed*, by Richard Wiener, John Wiley and Sons, 1988.

The reader may wish to consult *Data Structures Using MODULA-2*, by Richard Sincovec and Richard Wiener, John Wiley and Sons, 1986, Chapter 8, or any other appropriate data structures book for more details concerning the theory of search trees. This subject is only briefly reviewed in this section. In particular, the algorithms for insertion and deletion from a search table are presented in the above reference and are not discussed in this section.

Binary trees are among the most important data structures used in computer science and software development. They are used in syntax checking, searching, sorting, database management, game algorithms, and other important application areas.

A binary tree is a finite set of elements that is either empty or contains a root node and perhaps other nodes. These additional nodes are partitioned into two disjoint subsets, each of which is itself a binary tree. These two subsets are called the left subtree and the right subtree. Each node of a binary tree may have 0, 1, or 2 subtrees. If a node has no children, it is called a leaf node.

For our present purposes, is is assumed that each node of a binary tree has a key value.

A search tree is a binary tree with the property that all nodes that are left descendants of a given node have a key value smaller than the given node. All nodes that are right descendants of a given node have a key value larger than the given node. This property allows for a simple search of the binary tree (see Sincovec and Wiener referenced above).

A search table permits the storage, retrieval, and ordered display of data using a data structure stored in random access memory. The basic operations for a search table are insertion, deletion, lookup, and display. A search tree may be used to implement a search table.

As indicated at the beginning of this chapter, the search tree algorithms for insertion, deletion, and lookup are independent of the underlying base type but depend on a comparison function that compares two nodes with respect to their key values. This comparison function is passed as a parameter to function define and specified by the user building the search tree. Function define must be invoked before any of the other search tree functions.

Listing 4.9 presents the prototype for a generic search tree that contains arbitrary elements, all of the same type.

The structure TREE is a header node that contains several important fields. The field, root, points to the root node of the actual search tree. The field, elem_size, contains the size, in bytes, of the information to be stored in each NODE structure. The fields display and compare contain pointers to user-defined functions that are described below. A typedef was used to define TREE and NODE to make the programs easier to read. TREE and NODE become synonyms for struct tree and struct node.

Each structure, NODE, contains the actual packet of information, info, to be stored in the search table. The fields left and right are pointers to the two children of the given tree node.

Figure 4.2 shows the data structure of the generic search tree.

The two type definitions, display_type and compare_type, provide a template for the user-defined functions that must be supplied in function define. The generic tree package cannot assume responsibility for knowing how to compare two elements of the base type or knowing how to display the base type, because it does not know the base type.

The type, display_type, is a pointer to a function that returns nothing and has a single parameter, data, that points to void (any data type). This function displays some or all of the fields of the tree node based on the user's specifications.

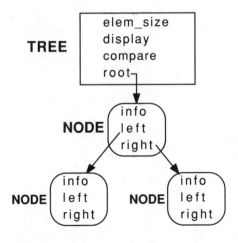

Figure 4.2 Data structure of generic search tree

The compare_type, is a pointer to a function that returns int and has two parameters, data1 and data2, that point to void (any data type). This function returns -1 if data1 is less than data2, returns 0 if data1 equals data2, and returns 1 if data1 is greater than data2. The user determines how two nodes are to be compared.

Function define provides the vehicle for binding the user defined functions disp, and compare to the header node of the generic tree. The element size, in bytes, is also bound to the header node using function define.

Function insertion allows a new node to be added to the search tree. Function deletion allows an existing node to be removed from the search tree. Function lookup determines whether a particular item is stored in the search tree. These three functions input a pointer to a particular tree and a pointer to the information to be added, deleted, or searched.

Function display_tree allows all the nodes of the tree to be displayed using the user-specified function, display.

Listing 4.9 Prototypes for generic tree

```
/* File: tree.h */

typedef void ( *display_type ) ( void *data );
/* Functions of display_type output the information
   fields of a node according to the user's specifications
*/

typedef int ( *compare_type ) ( void *data1,
                                 void *data2 );
/* Functions of compare_type return:
     -1 if element1 < element2
      0 if element1 = element2
      1 if element1 > element2
*/

typedef struct tree TREE;
typedef struct node NODE;

struct tree
{
  NODE *root;
  int elem_size;
  display_type display;
  compare_type compare;
};

struct node
{
```

```
  char *info;
  NODE *left, *right;
};


/* Define a new search tree
**
** ARGUMENTS
**    tree    - Pointer to a pointer to a TREE structure. The
**              address of a TREE pointer is sent into this
**              procedure.  The TREE pointer that is returned
**              must be used in all search tree functions.
**    size    - The size, in bytes, for each element to be
**              stored in the tree.
**    disp    - A user defined function for displaying a node
**              of the tree.
**    compare - A user defined function for comparing two
**              nodes of the tree.
**
**   RETURNS
**      nothing
*/
extern void define( TREE **tree,
                    int size,
                    display_type disp,
                    compare_type compare );



/* Inserts a node into a search tree
**
** ARGUMENTS
**    root - Pointer to search tree
**    item - Item to be inserted
**
** RETURNS
**    nothing
*/
extern void insertion( TREE *tree, char *item );



/* Deletes a node from the search tree
**
** ARGUMENTS
**    root - Pointer to search tree
**    item - Item to be deleted
**
** RETURNS
**    0 - Element to be deleted is not in tree
**    1 - Element is successfully deleted
*/
extern int deletion( TREE *tree, char *item );
```

(continued)

```
/* Displays all the nodes in a search tree
**
** ARGUMENTS
**    root - The root of the search tree to be displayed
**
** RETURNS
**    nothing
*/
extern void display_tree( TREE *root );


/* Searches for an item in a search tree
**
** ARGUMENTS
**    root - Root of the search tree to be searched
**    item - Item to be searched for in search tree
**
** RETURNS
**    0 - Item not found
**    1 - Item found
*/
extern int lookup( TREE *root, char *item );
```

Listing 4.10 presents the definition of the generic search tree functions.

The first function, create_node, in Listing 4.10 is hidden from the linker because of the static specifier. This function is called by function insertion. The generic character of the implementation is evident in this function.

A new node of type NODE is declared. Storage is allocated for both the node structure and its info field. A transfer of data from item to node is performed using the following code:

```
memcpy( node -> info, item, size );
```

The address of node is returned by function create_node.

Function define allocates storage for a new header node. It then binds elem_size and the user-defined functions disp and compare to the header node.

Functions insertion and deletion use the use-supplied function compare.

Function display_tree defines a local pointer, current, and initializes it to the address of the root node of the tree. Then function traverse is invoked. The user-defined function, display, is sent to traverse as its second parameter.

Static function, traverse, uses the code,

```
if ( current )
{
  traverse( current -> left, display );
  ( *display )( current -> info );
  traverse( current -> right, display );
}
```

to perform an in-order traversal of the tree. The "visit" operation consists of using the function pointer display to output the info field of each node in the tree.

Function lookup uses the user supplied function compare, as a traversal of the tree is performed. If a matchup is found the function returns 1, otherwise it returns 0.

Listing 4.10   Definitions for generic search tree

```
/* File: gentree.c */

#include <stdio.h>
#include <string.h>
#include <mem.h>
#include <alloc.h>
#include "tree.h"

/* Creates a new node in search tree
**
** ARGUMENTS
**    item - The information stored in node
**    size - The number of bytes of item
**
**    RETURNS
**       a pointer to NODE structure
*/
static NODE* create_node( char *item, int size )
{
  NODE *node;
  int i;

  node = ( NODE * ) malloc( sizeof( NODE ) );
  node -> info = ( char * ) malloc( size );
  memcpy( node -> info, item, size );
  return node;
}

/* Defines a new search tree
**
** ARGUMENTS
**    tree      - Pointer to a pointer to a TREE structure. The
**                address of a TREE pointer is sent into this
**                procedure.  The TREE pointer that is returned
**                must be used in all search tree functions.
**    size      - The size, in bytes, for each element to be
**                stored in the tree.
**    disp      - A user defined function for displaying a node
**                of the tree.
**    compare   - A user defined function for comparing two
**                nodes of the tree.                        (continued)
```

```
**
**   RETURNS
**      nothing
*/
void define( TREE **tree,
                int size,
                display_type disp,
                compare_type compare )
{
  *tree = ( TREE * ) malloc( sizeof( TREE ) );
  ( *tree ) -> root = NULL;
  ( *tree ) -> elem_size = size;
  ( *tree ) -> display = disp;
  ( *tree ) -> compare = compare;
}


/* Deletes a node from the search tree
**
** ARGUMENTS
**    root - Pointer to search tree
**    item - Item to be deleted
**
** RETURNS
**    0 - Element to be deleted is not in tree
**    1 - Element is successfully deleted
*/
int deletion( TREE *root, char *item )
{

  NODE *previous = NULL,
       *present = root -> root,
       *replace,
       *s,
       *parent;
  int found = 0;

  while ( present && !found )
  {
    if ( root -> compare( present -> info, item ) ==
        0 )
      found = 1;
    else
    {
      previous = present;
      if ( root -> compare( item, present -> info ) < 0 )
        present = present -> left;
      else
        present = present -> right;
    }
```

```
      }
    if ( found )
    {
      if ( present -> left == NULL )
        replace = present -> right;
      else
        if ( present -> right == NULL )
          replace = present -> left;
        else
        {
          parent = present;
          replace = present -> right;
          s = replace -> left;
          while ( s != NULL )
          {
            parent = replace;
            replace = s;
            s = replace -> left;
          }
          if ( parent != present )
          {
            parent -> left = replace -> right;
            replace -> right = present -> right;
          }
          replace -> left = present -> left;
        }
      if ( previous == NULL )
        root -> root = replace;
      else
        if ( present == previous -> left )
          previous -> left = replace;
        else
          previous -> right = replace;
      free( present -> info );
      free( present );
      return 1;
    }
    return 0;
}

/* Inserts a node into a search tree
**
** ARGUMENTS
**   root - Pointer to search tree
**   item - Item to be inserted
**
** RETURNS
**   nothing
*/                                                    (continued)
```

```
void insertion( TREE *root, char *item )
{
  NODE *parent = NULL,
       *current = root -> root;
  NODE *new_node;
  int found = 0;

  while ( current && !found )
  {
    if ( root -> compare( current -> info, item ) == 0 )
      found = 1;
    else
    {
      parent = current;
      if ( root -> compare( item, current -> info ) < 0 )
        current = current -> left;
      else
        current = current -> right;
    }
  }
  if ( found == 0 )
  {
    new_node = create_node( item, root -> elem_size );
    new_node -> left = new_node -> right = NULL;
    if ( parent == NULL )
    /* First node in the tree */
      root -> root = new_node;
    else
    {
      if ( root -> compare( item, parent -> info) < 0 )
        parent -> left = new_node;
      else
        parent -> right =new_node;
    }
  }
}


/* In-order traversal of search tree
**
** ARGUMENTS
**    current - Pointer to a search tree node
**    display - User defined function for displaying a tree
**              node
**
** RETURNS
**    nothing
*/
static void traverse( NODE *current,
                      display_type display )
```

```c
{
  if ( current )
  {
    traverse( current -> left, display );
    ( *display )( current -> info );
    traverse( current -> right, display );
  }
}

/* Displays all the nodes in a search tree
**
** ARGUMENTS
**    root - The root of the search tree to be displayed
**
** RETURNS
**    nothing
*/
void display_tree( TREE *root )
{
  NODE *current = root -> root;

  traverse( current, root -> display );
}

/* Searches for an item in a search tree
**
** ARGUMENTS
**    root - Root of the search tree to be searched
**    item - Item to be searched for in search tree
**
** RETURNS
**    0 - Item not found
**    1 - Item found
*/
int lookup( TREE *root, char *item )
{
  NODE *current = root -> root;
  int found = 0;

  while ( current && !found )
  {
    if ( root -> compare( current -> info, item ) == 0 )
      found = 1;
    else
    {
      if ( root -> compare( item, current -> info ) < 0 )
        current = current -> left;
      else
        current = current -> right;
    }
  }
}
```

(continued)

```
            }
        }
        return found;
    }
```

The reader should note that two equally valid syntax forms are used for invoking user specified functions in Listing 4.10. The function call,

```
root -> compare( item, parent -> info )
```

in function insertion is of the form,

```
function_name( parameters )
```

In function traverse, the function call,

```
( *display )( current -> info )
```

is of the form,

```
( *function_name )( parameter )
```

Listing 4.11 presents a test program that uses the generic search tree package.

A structure, RECORD, is defined with two members for test purposes. The first field, name, serves as the key field upon which the tree structure is built. The second field, id, contains a number of type float.

A tree, my_tree, is declared globally.

The two user-defined functions, display_record and my_compare are sent in as parameters to function define. The address of my_tree is sent as the first parameter to function define. The pointer to a RECORD structure, item, is reused to insert several items into the generic tree. One structure is then taken out of the tree. The tree is displayed.

Listing 4.11 Test program for generic search tree

```
#include <stdio.h>
#include <alloc.h>
#include <string.h>
#include "tree.h"

TREE *my_tree;

typedef struct record RECORD;

struct record
{
    char name[ 30 ];
    float id;
};
```

```
main()
{
  extern void display_record( void *info );

  extern int my_compare( void *item1, void *item2 );

  RECORD *item = ( RECORD * ) malloc( sizeof( RECORD ) );

  define( &my_tree, sizeof( RECORD ), display_record,
          my_compare );

  strcpy( item -> name, "Ccccc" );
  item -> id = 3.2345;
  insertion( my_tree, ( char * ) item );

  strcpy( item -> name, "Eeeee" );
  item -> id = 5.2345;
  insertion( my_tree, ( char * ) item );

  strcpy( item -> name, "Aaaaa" );
  item -> id = 1.2345;
  insertion( my_tree, ( char * ) item );

  strcpy( item -> name, "Ddddd" );
  item -> id = 4.2345;
  insertion( my_tree, ( char * ) item );

  strcpy( item -> name, "Fffff" );
  item -> id = 6.2345;
  insertion( my_tree, ( char * ) item );

  strcpy( item -> name, "Bbbbb" );
  item -> id = 2.2345;
  insertion( my_tree, ( char * ) item );

  strcpy( item -> name, "Ddddd" );
  item -> id = 4.2345;

  deletion( my_tree, ( char * ) item );

  display_tree( my_tree );
  printf( "\n\n" );
}


/*  User defined function for displaying nodes in search
**  tree.
**
** ARGUMENTS
**    info - Pointer to the information field of search tree
```

(continued)

```
**            node
**
** RETURNS
**    nothing
*/
void display_record( void *info )
{
  RECORD *temp = ( RECORD * ) info;

  printf( "\nName -> %s", temp -> name );
  printf( "\nid   ->  %f", temp -> id );
}


/* User defined function for comparing two nodes in the
** search tree.
**
** ARGUMENTS
**    item1, item2 - Pointers to items to compare
**
** RETURNS
**    -1 - item1 less than item2
**     0 - item1 equal to item2
**     1 - item1 greater than item2
*/
int my_compare( void *item1, void *item2 )
{
  RECORD *first = ( RECORD * ) item1;
  RECORD *second = ( RECORD * ) item2;

  return strcmp( first -> name, second -> name );
}
```

The output of Listing 4.11 is as follows:

```
Name -> Aaaaa
id   -> 1.234500
Name -> Bbbbb
id   -> 2.234500
Name -> Ccccc
id   -> 3.234500
Name -> Eeeee
id   -> 5.234500
Name -> Fffff
id   -> 6.234500
```

4.3 Generic AVL Trees

In this section the implementation details of functions insertion and deletion are changed to achieve a significant improvement in search-time performance. The motivation for this is that the search trees constructed using the functions given in Section 4.2 may be highly unbalanced. An extreme example of this occurs if the incoming data to be inserted is already perfectly ordered. The resulting search tree resembles a linked list. In such a case, the number of tree levels equals the number of nodes. This offsets the major advantage of a binary tree structure, namely, the logarithmic relationship between the number of levels and the number of nodes. This logarithmic relationship holds only when the binary tree is close to balanced.

In this section, a search tree is implemented as an AVL tree. An AVL tree, named after the two Russian mathematicians G.M. Adelson-Velskii and E.M. Landis, is a binary search tree constructed in such a way that for each node, the depth of the right subtree minus the depth of the left subtree is less than 1 in magnitude. The depth of a subtree is defined as the maximum distance, in levels, to the lowest leaf node in the subtree. This constraint assures tree balance. In order to achieve "AVL balance", rotations about various tree nodes are often required during either insertion or deletion. After using the AVL insertion or deletion functions given in this section, the resulting tree is an AVL tree.

AVL trees are almost balanced and thus reduce the number of levels in the tree for a given number of nodes. An extensive discussion of AVL trees, their properties, and algorithms is given in Chapter 9 of *Data Structures Using MODULA-2*, by Richard Sincovec and Richard Wiener, John Wiley and Sons, 1986. The reader may wish to consult this book or some other suitable reference to assist in understanding the complex algorithms used in implementing the insertion and deletion functions of this section.

Listings 4.11 and 4.12 present the modified prototype and definition of the generic search tree that includes the tree balancing code required to maintain AVL balance. Although the code in Listings 4.11 and 4.12 may be difficult to follow or understand without consulting outside references for a discussion of the AVL algorithms, this code forms the basis for an important reusable software component. The generic feature of the code allows search tables of any underlying data type to be efficiently constructed and maintained.

Listing 4.12 Prototypes for generic AVL tree

```
/* File: avl_tree.h */

typedef void ( *display_type ) ( void *data );
/* Functions of display_type output the information
   fields of a node according to the user's specifications
*/

typedef int ( *compare_type ) ( void *data1,
                                 void *data2 );
/* Functions of compare_type return:
     -1 if element1 < element2
      0 if element1 = element2
      1 if element1 > element2
*/
```
(continued)

```
typedef struct tree TREE;
typedef struct node NODE;

struct tree
{
  NODE *root;
  int elem_size;
  display_type display;
  compare_type compare;
};

struct node
{
  char *info;
  int bal;
  NODE *left, *right;
};


/* Define a new search tree
**
** ARGUMENTS
**    tree    - Pointer to a pointer to a TREE structure. The
**              address of a TREE pointer is sent into this
**              procedure.  The TREE pointer that is returned
**              must be used in all search tree functions.
**    size    - The size, in bytes, for each element to be
**              stored in the tree.
**    disp    - A user defined function for displaying a node
**              of the tree.
**    compare - A user defined function for comparing two
**              nodes of the tree.
**
** RETURNS
**    nothing
*/
extern void define( TREE **tree,
                    int size,
                    display_type disp,
                    compare_type compare );


/* Inserts a node into a search tree
**
** ARGUMENTS
**    root - Pointer to header node of search tree
**    item - Item to be inserted
**
** RETURNS
```

```
**    nothing
*/
extern void insertion( TREE *tree, char *item );


/* Deletes a node from the search tree
**
** ARGUMENTS
**    root - Pointer to header node of search tree
**    item - Item to be deleted
**
** RETURNS
**    0 - Element to be deleted is not in tree
**    1 - Element is successfully deleted
*/
extern int deletion( TREE *tree, char *item );


/* Displays all the nodes in a search tree
**
** ARGUMENTS
**    root - The header of the search tree to be displayed
**
** RETURNS
**    nothing
*/
extern void display_tree( TREE *root );


/* Searches for an item in a search tree
**
** ARGUMENTS
**    root - Header node of the search tree to be searched
**    item - Item to be searched for in search tree
**
** RETURNS
**    0 - Item not found
**    1 - Item found
*/
extern int lookup( TREE *root, char *item );
```

Listing 4.13 Definitions for generic AVL tree

```
/* File: avl_tree.c */

#include <string.h>
#include <mem.h>
#include <alloc.h>
#include "avl_tree.h"
```

(continued)

```
        int h = 1; /* Used in insertion and deletion to cut
                      off recursion when the rotations are
                      completed.
                */
NODE *q,
     *mark;



/* Creates a new node in search tree
**
** ARGUMENTS
**    item - The information stored in node
**    size - The number of bytes of item
**
**    RETURNS
**       a pointer to NODE structure
*/
static NODE* create_node( char *item, int size )
{
   NODE *node;
   int i;

   node = ( NODE * ) malloc( sizeof( NODE ) );
   node -> info = ( char * ) malloc( size );
   memcpy( node -> info, item, size );
   return node;
}



/* Defines a new search tree
**
** ARGUMENTS
**    tree    - Pointer to a pointer to a TREE structure. The
**              address of a TREE pointer is sent into this
**              procedure.  The TREE pointer that is returned
**              must be used in all search tree functions.
**    size    - The size, in bytes, for each element to be
**              stored in the tree.
**    disp    - A user defined function for displaying a node
**              of the tree.
**    compare - A user defined function for comparing two
**              nodes of the tree.
**
**    RETURNS
**       nothing
*/
void define( TREE **tree,
             int size,
             display_type disp,
             compare_type compare )
```

```c
{
  *tree = ( TREE * ) malloc( sizeof( TREE ) );
  ( *tree ) -> root = NULL;
  ( *tree ) -> elem_size = size;
  ( *tree ) -> display = disp;
  ( *tree ) -> compare = compare;
}


/* Performs tree rotations; Used by AVL_delete
**
** ARGUMENTS
**    *p - Pointer to root node of tree
**
** RETURNS
**    nothing
*/
static void balance1( NODE **p )
{
  NODE *p1, /* These are pointer tags */
       *p2;
  int b1,
      b2;

  switch ( ( *p ) -> bal )
  {
    case -1:
      ( *p ) -> bal = 0;
      break;
    case 0:
      ( *p ) -> bal = 1;
      h = 0;
      break;
    case 1:
      p1 = ( *p ) -> right;
      b1 = p1 -> bal;
      if ( b1 >= 0 )
      {
        /* single left rotate */
        ( *p ) -> right = p1 -> left;
        p1 -> left = *p;
        if ( b1 == 0 )
        {
          ( *p ) -> bal = 1;
          p1 -> bal = -1;
          h = 0;
        }
        else
        {
```

(continued)

```
              ( *p ) -> bal = 0;
               p1 -> bal = 0;
             }
            *p = p1;
         }
        else
        {
          /* double right left rotate */
          p2 = p1 -> left;
          b2 = p2 -> bal;
          p1 -> left = p2 -> right;
          p2 -> right = p1;
          ( *p ) -> right = p2 -> left;
          p2 -> left = *p;
          if ( b2 == 1 )
             ( *p ) -> bal = -1;
          else
             ( *p ) -> bal = 0;
          if ( b2 == -1 )
            p1 -> bal = 1;
          else
            p1 -> bal = 0;
          *p = p2;
          p2 -> bal = 0;
        }
    }
}


/* Performs tree rotations; Used by AVL_delete
**
** ARGUMENTS
**    *p - Pointer to root node of tree
**
** RETURNS
**    nothing
*/
static void balance2( NODE **p )
{
  NODE *p1,
       *p2;
  int b1,
      b2;

  switch ( ( *p ) -> bal )
  {
    case 1:
       ( *p ) -> bal = 0;
       break;
```

```c
      case 0:
        ( *p ) -> bal = -1;
        h = 0;
        break;
      case -1:
        p1 = ( *p ) -> left;
        b1 = p1 -> bal;
        if ( b1 <= 0 )
        {
          /* single right rotate */
          ( *p ) -> left = p1 -> right;
          p1 -> right = *p;
          if ( b1 == 0 )
          {
            ( *p ) -> bal = -1;
            p1 -> bal = 1;
            h = 0;
          }
          else
          {
            ( *p ) -> bal = 0;
            p1 -> bal = 0;
          }
          *p = p1;
        }
        else
        {
          /* double right left rotate */
          p2 = p1 -> right;
          b2 = p2 -> bal;
          p1 -> right = p2 -> left;
          p2 -> left = p1;
          ( *p ) -> left = p2 -> right;
          p2 -> right = *p;
          if ( b2 == -1 )
            ( *p ) -> bal = 1;
          else
            ( *p ) -> bal = 0;
          if ( b2 == 1 )
            p1 -> bal = -1;
          else
            p1 -> bal = 0;
          *p = p2;
          p2 -> bal = 0;
        }
    }
}
```

(continued)

```
/* Used by AVL_delete whenever a node with two children
** is deleted.
**
** ARGUMENTS
**    *r - Pointer to node to be deleted
**    *p - Pointer to the root node
**    size - The size, in bytes, of the tree elements
**
** RETURNS
**    nothing
*/
static void del( NODE **r, NODE **p, int size )
{
  int i;

  if ( ( *r ) -> right != NULL )
  {
    del( &( ( *r ) -> right ), &( *p ), size );
    if ( h )
      balance2 ( &( *r ) );
  }
  else
  {
    /* Transfer information from r -> info to p -> info */
    for ( i = 0; i < size; i++ )
      ( *p ) -> info[ i ] = ( *r ) -> info[ i ];
    mark = *r;
    *r = ( *r ) -> left;
    h = 1;
  }
}


/* Used by deletion
**
** ARGUMENTS
**    *w   - Information to be deleted
**    *p   - Pointer to root node
**    root - Pointer to header node
**
** RETURNS
**    0 - if information is not found
**    1 - if information is successfully deleted
*/
static int AVL_delete( char *w, NODE **p, TREE *root )
{
  if ( *p == NULL )
  {
```

```c
      h = 0;
      return 0;
    }
    else if ( root -> compare( w, ( *p ) -> info ) < 0 )
    {
      AVL_delete( w, &( ( *p ) -> left ), root );
      if ( h )
        balance1( &( *p ) );
    }
    else if ( root -> compare( w, ( *p ) -> info ) > 0 )
    {
      AVL_delete( w, &( ( *p ) -> right ), root );
      if ( h )
        balance2( &( *p ) );
    }
    else
    {
      if ( ( *p ) -> right == NULL )
      {
        q = *p;
        *p = q -> left;
        h = 1;
        free( q -> info );
        free( q );
      }
      else if ( ( *p ) -> left == NULL )
      {
        q = *p;
        *p = q -> right;
        h = 1;
        free( q -> info );
        free( q );
      }
      else
      {
        del( &( ( *p ) -> left ), &( *p ), root -> elem_size );
        if ( h )
          balance1( &( *p ) );
        free( mark -> info );
        free( mark );
      }
    }
    return 1;
}


/* Deletes a node from the search tree
**
** ARGUMENTS                                          (continued)
```

```
**    root - Pointer to header node of search tree
**    item - Item to be deleted
**
** RETURNS
**    0 - Element to be deleted is not in tree
**    1 - Element is successfully deleted
*/
int deletion( TREE *root, char *item )
{
  return AVL_delete( item, &( root -> root ), root );
}



/* Used by insertion
**
** ARGUMENTS
**    *w   - Information to be deleted
**    *p   - Pointer to root node
**    root - Pointer to header node
**
**    RETURNS
**      0 - if information is not found
**      1 - if information is successfully deleted
*/
static void AVL_insert( char *w, NODE **p, TREE *root )
{
  NODE *p1,
       *p2;

  if ( *p == NULL )
  {
    h = 1;
    *p = create_node( w, root -> elem_size );
    ( *p ) -> left = ( *p ) -> right = NULL;
    ( *p ) -> bal = 0;
  }
  else if ( root -> compare( w, ( *p ) -> info ) < 0 )
  {
    AVL_insert( w, &( ( *p ) -> left ), root );
    if ( h )
      switch ( ( *p ) -> bal )
      {
        case 1:
          ( *p ) -> bal = 0;
          h = 0;
          break;
        case 0:
          ( *p ) -> bal = -1;
          break;
```

```
          case -1:
            p1 = ( *p ) -> left;
            if ( p1 -> bal == -1 )
            {
              /* Single right rotation */
              ( *p ) -> left = p1 -> right;
              p1 -> right = *p;
              ( *p ) -> bal = 0;
              *p = p1;
            }
            else
            {
              /* left right rotation */
              p2 = p1 -> right;
              p1 -> right = p2 -> left;
              p2 -> left = p1;
              ( *p ) -> left = p2 -> right;
              p2 -> right = *p;
              if ( p2 -> bal == -1 )
                ( *p ) -> bal = 1;
              else
                ( *p ) -> bal = 0;
              if ( p2 -> bal == 1 )
                p1 -> bal = -1;
              else
                p1 -> bal = 0;
              *p = p2;
            }
            ( *p ) -> bal = 0;
            h = 0;
      }
}
else if ( root -> compare( w, ( *p ) -> info ) > 0 )
{
  AVL_insert( w, &( ( *p ) -> right ), root );
  if ( h )
    switch ( ( *p ) -> bal )
    {
      case -1:
        ( *p ) -> bal = 0;
        h = 0;
        break;
      case 0:
        ( *p ) -> bal = 1;
        break;
      case 1:
        p1 = ( *p ) -> right;
        if ( p1 -> bal == 1 )
        {
```

(continued)

```c
            /* Single left rotation */
            ( *p ) -> right = p1 -> left;
            p1 -> left = *p;
            ( *p ) -> bal = 0;
            *p = p1;
          }
          else
          {
            /* right left rotation */
            p2 = p1 -> left;
            p1 -> left = p2 -> right;
            p2 -> right = p1;
            ( *p ) -> right = p2 -> left;
            p2 -> left = *p;
            if ( p2 -> bal == 1 )
              ( *p ) -> bal = -1;
            else
              ( *p ) -> bal = 0;
            if ( p2 -> bal == -1 )
              p1 -> bal = 1;
            else
              p1 -> bal = 0;
            *p = p2;
          }
          ( *p ) -> bal = 0;
          h = 0;
      }
    else
      h = 0;
  }
  else
    h = 0;
}


/* Inserts a node into a search tree
**
** ARGUMENTS
**    root - Pointer to header node of search tree
**    item - Item to be inserted
**
** RETURNS
**    nothing
*/
void insertion( TREE *root, char *item )
{
  AVL_insert( item, &( root -> root ), root );
}
```

```
/* In-order traversal of search tree
**
** ARGUMENTS
**    current - Pointer to a search tree node
**    display - User defined function for displaying a tree
**              node
**
** RETURNS
**    nothing
*/
static void traverse( NODE *current,
                      display_type display )
{
  if ( current )
  {
    traverse( current -> left, display );
    ( *display )( current -> info );
    traverse( current -> right, display );
  }
}


/* Displays all the nodes in a search tree
**
** ARGUMENTS
**    root - The root of the search tree to be displayed
**
** RETURNS
**    nothing
*/
void display_tree( TREE *root )
{
  NODE *current = root -> root;

  traverse( current, root -> display );
}


/* Searches for an item in a search tree
**
** ARGUMENTS
**    root - Header node of the search tree to be searched
**    item - Item to be searched for in search tree
**
** RETURNS
**    0 - Item not found
**    1 - Item found
*/
```

(continued)

```
int lookup( TREE *root, char *item )
{
  NODE *current = root -> root;
  int found = 0;

  while ( current && !found )
  {
    if ( root -> compare( current -> info, item ) == 0 )
      found = 1;
    else
    {
      if ( root -> compare( item, current -> info ) < 0 )
        current = current -> left;
      else
        current = current -> right;
    }
  }
  return found;
}
```

Listing 4.14 presents a test program that exercises some of the functions in the generic AVL tree software component. Two trees, name_tree and number_tree, are defined. A series of insertions and deletions are performed on each tree. Although the same data is inserted and deleted from each tree, the comparison functions that are used to insert and delete data from the the tree are defined differently. Specifically, the tree, name_tree, uses the name field of the RECORD structure as a key field. The tree, number_tree, uses the id field of the RECORD structure as a key field.

Listing 4.14 Test program for generic AVL trees

```
#include <stdio.h>
#include <alloc.h>
#include <string.h>
#include "avl_tree.h"

TREE *name_tree,
     *number_tree;

typedef struct record RECORD;

struct record
{
  char name[ 30 ];
  int id;
};

main()
{
```

```c
extern void display_record( void *info );

extern int name_compare( void *item1, void *item2 );

extern int number_compare( void *item1, void *item2 );

RECORD *item = ( RECORD * ) malloc( sizeof( RECORD ) );

define( &name_tree, sizeof( RECORD ), display_record,
        name_compare );

define( &number_tree, sizeof( RECORD ), display_record,
        number_compare );

/* Insert data */
strcpy( item -> name, "Aaaaa" );
item -> id = 1;
insertion( name_tree, ( char * ) item );
insertion( number_tree, ( char * ) item );

strcpy( item -> name, "Bbbbb" );
item -> id = -2;
insertion( name_tree, ( char * ) item );
insertion( number_tree, ( char * ) item );

strcpy( item -> name, "Ccccc" );
item -> id = -3;
insertion( name_tree, ( char * ) item );
insertion( number_tree, ( char * ) item );

strcpy( item -> name, "Ddddd" );
item -> id = 4;
insertion( name_tree, ( char * ) item );
insertion( number_tree, ( char * ) item );

strcpy( item -> name, "Eeeee" );
item -> id = -5;
insertion( name_tree, ( char * ) item );
insertion( number_tree, ( char * ) item );

strcpy( item -> name, "Fffff" );
item -> id = 6;
insertion( name_tree, ( char * ) item );
insertion( number_tree, ( char * ) item );

strcpy( item -> name, "Ggggg" );
item -> id = -7;
insertion( name_tree, ( char * ) item );
insertion( number_tree, ( char * ) item );
```

(continued)

```c
        strcpy( item -> name, "Hhhhh" );
        item -> id = -8;
        insertion( name_tree, ( char * ) item );
        insertion( number_tree, ( char * ) item );

        strcpy( item -> name, "Iiiii" );
        item -> id = -9;
        insertion( name_tree, ( char * ) item );
        insertion( number_tree, ( char * ) item );

        strcpy( item -> name, "Jjjjj" );
        item -> id = 0;
        insertion( name_tree, ( char * ) item );
        insertion( number_tree, ( char * ) item );

        /* Display data */
        display_tree( name_tree );
        printf( "\n" );

        display_tree( number_tree );
        printf( "\n" );

        /* Delete data */
        strcpy( item -> name, "Ddddd" );
        item -> id = 4;
        deletion( name_tree, ( char * ) item );
        deletion( number_tree, ( char * ) item );

        strcpy( item -> name, "Ccccc" );
        item -> id = -3;
        deletion( name_tree, ( char * ) item );
        deletion( number_tree, ( char * ) item );

        strcpy( item -> name, "Bbbbb" );
        item -> id = -2;
        deletion( name_tree, ( char * ) item );
        deletion( number_tree, ( char * ) item );

        strcpy( item -> name, "Eeeee" );
        item -> id = -5;
        deletion( name_tree, ( char * ) item );
        deletion( number_tree, ( char * ) item );

        strcpy( item -> name, "Fffff" );
        item -> id = 6;
        deletion( name_tree, ( char * ) item );
        deletion( number_tree, ( char * ) item );
```

```c
        strcpy( item -> name, "Iiiii" );
        item -> id = -9;
        deletion( name_tree, ( char * ) item );
        deletion( number_tree, ( char * ) item );

        strcpy( item -> name, "Ggggg" );
        item -> id = -7;
        deletion( name_tree, ( char * ) item );
        deletion( number_tree, ( char * ) item );

        strcpy( item -> name, "Jjjjj" );
        item -> id = 0;
        deletion( name_tree, ( char * ) item );
        deletion( number_tree, ( char * ) item );

        /* Display data */
        display_tree( name_tree );
        printf( "\n" );

        display_tree( number_tree );
        printf( "\n" );

}

/*  User defined function for displaying nodes in search
**  tree.
**
** ARGUMENTS
**    info - Pointer to the information field of search tree
**           node
**
** RETURNS
**    nothing
*/
void display_record( void *info )
{
  RECORD *temp = ( RECORD * ) info;

  printf( "\nName -> %s", temp -> name );
  printf( "\nid   -> %d", temp -> id );
}

/* User defined function for comparing two nodes in the
** search tree based on name
**
** ARGUMENTS
**    item1, item2 - Pointers to items to compare
**
```

(continued)

```
**  RETURNS
**     -1 - item1 less than item2
**      0 - item1 equal to item2
**      1 - item1 greater than item2
*/
int name_compare( void *item1, void *item2 )
{
  RECORD *first = ( RECORD * ) item1;
  RECORD *second = ( RECORD * ) item2;

  return strcmp( first -> name, second -> name );
}

/* User defined function for comparing two nodes in the
** search tree based on id number
**
** ARGUMENTS
**     item1, item2 - Pointers to items to compare
**
** RETURNS
**     -1 - item1 less than item2
**      0 - item1 equal to item2
**      1 - item1 greater than item2
*/
int number_compare( void *item1, void *item2 )
{
  RECORD *first = ( RECORD * ) item1;
  RECORD *second = ( RECORD * ) item2;

  if ( first -> id == second -> id )
    return 0;
  else if ( first -> id < second -> id )
    return -1;
  else
    return 1;
}
```

The output of the test program in Listing 4.14 is as follows:

```
Name -> Aaaaa
id   -> 1
Name -> Bbbbb
id   -> -2
Name -> Ccccc
id   -> -3
Name -> Ddddd
id   -> 4
Name -> Eeeee
```

```
id    -> -5
Name -> Fffff
id    -> 6
Name -> Ggggg
id    -> -7
Name -> Hhhhh
id    -> -8
Name -> Iiiii
id    -> -9
Name -> Jjjjj
id    -> 0

Name -> Iiiii
id    -> -9
Name -> Hhhhh
id    -> -8
Name -> Ggggg
id    -> -7
Name -> Eeeee
id    -> -5
Name -> Ccccc
id    -> -3
Name -> Bbbbb
id    -> -2
Name -> Jjjjj
id    -> 0
Name -> Aaaaa
id    -> 1
Name -> Ddddd
id    -> 4
Name -> Fffff
id    -> 6

Name -> Aaaaa
id    -> 1
Name -> Hhhhh
id    -> -8

Name -> Hhhhh
id    -> -8
Name -> Aaaaa
id    -> 1
```

The reader should note how the display of the name_tree orders the data alphabetically by the name field, and how the display of the number_tree orders the data numerically by the id field.

5

A Potpourri of Basic Tools

This chapter presents and discusses a module of reusable software, with the prototype file util.h and the definition file util.c. Included in this module are functions for keyboard input, terminal output, cursor manipulation, timing, prompts and messages, and random number generation.

The original version of util.c was written using Turbo C, Version 1.0. Version 1.5 was released just prior to the completion of this book. Some of the functions contained in util.c are now available in Turbo C Version 1.5. These functions have not been removed from util.c because they are used in some of the code later in this book. Also the reader may wish to customize or modify this code to suit his or her special needs.

One could, of course, separate this general purpose utility file, util.c, into several smaller and more specialized files. Because the compiled Turbo C object code for util.c is relatively compact and because of the high potential frequency of usage of many of the functions contained within this module, the decision is made to group all the functions into a single module.

Many of the functions in util.c use DOS service calls or ROM BIOS calls. It is beyond the scope of this book to discuss these DOS service and ROM BIOS calls in great detail. The reader interested in a detailed and clear exposition of these operating system and BIOS calls may wish to consult the outstanding book, *Programming Guide to the IBM PC* by Peter Norton, Microsoft Press, 1985. Another excellent source of information, although less readable, is the DOS 3.x technical reference manual.

Listing 5.1 presents the prototype for the utility module. Listing 5.2 presents the definition of the utility module. All of the sections of this chapter make references to the code in these two listings.

Many of the utilities in Part 2 of the book use the functions of util.c.

Listing 5.1 Prototypes for utility module

```
/*
** Function prototypes for general purpose utilities
** File util.h
*/


/* Used in function rpttiming */
enum timetype { begin, end };


/*
*************************************************************
**      Keyboard handling functions                      **
*************************************************************
*/


/* Determines whether a key has been hit in the look ahead
** buffer.  This function is equivalent to Turbo C's
** kbhit function.
**
** ARGUMENTS
**    none
**
** RETURNS
**    0 - No key has been hit
**    1 - A key has been hit
*/
extern int keypressed( void );


/* Keyboard input with no echo.
** The constants given in util.h may be used to trap input.
** If flush = 0, the keyboard buffer is not flushed before
** the input.  If flush = 1, the keyboard buffer is flushed
** before the input.  Use flush = 1 if you wish to disable
** the look ahead buffer.
**
** Example : char ch;
**
**            get_key( &ch, 0 );
**            if ( ch == alt_p )
**              printf( "The key ALT_P has been hit." );
**
** ARGUMENTS
**    ch    - The numeric value of the input key.  If a
**            printable character is input, its ASCII value
**            is returned.  Otherwise, one of the special
**            constants given in util.h is returned.
```

```
**      flush - A value of:
**                  0 => Look ahead buffer not flushed before
**                        input.
**                  1 => Look ahead buffer flushed before input.
**
** RETURNS
**      nothing
*/
extern void get_key( unsigned char *ch, int flush );



/*
**************************************************************
**       Screen output functions                          **
**************************************************************
*/



/* Clear screen.  Version 1.5 now supports a function
** clrscr.
**
** ARGUMENTS
**      none
**
** RETURNS
**      nothing
*/
extern void clrscreen( void );



/* Writes a string with given attribute to terminal.
** The attributes are given in util.h.
** The output is bit-mapped and cannot be redirected
**
** ARGUMENTS
**      attrib - normal, reverse, highlight, or reverse
**      s      - String to be written to terminal
**
** RETURNS
**      nothing
*/
extern void writestring_attr( char* s, int attrib );



/*
**************************************************************
**        Cursor Manipulation                             **
**************************************************************
*/
```

(continued)

```
/* Get cursor coordinates
**
** ARGUMENTS
**    h, v - The horizontal and vertical coordinates of the
**           current cursor position.  The value of h ranges
**           from 0 to 79.  The value of v ranges from 0 to
**           24.
**
** RETURNS
**    nothing
*/
extern void getxy( unsigned *h, unsigned *v );


/* Set cursor coordinates
**
** ARGUMENTS
**    h, v - The horizontal and vertical coordinates of the
**           desired cursor position.  The value of h ranges
**           from 0 to 79.  The value of v ranges from 0 to
**           24.  The position 79, 24 is unattainable using
**           the present logic.
**
** RETURNS
**    nothing
*/
extern void gotoxy( unsigned h, unsigned v );


/* Removes the cursor
**
** ARGUMENTS
**    none
**
** RETURNS
**    nothing
*/
extern void remove_cursor( void );


/* Restores the cursor to its previous type
**
** ARGUMENTS
**    none
**
** RETURNS
**    nothing
*/
extern void restore_cursor( void );
```

```
/*
************************************************************
**      Timing                                          **
************************************************************
*/


/* Returns the current clock time in hours, minutes, seconds
** and hundreths of a second.
**
** ARGUMENTS
**    hour    - The current hour (0-23)
**    minute  - The current minute (0-59)
**    sec     - The current second (0-59)
**    hund    - The current hundreth (0-99)
**
** RETURNS
**    nothing
*/
extern void gtime( unsigned *hour,
                   unsigned *minute, unsigned *sec,
                   unsigned *hund );


/* Outputs the elapsed time between calls to
** rpttiming( begin) and rpttiming( end ).
**
** ARGUMENTS
**    p - Either begin or end
**
** RETURNS
**    nothing
*/
extern void rpttiming( enum timetype p );


/*
************************************************************
**   Random Number Generation                           **
************************************************************
*/


/* Returns a uniformly distributed random number between
** 0.0 and 1.0.  A random number generator exists in
** Version 1.5.
**
** ARGUMENTS
**    none
```

(continued)

```
**
** RETURNS
**    A real value between 0.0 and 1.0.
*/
extern float rand_real( void );



/* Random uniformly distributed integer in specified range
**
** ARGUMENTS
**    low  - The lower integer in the range
**    high - The upper integer in the range
**
** RETURNS
**    The random integer in the given range
*/
extern int random_int( int low, int high );



/*
*************************************************************
**      User Prompts and Messages                        **
*************************************************************
*/



/* Positions string in the middle of a screen line
**
** ARGUMENTS
**    s - The string to be centered.
**
** RETURNS
**    nothing
*/
extern void centermessage( char s[] );



/* Pauses program execution with the message,
** "Hit spacebar to continue ->"
** This message is displayed on the last line of the screen.
** Program execution resumes after the user has entered a
** space.
**
** ARGUMENTS
**    none
**
** RETURNS
**    nothing
*/
extern void spacebar( void );
```

```
/* Used to pause program execution and trap a character
** of either upper or lower case 'y' or 'n'.  If an upper
** or lower case 'y' is entered, the function returns 1.
** If an upper or lower case 'n' is entered, the function
** returns 0.
**
** ARGUMENTS
**    none
**
** RETURNS
**    0 - The character 'N' or 'n' is entered.
**    1 - The character 'Y' or 'y' is entered.
*/
extern int yes( void );


/* Attributes for function write_attrib */
#define normal 0x7
#define reverse 0x70
#define highlight 0x0F
#define underline 0x1


/* Function key definitions */
#define f1 128
#define f2 129
#define f3 130
#define f4 131
#define f5 132
#define f6 133
#define f7 134
#define f8 135
#define f9 136
#define f10 137
#define f11 205
#define f12 206


/* Key pad definitions and misc keys */
#define home 167
#define up_arrow 161
#define pg_up 165
#define left_arrow 164
#define right_arrow 163
#define end 168
#define down_arrow 162
#define pg_down 166
#define insert 180
#define delete 169
#define shift_tab 170
```

(continued)

```
#define ctrl_home 172
#define ctrl_end 173
#define ctrl_pg_up 174
#define ctrl_pg_down 175
#define ctrl_left_arrow 176
#define ctrl_right_arrow 177

/* Control key definitions */
#define ctrl_a 138
#define ctrl_b 139
#define ctrl_c 140
#define ctrl_d 141
#define ctrl_e 142
#define ctrl_f 143
#define ctrl_g 144
#define ctrl_j 145
#define ctrl_k 146
#define ctrl_l 147
#define ctrl_n 148
#define ctrl_o 149
#define ctrl_p 150
#define ctrl_q 151
#define ctrl_r 152
#define ctrl_s 153
#define ctrl_t 154
#define ctrl_u 155
#define ctrl_v 156
#define ctrl_w 157
#define ctrl_x 158
#define ctrl_y 159
#define ctrl_z 160
#define ret 171

/* Alt key definitions */
#define alt_a 178
#define alt_b 179
#define alt_c 181
#define alt_d 182
#define alt_e 183
#define alt_f 184
#define alt_g 185
#define alt_h 186
#define alt_i 187
#define alt_j 188
#define alt_k 189
#define alt_l 190
#define alt_m 191
#define alt_n 192
#define alt_o 193
```

```
#define alt_p 194
#define alt_q 195
#define alt_r 196
#define alt_s 197
#define alt_t 198
#define alt_u 199
#define alt_v 200
#define alt_w 201
#define alt_x 202
#define alt_y 203
#define alt_z 204
```

Listing 5.2   Definitions for utility module

```
/*
** General purpose utility package
** File util.c   Turbo C Version
*/

#define MONOCHROME /* Used in function restore_cursor */

#include <stdio.h>
#include <dos.h>
#include <string.h>
#include "util.h"

static const int max = 32767;

static int ins   = 0,
           first = 1;
static unsigned h1, h2, m1, m2, s1, s2, hund1, hund2;
static unsigned seed1, seed2;

#define F1 59
#define F2 60
#define F3 61
#define F4 62
#define F5 63
#define F6 64
#define F7 65
#define F8 66
#define F9 67
#define F10 68
#define F11 69
#define F12 70
#define HOME 71
#define UP_ARROW 72
#define PG_UP 73
```

(continued)

```
#define LEFT_ARROW 75
#define RIGHT_ARROW 77
#define END 79
#define DOWN_ARROW 80
#define PG_DOWN 81
#define INSERT 82
#define DELETE 83
#define SHIFT_TAB 15
#define CTRL_LEFT_ARROW 115
#define CTRL_RIGHT_ARROW 116
#define CTRL_END 117
#define CTRL_PG_DOWN 118
#define CTRL_HOME 119
#define CTRL_PG_UP 132
#define ALT_Q 16
#define ALT_W 17
#define ALT_E 18
#define ALT_R 19
#define ALT_T 20
#define ALT_Y 21
#define ALT_U 22
#define ALT_I 23
#define ALT_O 24
#define ALT_P 25
#define ALT_A 30
#define ALT_S 31
#define ALT_D 32
#define ALT_F 33
#define ALT_G 34
#define ALT_H 35
#define ALT_J 36
#define ALT_K 37
#define ALT_L 38
#define ALT_Z 44
#define ALT_X 45
#define ALT_C 46
#define ALT_V 47
#define ALT_B 48
#define ALT_N 49
#define ALT_M 50


/*
*************************************************************
**      Keyboard handling functions                       **
*************************************************************
*/
```

```c
static void convert ( unsigned char *ch )
{

   switch ( *ch )
   {
     case F1 : *ch = f1;
               break;
     case F2 : *ch = f2;
               break;
     case F3 : *ch = f3;
               break;
     case F4 : *ch = f4;
               break;
     case F5 : *ch = f5;
               break;
     case F6 : *ch = f6;
               break;
     case F7 : *ch = f7;
               break;
     case F8 : *ch = f8;
               break;
     case F9 : *ch = f9;
               break;
     case F10 : *ch = f10;
                break;
     case F11 : *ch = f11;
                break;
     case F12 : *ch = f12;
                break;
     case HOME : *ch = home;
                 break;
     case UP_ARROW : *ch = up_arrow;
                     break;
     case PG_UP : *ch = pg_up;
                  break;
     case LEFT_ARROW : *ch = left_arrow;
                       break;
     case RIGHT_ARROW : *ch = right_arrow;
                        break;
     case END : *ch = end;
                break;
     case DOWN_ARROW : *ch = down_arrow;
                       break;
     case PG_DOWN : *ch = pg_down;
                    break;
     case INSERT : *ch = insert;
                   ins = !ins;
                   break;
```

(continued)

```
case DELETE : *ch = delete;
                break;
case SHIFT_TAB : *ch = shift_tab;
                  break;
case CTRL_HOME : *ch = ctrl_home;
                  break;
case CTRL_END : *ch = ctrl_end;
                break;
case CTRL_PG_UP : *ch = ctrl_pg_up;
                   break;
case CTRL_PG_DOWN : *ch = ctrl_pg_down;
                      break;
case CTRL_LEFT_ARROW : *ch = ctrl_left_arrow;
                         break;
case CTRL_RIGHT_ARROW : *ch = ctrl_right_arrow;
                          break;
case ALT_A : *ch = alt_a;
              break;
case ALT_B : *ch = alt_b;
              break;
case ALT_C : *ch = alt_c;
              break;
case ALT_D : *ch = alt_d;
              break;
case ALT_E : *ch = alt_e;
              break;
case ALT_F : *ch = alt_f;
              break;
case ALT_G : *ch = alt_g;
              break;
case ALT_H : *ch = alt_h;
              break;
case ALT_I : *ch = alt_i;
              break;
case ALT_J : *ch = alt_j;
              break;
case ALT_K : *ch = alt_k;
              break;
case ALT_L : *ch = alt_l;
              break;
case ALT_M : *ch = alt_m;
              break;
case ALT_N : *ch = alt_n;
              break;
case ALT_O : *ch = alt_o;
              break;
case ALT_P : *ch = alt_p;
              break;
```

```
        case ALT_Q : *ch = alt_q;
                     break;
        case ALT_R : *ch = alt_r;
                     break;
        case ALT_S : *ch = alt_s;
                     break;
        case ALT_T : *ch = alt_t;
                     break;
        case ALT_U : *ch = alt_u;
                     break;
        case ALT_V : *ch = alt_v;
                     break;
        case ALT_W : *ch = alt_w;
                     break;
        case ALT_X : *ch = alt_x;
                     break;
        case ALT_Y : *ch = alt_y;
                     break;
        case ALT_Z : *ch = alt_z;
                     break;
        default: *ch = 0;
    }
}


/* Determines whether a key has been hit in the look ahead
** buffer.
**
** ARGUMENTS
**    none
**
** RETURNS
**    0 - No key has been hit
**    1 - A key has been hit
*/
int keypressed( void )
{
    union REGS regs;

    regs.h.ah = 0x0B;
    intdos( &regs, &regs );
    return ( regs.h.al == 255 );
}


/* Keyboard input with no echo.
** The constants given in util.h may be used to trap input.
** If flush = 0, the keyboard buffer is not flushed before
```

(continued)

```
** the input.  If flush = 1, the keyboard buffer is flushed
** before the input.  Use flush = 1 if you wish to disable
** the look ahead buffer.
**
** Example : char ch;
**
**              get_key( &ch, 0 );
**              if ( ch == alt_p )
**                 printf( "The key ALT_P has been hit." );
**
** ARGUMENTS
**    ch     - The numeric value of the input key.  If a
**             printable character is input, its ASCII value
**             is returned.  Otherwise, one of the special
**             constants given in util.h is returned.
**    flush - A value of:
**                 0 => Look ahead buffer not flushed after
**                      input.
**                 1 => Look ahead buffer flushed after input.
**
** RETURNS
**    nothing
*/
void get_key( unsigned char *ch, int flush )
{
  union REGS regs;

  if ( flush )
  {
    /* The C function fflush( stdin ) could be used here */
    regs.h.ah = 0xC;
    regs.h.al = 0x7;
  }
  else
    regs.h.ah = 0x7;
  intdos( &regs, &regs );
  *ch = regs.h.al;
  if ( *ch == 0 )
  {
    regs.h.ah = 0x7;
    intdos( &regs, &regs );
    *ch = regs.h.al;
    convert( ch );
  }
  else
  {
    switch ( *ch )
    {
```

```
case 1 : *ch = ctrl_a;
         break;
case 2 : *ch = ctrl_b;
         break;
case 3 : *ch = ctrl_c;
         break;
case 4 : *ch = ctrl_d;
         break;
case 5 : *ch = ctrl_e;
         break;
case 6 : *ch = ctrl_f;
         break;
case 7 : *ch = ctrl_g;
         break;
case 10: *ch = ctrl_j;
         break;
case 11: *ch = ctrl_k;
         break;
case 12: *ch = ctrl_l;
         break;
case 14: *ch = ctrl_n;
         break;
case 15: *ch = ctrl_o;
         break;
case 16: *ch = ctrl_p;
         break;
case 17: *ch = ctrl_q;
         break;
case 18: *ch = ctrl_r;
         break;
case 19: *ch = ctrl_s;
         break;
case 20: *ch = ctrl_t;
         break;
case 21: *ch = ctrl_u;
         break;
case 22: *ch = ctrl_v;
         break;
case 23: *ch = ctrl_w;
         break;
case 24: *ch = ctrl_x;
         break;
case 25: *ch = ctrl_y;
         break;
case 26: *ch = ctrl_z;
         break;
case 30: *ch = ret;
         break;
```

(continued)

```
          default : ;
       }
    }
}


/*
**************************************************************
**        Screen output functions                          **
**************************************************************
*/


/* Clear screen
**
** ARGUMENTS
**    none
**
** RETURNS
**    nothing
*/
void clrscreen( void )
{
   union REGS regs;

   /* clear screen */
   regs.h.ah = 6;                    /* window up */
   regs.h.al = 0;                    /* blanks entire screen */
   regs.h.ch = 0;                    /* upper row */
   regs.h.cl = 0;                    /* left column */

   /* The reader may wish to modify this code for terminals
      with more lines than 25.  See Peter Norton's book,
      PROGRAMMING THE IBM PC - pages 54, 55
   */
   regs.h.dh = 24;                   /* lower row */
   regs.h.dl = 79;                   /* right column */

   regs.h.bh = 7;                    /* filler attribute */
   int86( 0x10, &regs, &regs );
   /* home cursor */
   gotoxy( 0, 0 );
}


/* Writes a string with given attribute to terminal.
** The attributes are given in util.h.
** The output is memory-mapped and cannot be redirected
```

```
**
** ARGUMENTS
**    attrib - normal, reverse, highlight, or underline
**    s      - String to be written to terminal
**
** RETURNS
**    nothing
*/
void writestring_attr( char* s, int attrib )
{
  union REGS inregs, outregs;
  unsigned int x, y;

  inregs.h.ah = 0x9;
  inregs.x.cx = 1;
  inregs.h.bl = attrib;
  inregs.h.bh = 0;
  getxy( &x, &y );
  while ( *s )
  {
    gotoxy( x % 80, y + x / 80 );
    inregs.h.al = *s;
    s++;
    x++;
    int86( 0x10, &inregs, &outregs );
  }
  gotoxy( x % 80, y + x / 80 );
}



/*
*************************************************************
**          Cursor Manipulation                          **
*************************************************************
*/


/* Get cursor coordinates
**
** ARGUMENTS
**    h, v - The horizontal and vertical coordinates of the
**           current cursor position.  The value of h ranges
**           from 0 to 79.  The value of v ranges from 0 to
**           24.
**
** RETURNS
**    nothing
*/
```

(continued)

```c
void getxy( unsigned *h, unsigned *v )
{
  union REGS regs;

  regs.h.ah = 0x03;
  regs.x.bx = 0x0;
  int86( 0x10, &regs, &regs );
  *v = regs.h.dh;
  *h = regs.h.dl;
}


/* Set cursor coordinates
**
** ARGUMENTS
**    h, v - The horizontal and vertical coordinates of the
**           desired cursor position.  The value of h ranges
**           from 0 to 79.  The value of v ranges from 0 to
**           24.  The position 79, 24 is unattainable.
**
** RETURNS
**    nothing
*/
void gotoxy( unsigned h, unsigned v )
{
  union REGS regs;

  if ( ( h >= 0 ) && ( h <= 79 ) && ( v >= 0 ) && ( v <= 24 ) )
    if ( ( h != 79 ) || ( v != 24 ) )
    {
      regs.h.ah = 0x02;
      regs.h.bh = 0x0;
      regs.h.dl = h;
      regs.h.dh = v;
      int86( 0x10, &regs, &regs );
    }
}


/* Removes the cursor
**
** ARGUMENTS
**    none
**
** RETURNS
**    nothing
*/
void remove_cursor( void )
{
```

```
    union REGS regs;

    regs.h.ah= 0x01;
    regs.h.ch = 32;
    regs.h.cl = 0;
    int86( 0x10, &regs, &regs );
}


/* Restores the cursor to its previous type
**
** ARGUMENTS
**    none
**
** RETURNS
**    nothing
*/
void restore_cursor( void )
{
    union REGS regs;

    regs.h.ah = 0x01;
    #if defined( MONOCHROME )
    regs.h.ch = 12;
    regs.h.cl = 13;
    #elif
    regs.h.ch = 6;
    regs.h.cl = 7;
    #endif
    int86( 0x10, &regs, &regs );
}


/*
***************************************************************
**      Timing                                              **
***************************************************************
*/


/* Returns the current clock time in hours, minutes, seconds
** and hundreths of a second.
**
** ARGUMENTS
**    hour   - The current hour (0-23)
**    minute - The current minute (0-59)
**    sec    - The current second (0-59)
**    hund   - The current hundreth (0-99)
**
```
(continued)

```
**  RETURNS
**     nothing
*/
void gtime( unsigned *hour,
              unsigned *minute, unsigned *sec,
              unsigned *hund )
{
  union REGS inreg, outreg;

  inreg.h.ah = 0x2C;
  intdos( &inreg, &outreg );
  *sec = outreg.h.dh;
  *hund = outreg.h.dl;
  *hour = outreg.h.ch;
  *minute = outreg.h.cl;
}


/* Outputs the elapsed time between calls to
** rpttiming( begin) and rpttiming( end ).
**
** ARGUMENTS
**    p - Either begin or end
**
** RETURNS
**     nothing
*/
void rpttiming( enum timetype p )
{
  extern void gtime( unsigned *hour,
                       unsigned *minute, unsigned *sec,
                       unsigned *hund );

  if ( p == begin )
    gtime( &h1, &m1, &s1, &hund1 );
  if ( p == end )
  {
    gtime( &h2, &m2, &s2, &hund2 );
    if ( hund2 < hund1 )
    {
      hund2 += 100;
      s2 -= 1;
    }
    if ( s2 < s1 )
    {
      s2 += 60;
      m2 -= 1;
    }
    if ( m2 < m1 )
```

```
      {
        m2 += 60;
        h2 -= 1;
      }
      if ( h2 < h1 ) h2 += 24;
      printf("\n\n %d hours, %d minutes, %d seconds, %d
              hundreths\", h2 - h1, m2 - m1, s2 - s1, hund2 - hund1 );
  }
}


/*
*************************************************************
**   Random Number Generation                            **
*************************************************************
*/


/* Returns a uniformly distributed random number between
** 0.0 and 1.0.
**
** ARGUMENTS
**    none
**
** RETURNS
**    A real value between 0.0 and 1.0.
*/
float rand_real( void )
{
  extern void gtime( unsigned *hour,
                     unsigned *minute, unsigned *sec,
                     unsigned *hund );

  unsigned h, m, s, hu; /* Used for getting the current
                           clock time */
  unsigned c;
  int index;

  /* This code gets executed once */
  if ( first )
  {
    gtime( &h, &s, &m, &hu );
    seed1 = hu + m + 2 * s;
    seed2 = h + s * m + s;
    seed1 *= 2;
    seed2 *= 2;
    if ( seed1 > max ) seed1 -= max;
    if ( seed2 > max ) seed2 -= max;
```

(continued)

```
    /* Warm up the generator. r never used */
    first = 0;
    for ( index = 1; index <= 30; index++ )
      rand_real();
  }
  c = seed1 + seed2;
  if ( c > max ) c -= max;
  c *= 2;
  if ( c > max ) c -= max;
  seed1 = seed2;
  seed2 = c;
  return ( ( float ) c / 32767.0 );
}


/* Random uniformly distributed integer in specified range
**
** ARGUMENTS
**    low  - The lower integer in the range
**    high - The upper integer in the range
**
** RETURNS
**    The random integer in the given range
*/
int random_int( int low, int high )
{
  float r, t;
  int c;

  r = ( float ) high - ( float) low + 1.0;
  t = r * rand_real();
  c = ( int ) t;
  return ( low + c );
}


/*
***************************************************************
**      User Prompts and Messages                          **
***************************************************************
*/


/* Positions string in the middle of a screen line
**
** ARGUMENTS
**    s - The string to be centered.
**
** RETURNS
```

```
**    nothing
*/
void centermessage( char s[] )
{
  unsigned int x, y;

  getxy( &x, &y );
  gotoxy( 40 - strlen( s ) / 2, y );
  printf( "%s", s );
}


/* Pauses program execution with the message,
** "Hit spacebar to continue ->"
** This message is displayed on the last line of the screen.
** Program execution resumes after the user has entered a
** space.
**
** ARGUMENTS
**    none
**
** RETURNS
**    nothing
*/
void spacebar( void )
{
  unsigned char ch;

  gotoxy( 0, 24 );
  centermessage( "Hit spacebar to continue ->" );
  do
  {
    get_key( &ch, 1 );
  } while ( ch != ' ' );
}


/* Used to pause program execution and trap a character
** of either upper or lower case 'y' or 'n'.  If an upper
** or lower case 'y' is entered, the function returns 1.
** If an upper or lower case 'n' is entered, the function
** returns 0.
**
** ARGUMENTS
**    none
**
** RETURNS
**    0 - The character 'N' or 'n' is entered.
**    1 - The character 'Y' or 'y' is entered.
```
(continued)

```
*/
int yes( void )
/*  Returns 1 if true, 0 if false */
{
  unsigned char ch;

  do
  {
    get_key( &ch, 0 );
  } while (  ( ch != 'y' ) && ( ch != 'Y' ) && ( ch != 'n')
         && ( ch != 'N' )  );
  putch( ch );
  return (  ( ch == 'Y' ) || ( ch == 'y' )  );
}
```

5.1 *Keyboard Handling*

The two functions that comprise the keyboard handling functions of util.c
are keypressed and get_key. See Listing 5.2.

Function get_key supports "hot-key" input. "Hot-key" input is used here
to mean that the user does not have to type the "Enter" key after typing a
key. The second parameter of the function determines whether the type
ahead buffer is flushed before getting a character. The character that is
input is not echoed to the screen.

If the parameter flush is 1, the high byte of the ax register, ah, is set to
0xC. The low byte, al, is set to the number of the DOS service call that is used
for keyboard input. In get_key, DOS service call 0x7 is used. This service
provides direct keyboard input without echo. DOS service 0xC performs the
keyboard buffer flushing, if appropriate.

After the DOS service call 0x7 is performed, the character in the low
byte of ax is examined. If this character has the value 0, a special key has
been hit and another call to DOS 0x7 is made. This captures the scan code
of the special character. The function convert assigns an appropriate value
to ch. This value is returned to the calling program. The constants that are
defined in util.h may be used by the user to trap most of the special keys on
the keyboard.

Function keypressed is described in Chapter 3.

A test program that exercise all three functions is given in Listing 5.3.

Listing 5.3 Program to exercise keyboard handling functions in util.c

```
#include <stdio.h>
#include <conio.h>
#include "util.h"

main()
{
```

```
float r = 0.0;
unsigned char ch;

do
  r = r + 1.0;
while ( !keypressed() );
printf( "r = %f\n", r );

/* Trap a ctrl_w input */
printf( "\nEnter a key -> " );
/* Input character and flush keyboard buffer before input
*/
get_key( &ch, 1 );
putch( ch );
do
{
  if ( ch == ctrl_w )
    printf( "\nThe key ctrl_w has been hit.\n" );
  else
    printf( "\nStill waiting for the ctrl_w key.\n" );
  printf( "\nEnter a key -> " );
  get_key( &ch, 0 );
  putch( ch );
}
while ( ch != ctrl_w );
}
```

5.2   Screen Output

The functions in util.c that support screen output are clrscreen and writestring_attrib. See Listing 5.2.

The clrscreen function takes no parameters and clears the screen. A ROM BIOS call, 0x10, is used to accomplish this task. ROM BIOS service 6, for scrolling a window up, is used. The register settings required in this ROM BIOS call are given in the body of function clrscreen.

The writestring_attr function uses the ROM BIOS service call 9 to write a series of characters and attributes to the terminal. The initial cursor coordinates are obtained using a call to getxy. As each character in the input string is accessed, its value is assigned to the low byte of the ax register. The number of occurrences, 1, of each character is assigned to the cx register. The low byte of the bx register is assigned the attribute that is input. Because BIOS service 9 does not automatically advance the cursor, this is accomplished using a call to

```
gotoxy( x % 80, y + x / 80 );
```

A test program that exercises the functions clsrscreen and writestring_attr is given in Listing 5.4.

Listing 5.4   Test program to exercise screen output functions in util.c

```
#include <stdio.h>
#include "util.h"

main()
{
  clrscreen();
  writestring_attr( "This is normal", normal );
  printf( "\n" );

  writestring_attr( "This is reverse video", reverse );
  printf( "\n" );

  writestring_attr( "This is underline", underline );
  printf( "\n" );

  writestring_attr( "This is highlight", highlight );
  putch( '\n' );
}
```

5.3   *Cursor Manipulation*

The functions in util.c that support cursor manipulation are getxy, gotoxy, remove_cursor, and restore_cursor. See Listing 5.2.

Function getxy returns the horizontal and vertical position of the cursor. It uses ROM BIOS service 3 to accomplish this task. The results are returned in the dh and dl.

Function gotoxy contains error protection that insures that the values of h and v are within the range 0...79 and 0...24 respectively. Also the specific coordinate h = 79, v = 24 is prohibited using this implementation. ROM BIOS service 2 is used to accomplish this task.

Function remove_cursor uses ROM BIOS service 1 to set the cursor size to 0. The conditional compilation block,

```
#if defined( MONOCHROME )
regs.h.ch = 12;
regs.h.cl = 13;
#elif
regs.h.ch = 6;
regs.h.cl = 7;
#endif
```

is used to set the high and low bytes of register cx. If a monochrome adapter card is employed (as is the case in Listing 5.2 because MONOCHROME is defined at the top of the listing), the high and low bytes of register cx are assigned to 12 and 13. Otherwise, they are assigned to 6 and 7. Ideally, the program should automatically test for the presence of a monochrome card at run-time. This is illustrated in Section 11.3.

A test program that exercises functions getxy, gotoxy, remove_cursor, restore_cursor is given in Listing 5.5.

Listing 5.5   Test program to exercise cursor manipulation functions in util.c

```
#include <stdio.h>
#include "util.h"

main ()
{
  unsigned int x, y;
  char ch;

  clrscreen();
  gotoxy( 50, 12 );
  printf( "50, 12" );
  gotoxy( 60, 17 );
  getxy( &x, &y );
  printf( "%d, %d", x, y );
  remove_cursor();
  printf( "\n\nThe cursor is gone!  Enter a key: " );
  get_key( &ch, 1 );
  restore_cursor();
  printf( "\n\n\nThe cursor is restored!\n\n" );
}
```

5.4   Timing Functions

The functions in util.c that support timing are gtime and rpttiming. See Listing 5.2.

Function gtime returns the current clock time in hours, minutes, seconds, and hundreths of a second. This is accomplished using DOS service call 0x2C. The current second and hundreth of a second are returned in the high byte and low bytes of register dx. The current hour and minute are are returned in the high and low bytes of register cx.

Function rpttiming outputs the elapsed time between the invocation of rpttiming(begin) and rpttiming(end). This function is ideally suited for bench marking segments of code in an application.

A test program that exercises functions gtime and rpttiming is given in
Listing 5.6

Listing 5.6 Test program to exercise timing functions of util.c

```
#include <stdio.h>
#include "util.h"

main ()
{
  unsigned int hour, second, minute, hundreth;
  float operand1 = 3.0,
        operand2 = 4.0,
        product;
  int i;

  gtime( &hour, &minute, &second, &hundreth );
  printf( "The current time is: %d:%d:%d:%d\n",
          hour, minute, second, hundreth );

  rpttiming( begin );
  for ( i = 0; i < 10000; i++ )
    product = operand1 * operand2;
  rpttiming( end );
  printf( "\n\nThe value of product = %.0f\n", product );
}
```

5.5 Random Number Generation

The functions in util.c that support random number generation are rand_real
and random_int. See Listing 5.2.

Function rand_real returns a floating point number that is uniformly
distributed between 0.0 to 1.0. The algorithm ensures an exceedingly large
cycle length (that is, the cycle length determines how many values may be
generated before the sequence repeats itself). A call to gtime is made to
obtain the initial values of seed1 and seed2. Thirty calls are initially made
to rand_real to "warm-up" the generator. The for loop containing the 30 calls
to rand_real gets executed only one time in a given application.

The algorithm for random number generation is given by the code:

```
c = seed1 + seed2;
if ( c > max ) c -= max;
c *= 2;
if ( c > max ) c -= max;
seed1 = seed2;
seed2 = c;
return ( ( float ) c / 32767.0 );
```

The function random_int returns an integer that is uniformly distributed between low and high. The function rand_real is invoked to obtain the random integer.

A test program that exercises functions rand_real and random_int is given in Listing 5.7.

Listing 5.7 Test program to exercise random number generation functions of util.c

```c
#include <stdio.h>
#include <conio.h>
#include "util.h"

main ()
{
  int i;

  for ( i = 1; i <= 50; i++ )
    printf( "%5.2f", rand_real() );
  printf( "\n\n" );

  for ( i = 1; i <= 50; i++ )
    printf( "%5d", random_int( -100, 100 ) );
  putch( '\n' );
}
```

5.6 User Prompts and Messages

The functions in util.c that support user prompts and message are centermessage, spacebar, and yes.

Function centermessage first obtains the current cursor coordinate, x, y. It then uses,

```c
gotoxy( 40 - strlen( s ) / 2, y );
```

to center the message. If either the horizontal or vertical value sent into gotoxy is out of range, the gotoxy function protects against this error.

Function spacebar is useful for pausing program execution with the centered message, "Hit spacebar to continue —>" placed at the bottom of the screen.

Function yes is useful for pausing program execution and trapping either a 'Y' or 'y' or a 'N' or 'n' response to a yes/no query.

The test program in Listing 5.8 exercises functions centermessage, spacebar, and yes.

Listing 5.8 Test program to exercise the user prompts and message functions of util.c

```c
#include <stdio.h>
#include "util.h"

main()
{
    clrscreen();
    centermessage( "Test Program" );
    putch( '\n' );
    centermessage( "————————" );
    putch( '\n' );
    spacebar();
    clrscreen();
    gotoxy( 0, 10 );
    printf( "Is your answer yes or no (y/n)? " );
    if ( yes() )
        printf( "\nI thought you would answer yes.\n" );
    else
        printf( "\nI thought you would answer no.\n" );
}
```

Set Abstraction

This chapter presents the abstraction of a homogeneous set of discrete elements and its implementation in Turbo C.

A set is an unordered collection of elements. The principal operations on a set are insertion and test for membership.

In addition, there are various merging operations that combine two sets into a resultant set. Included among these merging operations are union, intersection, difference, and symmetric difference as well as others.

Only the merging operations of union and intersection are implemented here. The reader may wish to extend the set.c module to include other merging operations.

The objective is to limit the storage of each element in the set to a single bit. Since the only decision regarding each element is whether it is present or absent from the set, it should be possible to represent this information in a single bit.

Listings 6.1 and 6.2 present the function prototypes and definitions for the set abstraction.

The set data structure, given in Listing 6.2, has a static capacity of 32,000 elements.

Function insert computes an index using

```
element / 16
```

The denominator 16 is equal to the word size of the 80x86 machine in bits.

Function insert then uses the bitwise OR and assign operator, |=, and adds the bit 1 in position (element % 16). Because of the precedence of the operators, the expression

```
element % 16
```

is performed before the left shift. The assign and OR operator, |=, has the lowest precedence and is therefore performed last.

Consider an example. Suppose we wish to insert the number 16. The 0th index position holds the bits in positions 0 to 15. Thus the value, index = element / 16, produces index = 1. This is correct. The bit that must be enabled in this index location is given by the expression, element % 16 which evaluates to 0. This is also correct.

The function, in_set, which tests for set membership, reverses the process. After computing the appropriate index location, it determines whether the bit given by the expression, element % 16, is enabled (has the value 1). If it does, the element is in the set, otherwise the element is not in the set.

A test program that exercises the set abstraction is given in Listing 6.3.

Listing 6.1 Prototypes for set abstraction

```
#define CARDINALITY 32000

typedef unsigned set[ CARDINALITY / 16 ];

/* Make a set empty
**
**    ARGUMENTS
**       s - Set to empty
**
**    RETURNS
**       nothing
*/
void make_empty( set s );


/* Insert in set
**
** ARGUMENTS
**    element - unsigned integer
**
** RETURNS
**    nothing
*/
void insert( set s, unsigned element );


/* Determine whether element is in set
**
** ARGUMENTS
**    element - unsigned integer
**
** RETURNS
**    1 - Element in set, otherwise not in set
```

```
*/
int in_set( set s, unsigned element );


/* Union of two sets
**
** ARGUMENTS
**   resultant - The set formed by taking the union of
**               sets s1 and s2.
**   s1, s2    - The two operand sets used to form the
**               resultant set.
**
** RETURNS
**   nothing
*/
void set_union( set result, set s1, set s2 );


/* Intersection of two sets
**
** ARGUMENTS
**   resultant - The set formed by taking the intersection of
**               sets s1 and s2.
**   s1, s2    - The two operand sets used to form the
**               resultant set.
**
** RETURNS
**   nothing
*/
void intersection( set result, set s1, set s2 );
```

Listing 6.2 Definitions for set abstraction

```
#include "set.h"

/* Make a set empty
**
**   ARGUMENTS
**       s - Set to empty
**
**   RETURNS
**       nothing
*/
void make_empty( set s )
{
    int i;

    for ( i = 0; i < CARDINALITY / 16; i++ )
```

(continued)

```c
        s[ i ] = 0;
}


/* Insert in set
**
** ARGUMENTS
**    element - unsigned integer
**
** RETURNS
**    nothing
*/
void insert( set s, unsigned element )
{
    int index = element / 16;

    s[ index ] |= 1 << element % 16;
}


/* Determine whether element is in set
**
** ARGUMENTS
**    element - unsigned integer
**
** RETURNS
**    1 - Element in set, otherwise not in set
*/
int in_set( set s, unsigned element )
{
    int index = element / 16;

    return ( s[ index ] >> element % 16 ) & 1;
}


/* Union of two sets
**
** ARGUMENTS
**    resultant - The set formed by taking the union of
**                sets s1 and s2.
**    s1, s2    - The two operand sets used to form the
**                resultant set.
**
** RETURNS
**    nothing
*/
void set_union( set resultant, set s1, set s2 )
{
```

```
    int i;

  for ( i = 0; i < CARDINALITY / 16; i++ )
    resultant[ i ] = s1[ i ] | s2[ i ];
}


/* Intersection of two sets
**
** ARGUMENTS
**   resultant - The set formed by taking the intersection of
**               sets s1 and s2.
**   s1, s2    - The two operand sets used to form the
**               resultant set.
**
** RETURNS
**   nothing
*/
void intersection( set resultant, set s1, set s2 )
{
  int i;

  for ( i = 0; i < CARDINALITY / 16; i++ )
    resultant[ i ] = s1[ i ] & s2[ i ];
}
```

Listing 6.3 Test program for set abstraction

```
#include <stdio.h>
#include "set.h"

set s1, s2, s3;

main()
{
  int index;

  insert( s1, 12 );
  insert( s1, 15 );
  insert( s1, 16 );
  insert( s1, 17 );
  insert( s2, 11 );
  insert( s2, 16 );
  if ( in_set( s1, 11 ) )
    printf( "\nThe element 11 is in set 1.\n" );
  else
    printf( "\nThe element 11 is not in set 1.\n" );
  if ( in_set( s1, 12 ) )
    printf( "\nThe element 12 is in set 1.\n" );          (continued)
```

```
      else
        printf( "\nThe element 12 is not in set 1.\n" );
      set_union( s3, s1, s2 );
      printf(
      "\nThe elements in the union of sets 1 and 2 ->\n" );
      for ( index = 0; index < CARDINALITY; index++ )
        if ( in_set( s3, index ) )
          printf( "%d\n", index );
      intersection( s3, s1, s2 );
      printf(
      "\nThe elements in the intersection of 1 and 2 ->\n" );
      for ( index = 0; index < CARDINALITY; index++ )
        if ( in_set( s3, index ) )
          printf( "%d\n", index );
}
```

The output of the test program in Listing 6.3 is as follows:

```
The element 11 is not in set 1.


The element 12 is in set 1.


The elements in the union of sets 1 and 2 ->

11
12
15
16
17

The elements in the intersection of 1 and 2 ->

16
```

Part 2

Crafting Utilities

7

Stuffing the Keyboard Buffer

7.1 A Description of the Utility

The keyboard buffer, commonly called the "look ahead buffer," is provided by the MS-DOS or PC-DOS operating systems to allow a user to type ahead and have a program capture the characters at a later time. Unfortunately, the standard DOS keyboard buffer is limited to only 16 characters.

This chapter presents a utility that allows a programmer to stuff or preload this buffer with up to 15 characters that may be required in a given application that takes keyboard input. Normally this keyboard input would be provided in an interactive manner while the application is running. It may be useful to be able to "batch" the application by preloading the keyboard buffer with all the appropriate responses that the application requires.

For example, suppose the executable code for our keyboard stuffing utility were called stuff.exe. Furthermore, suppose that the application, my_prog, required that the responses 'Y', 'N', and <ESC> 'Q' be entered in the order given while the application is running. Using the stuff utility, a batch file, do.bat, could be written to accomplish this as follows:

```
stuff "YN\eQ"
my_prog
```

where the sequence \e indicates the escape key. Upon typing "do", the batch file program would stuff the characters, 'Y', 'N', <ESC>, and 'Q' into the keyboard buffer. The application program, my_prog, would not pause to wait for keyboard input but would capture these characters directly from the keyboard buffer.

7.2 *Technical Background and Algorithms*

The MS-DOS or PC-DOS operating systems implement the keyboard buffer using a 32 byte circular queue.

There are three memory locations that play an important role in controlling the keyboard buffer. These are: 0x41A, 0x41C, and 0x41E.

The first of these locations, 0x41A, stores information about the head of the circular queue. The second of these locations, 0x41C, stores information about the tail of the circular queue. The last of these locations, 0x41E, is the starting address of the keyboard buffer.

When a key is entered from the keyboard, the operating system assigns a two-integer code to the key. If the key is a normal printable character, the first integer is the ASCII code associated with the character. If the key is a special key, the operating system assigns a two-integer code to the character. The second integer is called the scan code. These codes are described in the DOS Technical Reference Manuals. The two-integer codes for a given key are inserted into the circular keyboard buffer queue by the operating system after a key is hit.

The keyboard buffer stuffing utility, stuff.c, must take control of managing the circular queue in the keyboard buffer. After each character is inserted (two-integer codes), the value of tail that is associated with the end of the queue must be updated. Also the byte offset that governs the position of the next two integer codes to be inserted must be updated.

The algorithm that accomplishes this is given in Listing 7.1.

Listing 7.1 Algorithm for insertion into the keyboard buffer

```
head = integer at memory address 0x41A
tail = integer at memory address 0x41C

if head = 60
then
  offset = 30
else
  offset = head MOD 30 /* MOD is the mod operation */

Put the first integer code into the address 0x41E + offset

head = head + 1
if head = 61
  offset = 31
else
  offset = head MOD 30

Put the second integer code into the address 0x41E + offset
```

```
head = head + 1
if head = 62
  head = 30
tail = tail + 2
```

7.3   Source Listing of stuff.c

Listing 7.2   Source listing of keyboard stuff utility

```c
/*
   This program accepts up to 15 characters on the command
   line and stuffs them into the keyboard buffer.

   File stuff.c

   Usage:  stuff string
*/

#include <stdio.h>
#include <stdlib.h>
#include <string.h>
#include <ctype.h>
#include <dos.h>

int index = 0;
int head,    /* Pointer to the beginning of circular queue */
    tail,    /* Pointer to the end of the circular queue */
    offset; /* Offset from 41E in the circular queue */
char buffer[ 20 ]; /* Holds the command line argument */


main( int argc, char* argv[] )
{
   extern void special_char( int first, int second );
   extern void ordinary_char( int ch );

   char ch;

   if ( argc != 2 )
   {
      printf( "%c", '\07' );
      printf( "\nCorrect usage: stuff string" );
```

(continued)

```c
      printf( "\n  \\e  -> escape key" );
      printf( "\n  \\c  -> return key" );
      printf( "\n  \\U  -> page up key" );
      printf( "\n  \\D  -> page down key" );
      printf( "\n  \\u  -> up arrow key" );
      printf( "\n  \\d  -> down arrow key" );
      printf( "\n  \\l  -> left arrow key" );
      printf( "\n  \\r  -> right arrow key" );
      printf( "\n  ^x  -> control x where x is any letter" );
      printf( "\n  @x  -> alt x where x is any letter" );
      printf( "\n  #x# -> Fx where F is a function key and" );
      printf( "\n          x is a numeral from 1 to 10" );
      printf( "\n   Example:  stuff \"\\eP\\c^L#3#\\D\"" );
      exit( 1 );
    }

    if ( strlen( argv[ 1 ] ) > 15 )
    {
      printf( "%c", '\07' );
      printf( "\n\nString length limited to 15 characters\n" );
      exit( 1 );
    }

    head = peek( 0, 0x41A );
    tail = peek( 0, 0x41C );

    strcpy( buffer, argv[ 1 ] );

    while ( buffer[ index ] )
    {
      if ( buffer[ index ] == '\\' &&
           buffer[ index + 1 ] == 'e' )
        /* ESC key */
        special_char( 27, 1 );
      else if ( buffer[ index ] == '\\' &&
                buffer[ index + 1 ] == 'c' )
        /* Enter key */
        special_char( 13, 28 );
      else if ( buffer[ index ] == '\\' &&
                buffer[ index + 1 ] == 'U' )
        /* Page up key */
        special_char( 0, 73 );
      else if ( buffer[ index ] == '\\' &&
                buffer[ index + 1 ] == 'D' )
        /* Page down key */
        special_char( 0, 81 );
      else if ( buffer[ index ] == '\\' &&
                buffer[ index + 1 ] == 'u' )
```

```c
        /* Up arrow key */
        special_char( 0, 72 );
      else if ( buffer[ index ] == '\\' &&
                buffer[ index + 1 ] == 'd' )
        /* Down arrow key */
        special_char( 0, 80 );
      else if ( buffer[ index ] == '\\' &&
                buffer[ index + 1 ] == 'l' )
        /* Left arrow key */
        special_char( 0, 75 );
      else if ( buffer[ index ] == '\\' &&
                buffer[ index + 1 ] == 'r' )
        /* Right arrow key */
        special_char( 0, 77 );
      else if ( buffer[ index ] == '#' && buffer[ index + 1 ] &&
                ( buffer[ index + 2 ] == '#' ||
                  buffer[ index + 3 ] == '#' ) )
      {
        /* One of the function keys */
        index++;
        switch ( buffer[ index ] )
        {
          case '1' :
            if ( buffer[ index + 1 ] == '0' )
            {
              index++;
              /* F10 key */
              special_char( 0, 68 );
            }
            else
              /* F1 key */
              special_char( 0, 59 );
            break;
          case '2' : special_char( 0, 60 );
                     break;
          case '3' : special_char( 0, 61 );
                     break;
          case '4' : special_char( 0, 62 );
                     break;
          case '5' : special_char( 0, 63 );
                     break;
          case '6' : special_char( 0, 64 );
                     break;
          case '7' : special_char( 0, 65 );
                     break;
          case '8' : special_char( 0, 66 );
                     break;
          case '9' : special_char( 0, 67 );
                     break;
```

(continued)

```c
          default:  printf( "\nUnimplemented function key\n" );
          exit( 1 );
    }
}
else if ( buffer[ index ] == '^' )
{
    /* One of the control keys */
    ch = tolower( buffer[ index + 1 ] );
    switch ( ch )
    {
      case 'a' : special_char( 1, 30 );
                break;
      case 'b' : special_char( 2, 48 );
                break;
      case 'c' : special_char( 3, 46 );
                break;
      case 'd' : special_char( 4, 32 );
                break;
      case 'e' : special_char( 5, 18 );
                break;
      case 'f' : special_char( 6, 33 );
                break;
      case 'g' : special_char( 7, 34 );
                break;
      case 'j' : special_char( 10, 36 );
                break;
      case 'k' : special_char( 11, 37 );
                break;
      case 'l' : special_char( 12, 38 );
                break;
      case 'n' : special_char( 14, 49 );
                break;
      case 'o' : special_char( 15, 24 );
                break;
      case 'p' : special_char( 16, 25 );
                break;
      case 'q' : special_char( 17, 16 );
                break;
      case 'r' : special_char( 18, 19 );
                break;
      case 's' : special_char( 19, 31 );
                break;
      case 't' : special_char( 20, 20 );
                break;
      case 'u' : special_char( 21, 22 );
                break;
      case 'v' : special_char( 22, 47 );
                break;
      case 'w' : special_char( 23, 17 );
                break;
```

```
        case 'x' : special_char( 24, 45 );
                   break;
        case 'y' : special_char( 25, 21 );
                   break;
        case 'z' : special_char( 26, 44 );
                   break;
        default:   printf( "\nUnimplemented control
                   character\n" );
                   exit( 1 );
    }
}
else if ( buffer[ index ] == '@' )
{
    /* One of the alt keys */
    ch = tolower( buffer[ index + 1 ] );
    switch ( ch )
    {
        case 'a' : special_char( 0, 30 );
                   break;
        case 'b' : special_char( 0, 48 );
                   break;
        case 'c' : special_char( 0, 46 );
                   break;
        case 'd' : special_char( 0, 32 );
                   break;
        case 'e' : special_char( 0, 18 );
                   break;
        case 'f' : special_char( 0, 33 );
                   break;
        case 'g' : special_char( 0, 34 );
                   break;
        case 'j' : special_char( 0, 36 );
                   break;
        case 'k' : special_char( 0, 37 );
                   break;
        case 'l' : special_char( 0, 38 );
                   break;
        case 'n' : special_char( 0, 49 );
                   break;
        case 'o' : special_char( 0, 24 );
                   break;
        case 'p' : special_char( 0, 25 );
                   break;
        case 'q' : special_char( 0, 16 );
                   break;
        case 'r' : special_char( 0, 19 );
                   break;
        case 's' : special_char( 0, 31 );
                   break;
```

(continued)

```
                case 't' : special_char( 0, 20 );
                           break;
                case 'u' : special_char( 0, 22 );
                           break;
                case 'v' : special_char( 0, 47 );
                           break;
                case 'w' : special_char( 0, 17 );
                           break;
                case 'x' : special_char( 0, 45 );
                           break;
                case 'y' : special_char( 0, 21 );
                           break;
                case 'z' : special_char( 0, 44 );
                           break;
                default:   printf( "\nUnimplemented alt character\n" );
                           exit( 1 );
            }
        }
        else
            ordinary_char( buffer[ index ] );
    }
    if ( tail > 60 )
        tail -= 32;
    poke( 0, 0x41C, tail );
}


/* Puts two integer codes into keyboard buffer
**
** ARGUMENTS
**    first, second - The integer codes of the key
**
** RETURNS
**    nothing
*/
void special_char( int first, int second )
{
    index += 2;
    if ( head == 60 )
        offset = 30;
    else
        offset = head % 30;
    pokeb( 0, 0x41E + offset, first );
    head++;
    if ( head == 61 )
        offset = 31;
    else
        offset = head % 30;
    pokeb( 0, 0x41E + offset, second );
```

```
    head++;
    if ( head == 62 )
      head = 30;
    tail += 2;
}


/* Puts a printable character into keyboard buffer
**
** ARGUMENTS
**    ch - Character to be put in the keyboard buffer
**
** RETURNS
**    nothing
*/
void ordinary_char( int ch )
{
  if ( head == 60 )
    offset = 30;
  else
    offset = head % 30;
  poke( 0, 0x41E + offset, ch );
  head += 2;
  if ( head == 62 )
    head = 30;
  tail += 2;
  index++;
}
```

7.4   *Discussion of Code*

The reader should refer to Listing 7.2.

The main program first tests to see whether the user has input exactly two command line arguments (the program name and the string of characters to be stuffed into the keyboard buffer). If the value of parameter, argc, is not equal to 2, the correct usage is displayed on the screen as follows and the program is terminated.

Correct usage: stuff string

```
\e  -> escape key
\c  -> return key
\U  -> page up key
\D  -> page down key
\u  -> up arrow key
\d  -> down arrow key
\l  -> left arrow key
```

(continued)

```
\r   -> right arrow key
^x   -> control x where x is any letter
@x   -> alt x where x is any letter
#x#  -> Fx where F is a function key and
        x is a numeral from 1 to 10
 Example: stuff "\eP\c^L#3#\D"
```

The values of head and tail are obtained from memory locations 0x41A and 0x41C. The string, argv[1], is copied to the string, buffer.

Within a loop that continues until all the characters in argv[1] have been processed, the program first tests for \e, then for \c, then for \U, then for \D, then for \u, then for \d, then for \l, then for \r. If any of these are found, the function special_char is called with the appropriate integer codes for the desired action.

The program then tests for #x# or #xx#, where x is a printable character. If such a sequence is found, the appropriate function key action is accomplished by sending the two integer codes to function special_char.

The program then tests for ^x, where x is a printable character. If such a sequence is found, the appropriate control key action is accomplished by sending the two integer codes to function special_char.

The program then tests for @x, where x is a printable character. If such a sequence is found, the appropriate alt key action is accomplished by sending the two integer codes to function special_char.

Finally, the program tests for an ordinary printable character. If such a character is found, the function ordinary_char is invoked.

The peek and poke functions, with prototypes in header file dos.h, are used to fetch and deposit words and bytes in specific memory locations.

7.5   *Application of Utility*

Many word processing systems, such as Microsoft WORD™, format text such that there are no newline characters (carriage-return, line-feed) after each line. Such newline characters occur only at the end of a paragraph. If a text file is generated with an ASCII program editor, it is common that each line is terminated with a newline character.

The purpose of this application is to convert a text file such as a letter, from ASCII format to WORD format.

The program, ltr, in Listing 7.3, is designed to input a text file and strip out the newline character at the end of each line except if one or more blank lines separate a given line from its successor line. In this case, the newline characters are left alone. It is assumed that the input text file is written flush left with no margin on any line. Some simple modifications to ltr.c would enable this program to strip out leading blanks at the beginning of each new line.

The goal of ltr.c is to automate the conversion of a letter written with an ASCII editor to a formatted WORD file that will then be printed. Normally after converting an ASCII file to a WORD file the user must enter WORD, format the file, and invoke the printer. The program ltr.c automates all of these tasks and offers the user turnkey conversion, formatting, and printing.

After conversion, ltr.c must stuff the sequence of characters L, (1 or 2 or 3), F3 into the keyboard buffer. These keys issue commands within WORD. This is done using the function, system, that allows an MS-DOS command to be issued from within a Turbo C program. The function call looks like,

```
system( "stuff 11#3#" ); /* stuff 11F3 into buffer */
```

Then, another call to function system invokes the Microsoft WORD program. Macros for formatting a letter, L 1 F3, L 2 F3, and L 3 F3 have already been defined in this word processing program. In fact, these macros format a letter, download an appropriate font to a laser jet printer, and invoke the printer, then exit the WORD program. Finally ltr.c invokes function system one last time to delete the Microsoft WORD created file .DOC. The net result of all of this is turnkey printing. The user never has to intervene in invoking WORD, formatting the text, invoking the printer, and exiting WORD. This is all automated by ltr.c by stuffing the keyboard buffer.

With relatively minor modification, the reader may wish to customize this program so that it works with another word processing system.

Listing 7.3 An application program for converting an ASCII file to a formatted letter in Microsoft WORD

```
/*
   This program allows an editor generated document,
   formatted flush left, to be converted to a WORD document
   and either formatted or sent to the printer in a turn-key
   manner.

   Usage:  ltr filename (1 or 2) [y]
               1 -> print and exit in a turn key manner
                       if y option is exercised, down load fonts
                       otherwise do not down load fonts.
               2 -> format letter in word but do not print
                       suitable for multiple page documents or
                       documents that the user wishes to touch up.
*/

#include <stdio.h>
#include <dos.h>
#include <string.h>

FILE *f1, *f2;
```

(continued)

```c
void error( void )
{
  printf( "%c", '\07' ); /* Ring bell */
  printf(
  "\n\nCorrect usage:  ltr filename 1 or 2 [ y ]" );
  printf(
  "\n\n  1 -> Turn key operation with printer" );
  printf(
  "\n\n  2 -> Set up letter but do not print " );
  printf(
  "\n\n  y -> Down load fonts (use the first time)\n" );
  exit( 1 );
}


main( int argc, char* argv[] )
{
  char out_file_name[ 13 ];
  char command[ 80 ];

  char *s;
  char ch;
  int count;
  int i;

  if ( argc < 3 )
  {
   error();
  }
  if ( strstr( argv[ 1 ], ".DOC" ) ||
       strstr( argv[ 1 ], ".doc" ) )
  {
    printf( "%c", '\07' ); /* Ring bell */
    printf(
    "\n\nFile name cannot end with the suffix .DOC\n\n" );
    exit( 1 );
  }
  if ( ( f1 = fopen( argv[ 1 ], "rt" ) ) != NULL )
  {
    strcpy( out_file_name, argv[ 1 ] );
    s = strchr( out_file_name, '.' );
    *s = '\0';
    strcat( out_file_name, ".DOC" );
    printf( "\n\n" );
    printf(
    "\n\nConverting %s to %s for use by Microsoft WORD\n\n",
    argv[ 1 ], out_file_name );
    f2 = fopen( out_file_name, "wt" );
    /* Read and write up to the colon at the end of Dear
       xxx: */
```

```
do
{
  ch = getc( f1 );
  putc( ch, f2 );
}
while ( !feof( f1 ) && ch != ':' );
/* Read and write past the next two cr's */
ch = getc( f1 );
putc( ch, f2 );
getc( f1 );
putc( ch, f2 );
/* Read and write while filtering out single cr's */
do
{
  ch = getc( f1 );
  if ( ch == '\n' )
  {
    count = 1;
    while ( !feof( f1 ) &&
              ( ch = getc( f1 ) ) == '\n' )
      count++;
    ungetc( ch, f1 );
    if ( count > 1 )
      for ( i = 0; i < count; i++ )
        putc( '\n', f2 );
    else
      putc( ' ', f2 );
  }
  else
    putc( ch, f2 );
}
while ( !feof( f1 ) );
putc( '\n', f2 );
fclose( f2 );
s = strstr( out_file_name, ".DOC" );
*s = '\0';
strcpy( command, "WORD " );
strcat( command, out_file_name );

if ( argv[ 2 ][ 0 ] == '1' )
  if ( argc == 4 )
    system( "stuff 11#3#" ); /* stuff 11F3 into WORD */
  else
    system( "stuff 13#3#" ); /* stuff 13F3 into WORD */
else if ( argv[ 2 ][ 0 ] == '2' )
  system( "stuff 12#3#" );    /* stuff 12F3 into WORD */
else
{
```

(continued)

```
        error();
        }
    system( command );
    strcat( out_file_name, ".DOC" );
    strcpy( command, "del " );
    strcat( command, out_file_name );
    if ( argv[ 2 ][ 0 ] == '1' )
        system( command );
  }
  else
  {
    printf( "%c", '\07' );
    printf( "\n\nThe file %s not found.\n", argv[ 1 ] );
  }
}
```

8

An Efficient Spelling Checker

8.1 A Description of the Utility

The spelling checker to be described in this chapter is extremely fast and memory efficient. However, it is not a full-feature spelling checker. Its output is a text file containing an alphabetized list of words from a given input text file that are not found in the spelling checker's dictionary. The user must scan this output file and determine the words that are actually misspelled. Using a text editor, the user can then search for these misspelled words and correct them.

Many full-feature spelling checkers display misspelled words in context, allow a user to correct the words in context, and provide the user with a list of words that are similar in spelling to the misspelled word. Such full-feature spelling checkers are also typically quite slow.

The spelling checker, Electric Spelling Express, described in this chapter is interesting because of the virtual hash algorithm that is used for dictionary storage and dictionary lookup. This algorithm, developed by the author, provides for lightning-fast dictionary access. As an example of this speed, a draft version of Chapter 4 of this book, containing 7507 words of text, and 2320 lines of text and occupying 45 single-spaced pages, takes 4.95 seconds to spell check on a COMPAQ DESKPRO 386® computer. The dictionary contains 29,341 root words. With the suffix logic used in the spelling checking algorithms, the effective number of words in the dictionary is well over double this value. Thus the throughput for spell checking Chapter 4 is 1516 words per second!

In addition to high speed, the virtual hashing algorithm is memory efficient. Only 2 bytes are required for each word stored in the dictionary. Words are encoded into unsigned integers and these integers are stored in the hash table (an array of unsigned integers). This permits much larger dictionaries to be constructed and stored in random access memory (RAM). The virtual hash algorithm is described and discussed in Section 8.2.

The use of Electric Spelling Express is now described.

Setup

The file SPELL.DTA contains an encoded form of a dictionary. The spelling checker suffix logic effectively expands the dictionary size so that it may check several times the number of base words actually contained in the dictionary.

The user should modify their autoexec.bat file by adding a SET SPELL path command to autoexec.bat. Specifically, SET SPELL should be set to the subdirectory that contains the dictionary file, SPELL.DTA as follows:

`SET SPELL=pathname`

where a legal MS-DOS pathname must be used.

After setting the environment pathname, the file SPELL.DTA should be copied to this subdirectory. The system must then be rebooted.

In the absence of any environment name, the program defaults to the pathname, c:\DICT.

Usage

`spell [ filename ] [ /h ]`

If a filename is not included on the command line, the program prompts for such a file name.

Normally, the spelling checker breaks hyphenated words into separate parts (for example, hy-phen-ate becomes the three words hy, phen, ate) and checks each of these separate parts as individual words. If the optional switch, /h, is on the command line, the spelling checker then merges all parts of a hyphenated word into a single word and checks it.

The output file that contains an alphabetized list of words not found in the dictionary is filename.SPL, where filename is the original file name prefix.

The file filename.SPL may be edited or sent to a printer for inspection.

Adding New Words to the Dictionary

The program, ADDWORDS, is used to expand the dictionary. The usage of ADDWORDS is

`ADDWORDS [ filename ] [ /s ]`

where filename is the name of any ASCII file that contains the words that you wish to add to the existing SPELL.DTA dictionary file. The ASCII file does not have to be formatted in any particular way. Spaces, tabs, or newline characters may be used as word terminators.

The program ADDWORDS prompts for the name of the ASCII file if you do not supply a name on the command line.

If the optional switch, /s, is enabled on the command line as a third parameter, then only words that begin with an asterisk, *, will be added to the dictionary (without the asterisk). The other words will be ignored. This option is useful in updating a list of misspelled words if this list contains some correctly spelled words that you wish to add to the dictionary.

The program reports the current number of root words stored in the SPELL.DTA file. This value will be correctly updated the next time you run the program after adding words.

The user should not add the plural of words such as trains (add train) or words that end in "ing" or "ed" or "er" since the suffix logic will take care of such occurrences. Only new root words should be added to the dictionary.

In order to protect the performance of the system, the ADDWORDS program limits the total number of words in SPELL.DTA to be 40,000.

When a word already contained in the dictionary is included in the file specified in ADDWORDS, the word is not duplicated in the dictionary.

When Electric Spelling Express runs, it reports its progress by writing to the screen the number of words checked, in increments of 1,000.

8.2 Technical Background and Algorithms

The central core of Electric Spelling Express is the virtual hash algorithm. It is used to construct and access a dictionary of words that are at least four characters in length. A separate small dictionary is used to store words of three characters or less. This small dictionary is combined with the virtual hash dictionary in the file SPELL.DTA.

The hash table used in virtual hashing is an array of unsigned integers.

The virtual hash algorithm encodes each word into two unsigned integers, a major key and a minor key. The major key is the index location in the hash array where the value, minor key, is placed.

In the event that two words produce the same major key, a simple linear chaining collision resolution strategy is used to locate a new major key for the word. This strategy consists of incrementing the value of the major key by one until either an empty array location is found or until a matchup is found between the minor key and a minor key already in the hash array. If an empty location is found, the minor key is inserted into this index location in the hash array. If a matchup is found, no insertion is performed since duplicate words are not allowed in the hash table.

In order for this or any hash function to be effective, it must scatter its data uniformly across the hash table. For virtual hashing, this means that the frequency distribution of major keys should be as uniform as possible within the range of allowable values. The term "hashing" is derived from the observation that a good hash function "hashs" or scrambles a word so that there is no apparent or obvious correlation between the word and its location in the hash table.

The success of virtual hashing in scrambling its major and minor keys is based on its similarity to well-known pseudo random number generators. These generators exploit the fact that when two multidigit numbers are multiplied, the interior digits are randomized.

In general terms, the virtual hash algorithm takes consecutive pairs of characters, forms them into 32 bit integers, multiplies these 32 bit integers and truncates the product to 32 bits. It then extracts groups of binary digits from the bit string of the products and uses these groups to form a new product for continued chain multiplication. At the end of this cycle of chain multiplication and bit extraction, 16 interior bits of the final 32 bit product are used to obtain the major key and 16 exterior bits are used to obtain the minor key.

Because unsigned integers are used to represent words, there is a possibility of error in checking a word that is not in the dictionary. The major and minor key of such a word may coincide with the major and minor key of a correctly spelled word that is in the dictionary. In such a case, the word that is not in the dictionary will be incorrectly processed as a correctly spelled word. The likelihood of such an error is very small. If there are 65,000 major key locations and 65,536 possible values for a minor key, the odds are roughly $1 / (65,000 \times 65,536)$ that such an error will occur.

Listing 8.1 contains pseudo code for the virtual hash algorithm. Listing 8.2 contains pseudo code for the linear chaining collision resolution algorithm that finds a new major key for a word in the event that the hash array location for the original major key is already occupied.

Listing 8.1 Virtual hash algorithm

```
Compute( input: word, output: minorkey, output: majorkey )

len = length of the word
if len is odd
then
  number_of_iterations = ( len - 1 ) / 2 - 2
else
  number_of_iterations = len /2 - 2
long integer w1 = makelong( w[ 0 ], w[ 1 ] )
long integer w2 = makelong( w[ 2 ], w[ 3 ] )
long integer w3 = w1 * w2
integer hiwd = high word of w3
integer lowd = low word of w3
integer lobyte = bits 15 to 8 of hiwd
integer hibyte = bits 7 to 0 of lowd
for iteration = 1 to number_iterations loop
  w1 = makelong( 0, makeword( hibyte, lobyte ) )
  w2 = makelong( w[ 2 * iteration + 2 ],
      w[ 2 * iteration + 3 ]
  w3 = w1 * w2
  hiwd = hilong( w3 )
  lowd = lolong( w3 )
```

```
    lobyte = bits 15 to 8 of hiwd
    hibyte = bits 7 to 0 of lowd
end loop
if length of word is odd
then
    w1 = makelong( w[ 1 ], makeword( hibyte, lobyte )
    w2 = makelong( w[ 0 ], w[ length of word - 1 ] )
    w3 = w1 * w2
end if
hiwd = lilong( w3 )
lowd = lolong( w3 )
lobyte = bits 15 to 8 of hiwd
hibyte = bits 7 to 0 of lowd
majorkey = makeword( hibyte, lobyte )
lobyte = bits 7 to 0 of hiwd
hibyte = bits 15 to 8 of lowd
minorkey = makeword( hibyte, lobyte )
```

The C language is ideally suited to implement the virtual hash algorithm given in Listing 8.1. Some of the operations may be implemented as macros and others as functions. The reader who has limited experience with C's bit manipulation capability should carefully study the bit manipulation macros and functions presented with the code listing of the next section. Included are macros and functions for building long integers from two ordinary integers, extracting a specified number of bits from a particular bit location within an integer, extracting the high and low words from a long integer, extracting the high and low bytes from an integer, and forming an integer from two bytes.

These operations can be performed very efficiently in Turbo C. This accounts for the high speed of the virtual hashing algorithm.

Listing 8.2 Linear chaining collision resolution

```
Find_hash_index( input/output: majorkey )

found = false
while ( table[ majorkey ] is not empty and found = false )
loop
    if table[ majorkey ] = minorkey
    then
        found = true
    else
        majorkey = majorkey + 1 mod ( maxindex + 1 )
    end if
end loop
if found = false
then
    table[ majorkey ] = minorkey
end if
```

The linear chaining algorithm given in Listing 8.2 requires that there is at least one empty location left in the hash array (table) at all times. In practice, the number of empty locations should be at least 25% of the table in order to lower the search time associated with locating a new major key due to collisions.

The reader may wish to consult the textbook, *Data Structures Using MODULA-2*, by Richard Sincovec and Richard Wiener, John Wiley and Sons, 1986 for more details concerning both the virtual hashing algorithm and linear chaining.

8.3 Source Listing of spell.c

The source code for the main spelling checker file, spell.c, is given in Listing 8.3. In recognition of the assistance provided by the author's son, Erik Wiener, in developing and testing this and other software utilities in this book, Erik's name is part of the title block.

The files fileio.h and fileio.c are given in the Appendix.

Listing 8.3 Spelling checker source code

```
/*

   Electric Spelling Express

   Compiled using Turbo C's compact memory model and linked
   with the files util.obj and fileio.obj  These files are
   presented and discussed in Chapters 5 and the Appendix.

   File: spell.c
*/

#include <stdio.h>
#include <ctype.h>
#include <stdlib.h>
#include <string.h>
#include <alloc.h>
#include "util.h"
#include "fileio.h"

/* Constants for small table lookup */
#define c2 26
#define c3 676
#define c4 96

#define getbits( x, pos, nbits ) ( x >> pos + 1 - nbits ) \
                 & ~( ~0 << nbits )

/* Define the size of the tables */
```

```c
#define buffersize 100000
#define hashsize 65000
#define smallsize 18280

int hyphenation;
/*
   1 -> close hyphenated words,
   0 -> break hyphenated words
*/

/* Tables */
unsigned int huge *hash;        /* Hash table.             */
char huge *buffer;              /* Buffer that holds words. */
unsigned small[ smallsize ];    /* Table of small words.   */

unsigned distinct_words;        /* Number of distinct words
                                   not found in file.      */
unsigned nwords = 0;            /* Number of words checked
                                   in file.                */

/* File handles or pointers */
int fp;                         /* Handle of file to spell
                                   check.                  */
int h;                          /* Handle of hash table
                                   file.                   */
FILE *output;                   /* File pointer to output
                                   text file.              */

/* Path names */
char filename[ 65 ],
     origfile[ 65 ];

/* Used for timing */
unsigned hour1, minute1, second1, hund1,
         hour2, minute2, second2, hund2;

/* Binary tree structure used for holding words not in
   dictionary.    */
typedef struct tree TREE;

struct tree
{
  char *word;
  TREE *left;
  TREE *right;
};

TREE *root; /* The root node of the tree that holds words
               that are not in the dictionary.           */
```

```
/* Allocate tree node
**
** ARGUMENTS
**    none
**
** RETURNS
**    pointer to tree node
*/
TREE *alloc_node()
{
  return ( TREE * ) malloc( sizeof( TREE ) );
}



/* Allocate memory for and save string s
**
** ARGUMENTS
**    s - String to be saved
**
** RETURNS
**    pointer to string that is saved
*/
char *strsave( char *s )
{
  char *p;

  if ( ( p = malloc( strlen( s ) + 1 ) ) != 0 )
  {
    strcpy( p, s );
    return p;
  }
  else
    return 0;
}



/*
** Insert word in binary tree
**
** ARGUMENTS
**    w - word to insert in binary tree
**
** RETURNS
**    0 - insertion unsuccessful
**    1 - insertion successful
*/
int insert_word( char *w )
{
```

```c
    TREE *current, *previous;

    if ( root == 0 )
    {
      if ( ( root = alloc_node() ) != 0 )
        if ( ( root -> word = strsave( w ) ) != 0 )
        {
          root -> left = root -> right = 0;
          distinct_words++;
          return 1;
        }
        else
          return 0;
      else
        return 0;
    }
    else
    {
      previous = 0;
      current = root;
      while ( current != 0 )
      {
        previous = current;
        if ( strcmp( w, current -> word ) < 0 )
          current = current -> left;
        else if ( strcmp( w, current -> word ) > 0 )
          current = current -> right;
        else
          return 1;
      }
      if ( ( current = alloc_node() ) != 0 )
      {
        distinct_words++;
        if ( ( current -> word = strsave( w ) ) != 0 )
        {
          current -> left = current -> right = 0;
          if ( strcmp( w, previous -> word ) < 0 )
            previous -> left = current;
          else
            previous -> right = current;
          return 1;
        }
        else
          return 0;
      }
      else
        return 0;
    }
}
```

```
/* Display alphabetized list of words in tree containing
** words not in dictionary.
**
** ARGUMENTS
**    p - pointer to tree containing words not in dictionary
**
** RETURNS
**    nothing
*/
void display( TREE *p )
{
  static int word_count = 0;

  if ( p != 0 )
  {
    display( p -> left );
    fprintf( output, "%-19s", p -> word );
    if ( ++word_count == 4 )
    {
      fprintf( output, "\n" );
      word_count = 0;
    }
    display( p -> right );
  }
}


/* Create a word from two individual integers.
** Combines the upper 8 bits of card1 with the lower 8 bits
** of card2.
**
** ARGUMENTS
**    card1, card2 - Two integers that are combined to create
**                   a word
**
** RETURNS
**    word (unsigned integer)
*/
unsigned int makeword( unsigned int card1,
                       unsigned int card2 )
{
  return ( ( card1 << 8 ) | ( card2 & 0x00FF ) );
}


/* Extracts the upper 16 bits of a long integer
**
** ARGUMENTS
**    l - long integer
```

```
**
** RETURNS
**    unsigned integer that represents upper 16 bits of l
*/
unsigned int hilong( long l )
{
  return ( ( l >> 16 ) & ( 0xFFFF ) );
}


/* Create a long integer from two integers
**
** ARGUMENTS
**    card1, card2 - Two integers used to form a long integer
**
** RETURNS
**    long integer
*/
long makelong( unsigned card1, unsigned card2 )
{
  long temp1, temp2;

  temp1 = ( long ) card1;
  temp2 = ( long ) card2;
  return ( ( temp1 << 16 ) | temp2 );
}



/* Extracts the lower 16 bits of a long integer
**
** ARGUMENTS
**    l - long integer
**
** RETURNS
**    unsigned integer that is the lower 16 bits of l
*/
unsigned int lolong ( long l )
{
  return ( ( l ) & ( 0xFFFF ) );
}



/* Virtual hash algorithm
** Returns the minor key and major key of a word using the
** virtual hash algorithm developed by Richard Wiener
**
** ARGUMENTS
**    w          - The word to be hashed
```

```
**     minorkey - The unsigned integer to be checked in
**                hash table.  Value is returned by function.
**     majorkey - The index location in hash table.  Value is
**                returned by function.
**
** RETURNS
**    nothing
*/
void compute( char *w,
              unsigned *minorkey,
              unsigned *majorkey )
{
  int even;         /* True if the word has an even number
                       of characters.                       */
  int temp;         /* Temporary integer variable.          */
  int iteration;    /* Loop counter.                        */
  int numberit;     /* Number of iterations of major loop. */
  long w1,
       w2,
       w3;          /* Long integers used in chain
                       multiplication.                      */
  unsigned hiwd,
           lowd,
           hibyte,
           lobyte; /* High and low words and bytes.         */

  int len = strlen( w );

  if ( len % 2 == 1 )
  {
    temp = len - 1;
    even = 0;
  }
  else
  {
    temp = len;
    even = 1;
  }
  numberit = temp / 2 - 2;
  w1 = makelong( w[ 0 ], w[ 1 ] );
  w2 = makelong( w[ 2 ], w[ 3 ] );
  w3 = w1 * w2;
  hiwd = hilong( w3 );
  lowd = lolong( w3 );
  lobyte = getbits( hiwd, 15, 8 );
  hibyte = getbits( lowd, 7, 8 );
  for ( iteration = 1; iteration <= numberit; iteration++ )
  {
```

```
      temp = 0;
      w1 = makelong( temp, makeword( hibyte, lobyte ) );
      w2 = makelong( w[ 2 * iteration + 2 ],
                     w[ 2 * iteration + 3 ] );
      w3 = w1 * w2;
      hiwd = hilong( w3 );
      lowd = lolong( w3 );
      lobyte = getbits( hiwd, 15, 8 );
      hibyte = getbits( lowd, 7, 8 );
    }
    if ( ! even )
    {
      w1 = makelong( w[ 1 ], makeword( hibyte, lobyte ) );
      w2 = makelong( w[ 0 ], w[ len - 1 ] );
      w3 = w1 * w2;
    }
    hiwd = hilong( w3 );
    lowd = lolong( w3 );
    lobyte = getbits( hiwd, 15, 8 );
    hibyte = getbits( lowd, 7, 8 );
    *majorkey = makeword( hibyte, lobyte );
    lobyte = getbits( hiwd, 7, 8 );
    hibyte = getbits( lowd, 15, 8 );
    *minorkey = makeword( hibyte, lobyte );
}


/* Check word against dictionary
**
** ARGUMENTS
**    w - word to be checked
**
** RETURNS
**    0 - word not in dictionary
**    1 - word in dictionary
*/
int check_word( char *w )
{
  unsigned majorkey, minorkey, tablevalue, len;

  if ( strlen( w ) != 0 )
  {
    len = strlen( w );
    if ( len <= 3 )
    {
      /* Check word against small table */
      if ( len == 1 )
        return ( small[ w[ 0 ] - c4 ] );
```

```
            else
              if ( len == 2 )
                return ( small[ w[ 0 ] - c4 +
                        c2 * ( w[ 1 ] - c4 ) ] );
              else
                return ( small[ w[ 0 ] - c4 +
                        c2 * (w[ 1 ] - c4 ) +
                        c3 * ( w[ 2 ] - c4 ) ] );
          }
        else
          {
            /* Check word against large table using virtual
               hashing.                                         */
            compute( w, &majorkey, &minorkey );
            if ( majorkey > 64999 )
              /* Make table a circular structure.               */
              majorkey = 1;
            tablevalue = hash[ majorkey ];
            /* Linear chaining collision resolution.            */
            while (   ( tablevalue != 0 ) &&
                      ( tablevalue != minorkey )   )
              {
                majorkey = ( majorkey + 1 ) % hashsize;
                if ( majorkey > 64999 )
                  majorkey = 1;
                tablevalue = hash[ majorkey ];
              }
            return ( tablevalue == minorkey );
          }
      }
}


/* Get next word in input text buffer
**
** ARGUMENTS
**    size - Number of bytes in buffer
**    w    - The next word that is returned
**
** RETURNS
**    0 - No word obtained
**    1 - Word obtained
*/
int get_next_word( long size, char w[] )
{
    long start, finish, len, i;
    char *source, *dest;
    char temp[ 60 ];
    static long pos = 0;   /* Location in input buffer */
```

```
    /* Move to beginning of a word */
    while (  ( pos < size ) &&
            ( ! isalpha( buffer[ pos ] ) )  )
      pos++;
    if ( pos >= size )
    {
      return 0;
    }
    else
    {
      start = pos;
      /* Move to the end of a word */
      while (  ( pos < size ) &&
              ( isalpha( buffer[ pos ] ) )  )
        pos++;
      finish = pos;
      len = finish - start;
      source = ( char * ) &buffer[ start ];
      dest = w;
      memmove( dest, source, len );
      w[ len ] = 0;
      if ( hyphenation )
      {
        /* Trap words that are hyphenated */
        if ( pos < size && buffer[ pos ] == '-' )
        {
          if ( get_next_word( size, temp ) )
            strcat( w, temp );
        }
      }
      for ( i = 0; i < strlen( w ); i++ )
        w[ i ] = tolower( w[ i ] );
      return 1;
    }
}


/* Put program title on screen
**
** ARGUMENTS
**    none
**
** RETURNS
**    nothing
*/
void title()
{
  int i;
```

```
              clrscreen();
              writestring_attr( "HIT-AND-RUN SOFTWARE:", reverse );
              writestring_attr(
              "                                                    ",
              reverse );
              writestring_attr( "Version 1.1    ", reverse );
              gotoxy( 0, 1 );
              writestring_attr(
              "  Richard Wiener              ELECTRIC SPELLING EXPRESS"
              "              Copyright (C)   ", reverse );
              gotoxy( 0, 2 );
              writestring_attr(
              "  Erik Wiener                                    "
              "                         July, 1987           ",
                 reverse );
              gotoxy( 0, 3 );
              writestring_attr(
              "╔═════════════════════════════════════════════════"
              "═════════════════════════════╗", normal );
              for ( i = 4; i <= 20; i++ )
              {
                gotoxy( 0, i );
                writestring_attr( "║", normal );
                gotoxy( 79, i );
                writestring_attr( "║", normal );
              }
              gotoxy( 0, 13 );
              writestring_attr(
              "╟─────────────────────────────────────────────────"
              "─────────────────────────────╢", normal );
              gotoxy( 36, 13 );
              writestring_attr( "MESSAGES", normal );
              gotoxy( 0, 17 );
              writestring_attr(
              "╟─────────────────────────────────────────────────"
              "─────────────────────────────╢", normal );
              gotoxy( 31, 17 );
              writestring_attr( "EXPRESS INFORMATION", normal );

              gotoxy( 0, 21 );
              writestring_attr(
              "╚═════════════════════════════════════════════════"
              "═════════════════════════════╝", normal );
              }


              /* Put error message on screen
              **
              ** ARGUMENTS
```

```
**     str1, str2 - Error messages
**
** RETURNS
**     nothing
*/
void error( char* str1, char* str2 )
{
  gotoxy( 5, 15 );
  printf( "ERROR: " );
  printf( str1, str2 );
  gotoxy( 0, 23 );
  restore_cursor();
  exit( 1 );
}


/* Put clock time on the screen
**
** ARGUMENTS
**     none
** RETURNS
**     nothing
*/
void put_time()
{
  int sec;

  if ( hund2 < hund1 )
  {
    hund2 += 100;
    second2 -= 1;
  }
  if ( second2 < second1 )
  {
    second2 += 60;
    minute2 -= 1;
  }
  if ( minute2 < minute1 )
  {
    minute2 += 60;
  }
  sec = second2 - second1 + ( minute2 - minute1 ) * 60;
  gotoxy( 3, 5 );
  printf( "Time: %d.%d seconds", sec, hund2 - hund1 );
}


/* Used by checkspelling */
void op1()
{
```

```
        int len;
        char word[ 60 ], temp[ 60 ];

        len = strlen( word );
        if ( word[ len - 1 ] == 's' )
        {
          strcpy( temp, word );
          temp[ len - 1 ] = '\0';
          if ( !check_word( temp ) )
          {
            if ( insert_word( word ) == 0 )
              error(
              "Heap overflow in tree", "" );
          }
        }
        else
        {
          if ( ( len > 3 )  &&
               ( ( word[ len - 2 ] == 'e' &&
                   word[ len - 1 ] == 'r' ) ||
                 ( word[ len - 2 ] == 'e' &&
                   word[ len - 1 ] == 'd' ) )  )
          {
            strcpy( temp, word );
            temp[ len - 2 ] = '\0';
            if ( ! check_word( temp ) )
            {
              if ( insert_word( word ) == 0 )
                error( "Heap overflow in tree", "" );
            }
          }
          else
          {
            if (  ( len > 3 ) &&
                  ( word[ len - 3 ] == 'i' &&
                    word[ len - 2 ] == 'n' &&
                    word[ len - 1 ] == 'g' )  )
            {
              strcpy( temp, word );
              temp[ len - 3 ] = '\0';
              if ( ! check_word( temp ) )
              {
                strcat( temp, "e" );
                if ( !check_word( temp ) )
                {
                  if ( insert_word( word ) == 0 )
                    error(
                      "Heap overflow in tree", "" );
                }
```

```
            }
        }
        else
          if ( insert_word( word ) == 0 )
            error( "Heap overflow in tree", "" );
      }
  }
}


/* Controls spelling checking
**
** ARGUMENTS
**    none
**
** RETURNS
**    nothing
*/
void check_spelling()
{
  int result = 1;
  unsigned j;
  long size;
  unsigned nbytes;
  char word[ 60 ];

  do
  {
    j = size = 0;
    do
    {
      nbytes = readfile( fp, buffersize / 4,
                         ( char * ) ( buffer +
                           j++ * buffersize / 4 ) );
      size += nbytes;
    }
    while ( j < 4 && nbytes == buffersize / 4 );
    get_next_word( size, word );
    nwords++;
    if ( !check_word( word ) )
      op1();
    while ( result )
    {
      result = get_next_word( size, word );
      if ( result )
      {
        nwords++;
        if ( nwords % 1000 == 0 )
        {
```

```
                    gotoxy( 71, 4 );
                    printf( "%d", nwords );
                }
                if ( !check_word( word ) )
                    op1();
            }
        }
    }
    while ( size == buffersize );
}


/* Write words not in dictionary to output file
**
** ARGUMENTS
**    none
**
** RETURNS
**    nothing
*/
void write_output()
{
    char *dot;

    strcpy( origfile, filename );
    dot = strchr( filename, '.' );
    if ( dot )
        *dot = '\0';
    strcat( filename, ".SPL" );
    gotoxy( 17, 15 );
    printf( "Potentially misspelled words in file %s",
            filename );
    output = fopen( filename, "wt" );
    fprintf( output,
    "ELECTRIC SPELLING EXPRESS" );
    fprintf( output, "\n\n" );
    fprintf( output,
        "%-30sWord Count: %-19uMisspelled: %-19u\n",
        origfile, nwords, distinct_words );
    fprintf( output,
    "_____"
    "_____ \n\n" );
    display( root );
    fclose( output );
}


main( int argc, char* argv[] )
{
```

```c
    unsigned i;                      /* Loop index variable.   */
    unsigned num_table_words = 0; /* Number of words in hash
                                      table.               */
    char *env_pathname;              /* Pathname of subdirectory
                                        containing SPELL.DTA.  */
    char dictname[ 80 ];             /* File name containing
                                        dictionary.          */

    title();

    /* Determine whether hyphenation logic is on.            */
    if ( argc == 3 && strcmp( argv[ 2 ], "//h" ) )
      hyphenation = 1;


    /* Get file name to spell check from the command line.  */
    if ( argc >= 2 )
      strcpy( filename, argv[ 1 ] );
    else
    {
      /* Prompt the user for the name of the text file to
         spell check.                                        */
      gotoxy( 5, 7 );
      printf(
      "Enter the file to check for spelling (CR to exit): " );
      gets( filename );
      if ( filename[ 0 ] == 0 )
      {
        gotoxy( 0, 23 );
        exit( 1 );
      }
    }
    gotoxy( 5, 7 );
    printf("         ");
    if ( ( fp = openfile( filename ) ) == 2 )
      error( "\a%s not found", filename );
    gotoxy( 27, 18 );
    printf( "Load:" );
    gotoxy( 27, 19 );
    printf( "Capacity: 40000 words" );
    gotoxy( 27, 20 );
    printf( "Condition: " );
    gotoxy( 38, 20 );
    writestring_attr( "INITIALIZING", reverse );
    remove_cursor();


    /* Allocate space for RAM buffer that contains
       the first 100,000 bytes of the text file.           */
```

```
      if ( ( buffer = ( char huge * ) farmalloc( buffersize ) )
           == 0 )
        error( "\aNot enough memory for buffer", "" );

      /* Allocate space for hash table.                          */
      if ( ( hash = ( unsigned huge * )
             farmalloc( hashsize * sizeof( int ) ) ) == 0 )
        error( "\aNot enough memory for hash table", "" );

      /* Get environment path.                                   */
      env_pathname = getenv( "SPELL" );
      if ( env_pathname == 0 )
      {
        /* Default if no environment name is set                 */
        env_pathname = ( char * ) malloc( 20 );
        strcpy( env_pathname, "c:\\DICT" );
      }

      /* Get path name of SPELL.DTA file.                        */
      strcpy( dictname, env_pathname );
      strcat( dictname, "\\SPELL.DTA" );

      /* Open hash table file */
      h = openfile( dictname );
      if ( h == 2 )
        error( "\SPELL.DTA not found in %s", env_pathname );

      /* Read hash table from disk into hash array.              */
      for ( i = 0; i < 5; i++ )
        readfile( h, 13000 * sizeof( int ),
                  ( unsigned int * ) ( hash + 13000 * i ) );

      /* Read small table from disk, close hash file.            */
      readfile( h, smallsize * sizeof( int ), small );
      closefile( h );

      /* Count the number of words in the hash table.            */
      for ( i = 0; i < hashsize; i++ )
        if ( hash[ i ] )
          num_table_words++;

      gotoxy( 33, 18 );
      printf( "%d words", num_table_words );
      gotoxy( 38, 20 );
      writestring_attr( "READY", reverse );
      writestring_attr( "       ", normal );
      restore_cursor();
      gotoxy( 3, 4 );
      printf( "Checking: %s", filename );
```

```
gotoxy( 56, 4 );
printf( "Words checked: 0" );
gotoxy( 38, 20 );
writestring_attr( "RUNNING", reverse );
remove_cursor();
printf( "\a" );

/* Start timer.                                            */
gtime( &hour1, &minute1, &second1, &hund1 );
check_spelling();

/* End timer.                                              */
gtime( &hour2, &minute2, &second2, &hund2 );

printf( "\n%c", '\a' );
gotoxy( 71, 4 );
printf( "%d", nwords );
gotoxy( 38, 20 );
writestring_attr( "DONE", reverse );
writestring_attr( "    ", normal );
gotoxy( 41, 5 );
printf(
"Potentially misspelled words: %d", distinct_words );
put_time();

/* Write output file containing words not in the
   dictionary.                                             */
write_output();
restore_cursor();
gotoxy( 0, 23 );
}
```

The source code for the addwords.c program is given in Listing 8.4. Because much of this code is the same as the code for spell.c, only new code is shown.

Listing 8.4   Add words source code

```
/*
This program adds words to the dictionary file, SPELL.DTA

Compile in Turbo C's compact memory model and link with
files util.obj and fileio.obj

File: addwords.c
*/

#include <stdio.h>
#include <stdlib.h>
```

```
#include <ctype.h>
#include <string.h>
#include <alloc.h>
#include "util.h"
#include "fileio.h"

#define getbits( x, pos, nbits ) ( x >> pos + 1 - nbits ) \
        & ~( ~0 << nbits )

/* Table sizes */
#define buffersize 100000
#define hashsize 65000
#define smallsize 18280

/* Constants for small table lookup */
#define c2 26
#define c3 676
#define c4 96

/* Tables */
unsigned int huge *hash;        /* Hash table.            */
char huge *buffer;              /* Buffer that holds words. */
unsigned small[ smallsize ];    /* Table of small words.   */

long pos = 0;                   /* Used in get_next_word and
                                   add_to_table.         */
long size;                      /* Number of bytes in
                                   buffer.               */

/* Subdirectory path names.                              */
char *env_pathname;
char dictname[ 64 ];

unsigned num_table_words;       /* Number of words in hash
                                   table.                */

/* File handle for hash file.                            */
int h;

unsigned words_added;           /* Number of words added
                                   to dictionary.        */

int star;
/*
   1 -> Add only words that begin with *
   0 -> Add all words
*/
```

```
/* Put error message on screen
**
** ARGUMENTS
**    str1, str2 - Error messages
**
** RETURNS
**    nothing
*/
void error( char* str1, char* str2 )
{
  /* See Listing 8.3 for function body */
}



/* Create a word from two individual integers.
** Combines the upper 8 bits of card1 with the lower 8 bits
** of card2.
**
** ARGUMENTS
**    card1, card2 - Two integers that are combined to create
**                   a word
**
** RETURNS
**    word (unsigned integer)
*/
unsigned int makeword( unsigned card1, unsigned card2 )
{
  /* See Listing 8.3 for function body */
}



/* Create a long integer from two integers
**
** ARGUMENTS
**    card1, card2 - Two integers used to form a long integer
**
** RETURNS
**    long integer
*/
long makelong( unsigned card1, unsigned card2 )
{
  /* See Listing 8.3 for function body */
}



/* Extracts the upper 16 bits of a long integer
**
** ARGUMENTS
**    l - long integer
```

```
**
** RETURNS
**     unsigned integer that represents upper 16 bits of 1
*/
unsigned int hilong ( long l )
{
   /* See Listing 8.3 for function body */
}


/* Extracts the lower 16 bits of a long integer
**
** ARGUMENTS
**     l - long integer
**
** RETURNS
**     unsigned integer that is the lower 16 bits of 1
*/
unsigned int lolong( long l )
{
   /* See Listing 8.3 for function body */
}


/* Virtual hash algorithm
** Returns the minor key and major key of a word using the
** virtual hash algorithm developed by Richard Wiener
**
** ARGUMENTS
**    w        - The word to be hashed
**    minorkey - The unsigned integer to be checked in
**               hash table.  Value is returned by function.
**    majorkey - The index location in hash table.  Value is
**               returned by function.
**
** RETURNS
**    nothing
*/
void compute( char *w,
              unsigned *minorkey,
              unsigned *majorkey )
{
   /* See Listing 8.3 for function body */
}


/*
** Insert word in hash table
**
```

```
**  ARGUMENTS
**     w - word to insert in hash table
**
**  RETURNS
**     0 - insertion unsuccessful
**     1 - insertion successful
*/
void insert_in_table( char *w )
{
  unsigned int majorkey, minorkey, tablevalue, len;

  if ( strlen( w ) != 0 )
  {
    len = strlen( w );
    if ( len <= 3 )
    {
      /* Add to small table */
      if ( len == 1 ) small[ w[ 0 ] - c4 ] = 1;
      else
        if ( len == 2 )
          small[ w[ 0 ] - c4 + c2 * ( w[ 1 ] - c4 ) ] = 1;
        else
          small[ w[ 0 ] - c4 + c2 * (w[ 1 ] - c4 ) +
                      c3 * ( w[ 2 ] - c4 ) ] = 1;
    }
    else
    {
      /* Use virtual hashing and add to hash array */
      compute( w, &majorkey, &minorkey );
      if ( majorkey > 64999 )
        majorkey = 1;
      tablevalue = hash[ majorkey ];
      while (  ( tablevalue != 0 ) &&
               ( tablevalue != minorkey )  )
      {
        majorkey = ( majorkey + 1 ) % hashsize;
        if ( majorkey > 64999 )
          majorkey = 1;
        tablevalue = hash[ majorkey ];
      }
      if ( tablevalue == minorkey )
        return;
      else
      {
        hash[ majorkey ] = minorkey;
        num_table_words++;
        words_added++;
        if ( words_added % 100 == 0 )
        {
```

```
            gotoxy( 69, 4 );
            printf( "%d", words_added );
            gotoxy( 33, 18 );
            printf( "%d words", num_table_words );
        }
      }
    }
  }
}


/* Get next word in input text buffer
**
** ARGUMENTS
**    size - Number of bytes in buffer
**    w    - The next word that is returned
**
** RETURNS
**    0 - No word obtained
**    1 - Word obtained
*/
int get_next_word( long size, char w[] )
{
  /* See Listing 8.3 for function body */
}


/* Add words in filename to the hash table
**
** ARGUMENTS
**    filename - File containing words to be addes
**
** RETURNS
**    nothing
*/
void add_to_table( char *filename )
{
  int fp;              /* File handle.                    */
  char word[ 60 ];     /* Storage for a word.             */
  int nbytes;          /* Number of bytes read with
                          readfile.                       */
  int result = 1;
  int i = 0;           /* Loop index.                     */

  size = 0;
  /* Check to see whether filename exists. */
  if (  ( fp = openfile( filename ) ) == 2  )
    error( "\a%s not found", filename );
  do
  {
```

```
          nbytes = readfile( fp, buffersize / 4,
                             ( char * ) buffer +
                             buffersize / 4 * i++ ) );
      size += nbytes;
   }
   while ( i < 4 && nbytes == buffersize / 4 );
   get_next_word( size, word );
   insert_in_table( word );
   while ( result && num_table_words < 40000 )
   {
      result = get_next_word( size, word );
      if ( result )
        insert_in_table( word );
   }
   closefile( fp );
   pos = 0;
}


void title()
{
   int i;

   clrscreen();
   writestring_attr( "HIT-AND-RUN SOFTWARE:", reverse );
   writestring_attr(
   "                                                  ",
   reverse );
   writestring_attr( "Version 1.01", reverse );
   gotoxy( 0, 1 );
   writestring_attr(
   "  Richard Wiener                ELECTRIC SPELLING EXPRESS"
   "           Copyright (C)  ", reverse );
   gotoxy( 0, 2 );
   writestring_attr(
   "  Erik Wiener                        Dictionary Modifier   "
   "           July, 1987     ", reverse );
   gotoxy( 0, 3 );
   writestring_attr(
   "╔═══════════════════════════════════════════════════╗ "
   "═════════════════════════════════════════════╗ ", normal );
   for ( i = 4; i <= 20; i++ )
   {
      gotoxy( 0, i );
      writestring_attr( "║", normal );
      gotoxy( 79, i );
      writestring_attr( "║", normal );
   }
```

```c
      gotoxy( 0, 13 );
      writestring_attr(
        "|┌────────────────────────────────────────"
        "───────────────────────────────┤|", normal );
      gotoxy( 36, 13 );
      writestring_attr( "MESSAGES", normal );
      gotoxy( 0, 17 );
      writestring_attr(
        "|┌────────────────────────────────────────"
        "───────────────────────────────┤|", normal );
      gotoxy( 31, 17 );
      writestring_attr( "EXPRESS INFORMATION", normal );

      gotoxy( 0, 21 );
      writestring_attr(
        "|└────────────────────────────────────────"
        "───────────────────────────────┘|", normal );
}


main( int argc, char *argv[] )
{
  unsigned int i;
  int newfile;
  char letter;
  char *filename;

  title();
  gotoxy( 27, 18 );
  printf( "Load:" );
  gotoxy( 27, 19 );
  printf( "Capacity: 40000 words" );
  gotoxy( 27, 20 );
  printf( "Condition: " );
  gotoxy( 38, 20 );
  writestring_attr( "INITIALIZING", reverse );
  remove_cursor();

  /* Allocate space for hash array.                    */
  if ( ( hash = ( unsigned huge * )
    farmalloc( hashsize * sizeof( int ) ) ) == 0 )
    error( "\aNot enough memory to load dictionary", "" );

  /* Allocate space for buffer array.                  */
  if ( ( buffer =
      ( char huge * ) farmalloc( buffersize ) ) == 0 )
    error( "\aNot enough memory to load file", "" );
```

```
/* Get subdirectory where SPELL.DTA is stored.          */
env_pathname = getenv( "SPELL" );
if ( env_pathname == 0 )
{
  /* Default if no environment name is set */
  env_pathname = ( char * ) malloc( 20 );
  strcpy( env_pathname, "c:\\DICT" );
}
strcpy( dictname, env_pathname );
strcat( dictname, "\\SPELL.DTA" );

/* Open dictionary file.                                 */
h = openfile( dictname );
if ( h == 2 )
{
  /* If dictionary does not exist, initialize tables to
     blank.      */
  for ( i = 0; i < hashsize; i++ )
    hash[ i ] = 0;
  for ( i = 0; i < smallsize; i++ )
    small[ i ] = 0;
}
else
{
  /* Read dictionary files from disk.                    */
  for ( i = 0; i < 5; i++ )
    readfile( h, 13000 * sizeof( int ), hash + 13000 * i );
  readfile( h, smallsize * sizeof( int ), small );
  closefile( h );
}

/* Count the number of words currently in the hash
   array.                                                */
num_table_words = 0;
for ( i = 0; i < hashsize; i++ )
  if ( hash[ i ] )
    num_table_words++;

gotoxy( 33, 18 );
printf( "%d words", num_table_words );
gotoxy( 38, 20 );
writestring_attr( "READY", reverse );
writestring_attr( "       ", normal );
restore_cursor();

/* Test to see whether a command string /s exists.      */
if ( argc == 3 && strcmp( argv[ 2 ], "//s" ) )
  star = 1;
```

```c
/* Test to see whether a file name exists.             */
if ( argc >= 2 )
  strcpy( filename, argv[ 1 ] );
else
{
  /* Prompt user for file name.                        */
  gotoxy( 5, 7 );
  printf(
  "Enter the file to add to dictionary (CR to exit): " );
  gets( filename );
  if ( filename[ 0 ] == 0 )
  {
    gotoxy( 0, 23 );
    exit( 1 );
  }
}
if ( !star )
{
  printf(
  "\n\nAdd all the words in %s (y/n) ", filename );
  if ( ! yes() )
  {
    printf(
    "\nUse /s, to add words that begin with *" );
    exit( 0 );
  }
}
gotoxy( 3, 4 );
printf( "Adding: %s", filename );
gotoxy( 56, 4 );
printf( "Words added: 0" );
gotoxy( 38, 20 );
writestring_attr( "RUNNING", reverse );
remove_cursor();
add_to_table( filename );
gotoxy( 69, 4 );
printf( "%d", words_added );
gotoxy( 33, 18 );
printf( "%d words", num_table_words );

/* Write the new hash table to disk and close file.    */
h = lookupfile( dictname, &newfile );
for ( i = 0; i < 5; i++ )
  writefile( h, 13000 * sizeof( int ), hash + i * 13000 );
writefile( h, smallsize * sizeof( int ), small );
closefile( h );
```

```
        gotoxy( 38, 20 );
        writestring_attr( "DONE", reverse );
        writestring_attr( "     ", normal );
        restore_cursor();
        gotoxy( 0, 23 );
}
```

8.4 Discussion of Code

The code in Listings 8.3 and 8.4 is heavily annotated with comments to aid the reader in understanding it.

There is a set of important macros and functions used to extract bits from words, combine words into long integers, and so forth, in spell.c. A few of these important functions are examined first.

An important macro used in spell.c is

```
#define getbits( x, pos, nbits ) ( x >> pos + 1 - nbits ) \
                 & ~( ~0 << nbits )
```

This macro takes a word x, a position in the bit string of x (pos 0 refers to the rightmost bit, pos 15 the leftmost bit), and the number of bits to extract from left to right from the given position. A new word x is returned with the appropriate bit pattern. The backslash character is used on the first line of the macro to indicate that the macro continues on the next line.

Function makelong, that combines two unsigned integers into a long integer, has code given as follows:

```
long makelong( unsigned card1, unsigned card2 )
{
    long temp1, temp2;

    temp1 = ( long ) card1;
    temp2 = ( long ) card2;
    return ( ( temp1 << 16 ) | temp2 );
}
```

The parameters, card1 and card, are converted with a type cast to type long. Then the first parameter is shifted to the left by 16 bits and "or'd" with the second parameter. The resulting long integer has card2 as its high word and card1 as its low word.

Function hilong, that extracts an unsigned integer from the high word of a long integer is given as:

```
unsigned int hilong( long l )
{
    return ( ( l >> 16 ) & ( 0xFFFF ) );
}
```

The long integer, l, is shifted to the right by 16 bits and "and'd" with the digit 0xFFFF (a string of 1's).

The memory model and some of the data structures are worth commenting on. A compact memory model is chosen because the combined storage for the data and code occupy more than one segment, but the code can easily be fit into one segment. If the code required more than one segment, a large memory model would be required. In general, a Turbo C programmer should use the smallest memory model appropriate for the application.

The hash array, hash, and the buffer for the text file are declared as follows:

```
unsigned int huge *hash;
char huge *buffer;
```

The huge storage specifier allows each of these structures to occupy more than one 64K heap segment. The actual memory storage for these two structures are allocated as follows:

```
if ( ( buffer = ( char huge * ) farmalloc ( buffersize ) )
     == 0 )
  error ( "\aNot enough memory for buffer", "" );

if ( ( hash = ( unsigned huge * )
        farmalloc ( hashsize * sizeof ( int ) ) ) == 0 )
  error ( "\aNot enough memory for hash table", "" );
```

The code for loading the 166,560 byte data file, SPELL.DTA, is examined next. The first 130,000 bytes of SPELL.DTA contains the 65,000 unsigned integers. The remaining 36,560 bytes contains the small table that stores words of less than 4 characters in length.

```
for ( i = 0; i < 5; i++ )
  readfile( h, 13000 * sizeof( int ),
            ( unsigned int * ) ( hash + 13000 * i ) );
readfile( h, smallsize * sizeof( int ), small );
```

Using the readfile function presented in Chapter 6, one fifth of the hash array is loaded at once. The MS-DOS system currently prohibits a block of more than 32,767 bytes to be loaded at once. After loading the hash array, the remaining smallsize * sizeof(int) bytes are loaded into the small array.

The code for spell checking is examined next. This code is reproduced from Listing 8.3 and is given in Listing 8.5.

Listing 8.5 Function check_spelling

```
void check_spelling()
{
  int result = 1;
  int len;
```

```
unsigned j;
long size;
unsigned nbytes;
char word[ 60 ], temp[ 60 ];

do
{
  j = size = 0;
  do
  {
    nbytes = readfile( fp, buffersize / 4,
                        ( char * ) ( buffer +
                        j++ * buffersize / 4 ) );
    size += nbytes;
  }
  while ( j < 4 && nbytes == buffersize / 4 );
  get_next_word( size, word );
  nwords++;
  if ( !check_word( word ) )
  {
    len = strlen( word );
    if ( word[ len - 1 ] == 's' )
    {
      strcpy( temp, word );
      temp[ len - 1 ] = '\0';
      if ( !check_word( temp ) )
      {
        if ( insert_word( word ) == 0 )
          error(
          "Heap overflow in tree", "" );
      }
    }
    else
      if ( ( len > 3 ) &&
           ( ( word[ len - 2 ] == 'e' &&
               word[ len - 1 ] == 'r' ) ||
             ( word[ len - 2 ] == 'e' &&
               word[ len - 1 ] == 'd' ) ) )
      {
        strcpy( temp, word );
        temp[ len - 2 ] = '\0';
        if ( ! check_word( temp ) )
        {
          if ( insert_word( word ) == 0 )
            error( "Heap overflow in tree", "" );
        }
      }
```

```
                  else
                    if (    ( len > 3 ) &&
                            ( word[ len - 3 ] == 'i' &&
                              word[ len - 2 ] == 'n' &&
                              word[ len - 1 ] == 'g' )  )
                  {
                    strcpy( temp, word );
                    temp[ len - 3 ] = '\0';
                    if ( ! check_word( temp ) )
                    {
                      strcat( temp, "e" );
                      if ( !check_word( temp ) )
                      {
                        if ( insert_word( word ) == 0 )
                          error(
                            "Heap overflow in tree", "" );
                      }
                    }
                  }
                  else
                    if ( insert_word( word ) == 0 )
                      error( "Heap overflow in tree", "" );
          }
          while ( result )
          {
            result = get_next_word( size, word );
            if ( result )
            {
              nwords++;
              if ( nwords % 1000 == 0 )
              {
                gotoxy( 71, 4 );
                printf( "%d", nwords );
              }
              if ( !check_word( word ) )
              {
                len = strlen( word );
                if ( word[ len - 1 ] == 's' )
                {
                  strcpy( temp, word );
                  temp[ len - 1 ] = '\0';
                  if ( ! check_word( temp ) )
                  {
                    if ( insert_word( word ) == 0 )
                      error( "Heap overflow in tree", "" );
                  }
                }
```

```
      else
        if ( ( len > 3 ) &&
             (    ( word[ len - 2 ] == 'e' &&
                    word[ len - 1 ] == 'r' ) ||
                  ( word[ len - 2 ] == 'e' &&
                    word[ len - 1 ] == 'd' ) )  )
        {
          strcpy( temp, word );
          temp[ len - 2 ] = '\0';
          if ( ! check_word( temp ) )
          {
            if ( insert_word( word ) == 0 )
              error( "Heap overflow in tree", "" );
          }
        }
        else
          if (    ( len > 3 ) &&
                  ( word[ len - 3 ] == 'i' &&
                    word[ len - 2 ] == 'n' &&
                    word[ len - 1 ] == 'g' )  )
          {
            strcpy( temp, word );
            temp[ len - 3 ] = '\0';
            if ( ! check_word( temp ) )
            {
              strcat( temp, "e" );
              if ( !check_word( temp ) )
              {
                if ( insert_word( word ) == 0 )
                  error( "Heap overflow in tree", "" );
              }
            }
          }
          else
          {
            if ( insert_word( word ) == 0 )
              error( "Heap overflow in tree", "" );
          }
      }
    }
  }
}
while ( size == buffersize );
}
```

Function spelling_checking, given in Listing 8.5, gets words from the 100,000 byte buffer of characters. This approach promotes much faster throughput when compared with reading words directly from the input text file.

A do-while loop that terminates when the number of bytes read into the RAM buffer is not equal to 100,000 bytes controls function spelling_checking. If the input text file is smaller than 100,000 bytes, this loop is executed only once.

For input files that are larger than 100,000 bytes, if a word is broken at the 100,000 byte limit, there is no provision in this version of the spelling checker to lace the seams of the next 100,000 byte buffer with the previous buffer and reconstruct the word that is caught on the 100,000 byte boundary. This is based on the assumption that the odds are overwhelming that such a word will not be misspelled. For example, suppose that the word caught on the 100,000 byte boundary were the word boun — dary, the output file would report boun as misspelled and dary as misspelled. No serious damage would have been done because no incorrect word would have actually slipped through the sieve!

An interior while loop that begins with

```
while( result )
{
   ...
}
```

fetches words from the buffer until all such words have been exhausted. If the number of characters read into the buffer (given by variable size), equals 100,000, another buffer is read in.

If a word ends with the character 's' and is not found in the dictionary, the 's' is stripped out and the resulting root word is tested. If it is in the dictionary, the word ending in 's' is accepted.

If a word ends in "er" or "ed" and is not found in the dictionary, these characters are stripped out and the resulting word is tested. If it is in the dictionary, the word ending in either "ed" or "es" is accepted.

If a word ends in "ing" and is not found in the dictionary, these characters are stripped out and the resulting word is tested. If it is in the dictionary, the word ending in "ing" is accepted. If it is not in the dictionary, an 'e' is appended to the word. If this word is in the dictionary, the word ending in "ing" is accepted.

This suffix logic just described is a two-edged sword. One the one hand it significantly expands the number of words that can be checked from the dictionary of root words. But unfortunately, it also introduces the possibility that some incorrectly spelled words will be accepted. For example, the word treeer will be accepted. This is because the last two characters, "er" will be stripped out leaving the correctly spelled word tree that will be accepted. Is the trade-off of increasing the effective size of the dictionary worth the risk of occasionally allowing a truly misspelled word to slip through the sieve? The author believes the answer is yes.

As words are identified that are not in the dictionary, these words are inserted into the binary tree by invoking the function insert_word. Each such insertion requires some heap overhead and is therefore error protected. If the function insert_word returns a value 0, there is no further room in the heap to store this word, and an appropriate error message is emitted.

In principle, there is no limit on the size of the text file that may be spell checked. As indicated before, 100,000 byte chunks of a large input file are input at a given time and tested.

What about building the dictionary? The program addwords.c, given in Listing 8.4, allows the user to input an ASCII text file containing words to be inserted into the dictionary. In principle, the user may "bootstrap" a dictionary by spell-checking a large file of correctly spelled words. Initially, every correctly spelled word in this file will be identified as misspelled and listed in the .SPL file. The user may then feed this list of misspelled words back into the dictionary using program addwords.c. These words will have been effectively added to the dictionary. This process may be repeated with additional files. The user's dictionary thus becomes trained to the vocabulary typically used by the user.

Of course, a much better approach is to obtain a text file of words that comprise a real dictionary. The addwords program may then be used to convert these words into a SPELL.DTA file. Even after a real dictionary is used to build SPELL.DTA, the user should refine this dictionary from time to time using the /s command line option in addwords. This option allows the user to flag correctly spelled words in the list given in a *.SPL file with an asterisk. These correctly spelled words can then be fed back into the dictionary by running addwords with the /s option. The user's dictionary will eventually become specialized to include the special class of technical words that perhaps are not found in an ordinary dictionary.

As indicated in Section 8.2, the addwords program limits the number of words that may be in the hash array to 40,000 words using the code segment

```
while ( result && num_table_words < 40000 )
{
  result = get_next_word( size, word );
  if ( result )
    insert_in_table( word );
}
```

This artificial limit is imposed to ensure that the hash array has sufficient free space to limit the length of the collision chains. It is expected that, as the limit of 40,000 words is approached, the performance of the spelling checker will drop slightly.

9

File Compression and Decompression Utility

9.1 A Description of the Utility

The file compression utility, arc.c, to be described in this chapter, encodes a set of one or more text files (ASCII files) and compresses them. For large text files, the degree of compression is between 40 and 60%. The use of arc.c can result in the savings of a significant amount of disk storage.

The user of arc.c can specify one or more files on the command line when the program is invoked. MS-DOS currently restricts command lines to be smaller than 256 characters.

As an alternative, the user can include a "/d" after the program name and then specify a wild card pattern such as ".c". In such a case, all files on the current subdirectory that end in ".c" will be compressed into an archive file.

The program prompts the user to name the archive file. It then compresses all the individual files into a single archive file. Later, when this archive file is decompressed using the utility, darc.c, the individual uncompressed files that comprise the original set are restored.

Progress statistics are reported on the screen as the arc.c utility does its work. A running total of the number of bytes compressed is given in increments of 2,000 bytes. When several large files are compressed as a set, the total number of bytes can be quite large.

The usage is

```
arc /d wildcard
    — Archive all files with wildcard pattern.
```

or

```
arc filename1 filename2 .. filenameN
```

9.2 Technical Background and Algorithm for File Compression

9.2.1 General Discussion of Huffman trees

The basis for text compression presented here is the famous Huffman tree algorithm. Although this algorithm is described in this section, the reader may wish to consult a data structures or algorithm design book for more details. One such book that contains an extensive discussion of Huffman trees is *Data Structures Using PASCAL*, Tennenbaum and Augenstein, Prentice-Hall, 1981.

The Huffman algorithm determines a bit-string (a sequence of 0's and 1's) for every character in the input file. The utility, arc.c, assumes that there are 256 possible characters that can be encountered in a given text file. These include printable as well as nonprintable characters and the upper IBM graphics characters.

A frequency distribution (histogram) that determines the frequency of occurrence for each character in the input file must be computed first. This distribution forms the basis for constructing the Huffman tree. The characters that occur the most frequently are assigned short bit-strings. The characters that occur infrequently are assigned longer bit-strings.

A Huffman tree is a binary tree consisting of branches that represent 0's or 1's. The closer a node is to the root of the tree (the geometric top of the tree), the smaller the corresponding bit-string is for the node. For example, for a text file consisting of the characters: AAAABBBCCD, the Huffman tree is given in Figure 9.1.

Let us examine Figure 9.1 carefully. The character with the lowest frequency of occurrence is D. It is combined with the second least frequently occurring character, C, to form a parent node $, with a combined frequency

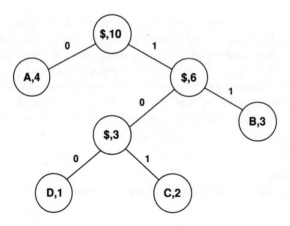

Figure 9.1 Huffman tree for AAAABBBCCD

of 1 + 2 = 3. This node, $, is combined with the node with the next lowest frequency of occurrence, B, to form the parent node $, with frequency 6. This node $ is combined with the final node, A, to form the root node $, with frequency 10. Huffman trees are built from the bottom, up by combining nodes of lowest frequency to form a parent node that is assigned a frequency equal to the sum of its children.

This method of construction assures that the most frequently occurring node is closest to the top of the tree. The node that occurs least frequently is at the bottom of the tree. Indeed the frequency of occurrence of a given node is inversely proportional to the depth of the node in the tree. If the bit 1 is associated with a right child and the bit 0 with a left child, the following codes can be gleaned from the Huffman tree of Figure 9.1:

```
A -> 0
B -> 11
C -> 101
D -> 100
```

For an alphabet of four characters (that is, A, B, C, and D) it would normally require two bits to represent each character. It would therefore normally take 20 bits to represent the sequence **AAAABBBCCD**.

Using the Huffman codes given above, it would take 4 + 6 + 6 + 3 = 19 bits to represent the same sequence. In this case the degree of compression is only 5%. For bigger files with an alphabet of 256 characters (8 bits per character), the gain is significantly greater.

Another example of a Huffman tree is shown in Figure 9.2. This tree represents the more complex sequence:

HGGFFFEEEEDDDDDCCCCCCBBBBBBBAAAAAAAA

The Huffman tree in Figure 9.2 is constructed as follows: The lowest frequency character, H is combined with the second lowest frequency character, G. The parent node, $, is assigned a frequency of 1 + 2 = 3, the sum of the frequencies of the children.

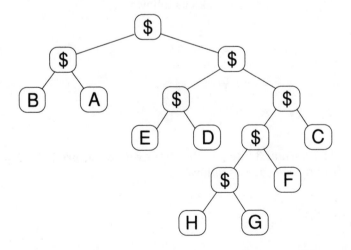

Figure 9.2 More complex Huffman tree

The next lowest frequency character, F, is combined with the next lowest frequency character, $, to form a parent node, $, with the assigned frequency 3 + 3 = 6.

The next lowest frequency character, E (frequency 4), is combined with the next lowest frequency character, D (frequency 5), to form a parent node, $, with the assigned frequency 11.

The reader is encouraged to continue this pattern and verify that the Huffman tree shown in Figure 9.2 is correct.

From the Huffman tree of Figure 9.2, the following codes can be assigned to the various characters in the tree:

a -> 01
b -> 00
c -> 111
d -> 101
e -> 100
f -> 1101
g -> 11001
h -> 11000

It would normally require 3 bits to represent an eight-character alphabet (A, B, C, D, E, F, G, and H). Therefore, the sequence HGGFFFEEEEDDDDDCCCCCCBBBBBBBBAAAAAAAAA would normally take 36 * 3 = 108 bits to represent.

Using the Huffman codes given above, this sequence takes 8 * 2 + 7 * 2 + 6 * 3 + 5 * 3 + 4 * 3 + 3 * 4 + 2 * 5 + 1 * 5 = 102 bits. This also is only a modest improvement. The reason why the improvement is so small is that the frequency distribution of characters is relatively uniform. The Huffman codes become more efficient when the frequency distribution of the characters is much more skewed.

As a final example, suppose that the text file contains 100 A's, 40 B's, 15 C's, 5 D's, 4 E's, 3 F's, 2 G's, 1 H.

The Huffman tree looks as follows:

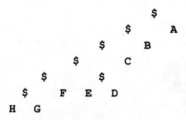

The normal 3 bits per character would require 170 * 3 = 510 bits. The Huffman codes are as follows:

A -> 1
B -> 01
C -> 001
D -> 00011
E -> 00010

```
F -> 00011
G -> 000000
H -> 000001
```

The number of bits required to represent the sequence is: 140 * 1 + 40 * 2 + 15 * 3 + 5 * 5 + 4 * 5 + 3 * 5 + 2 * 6 + 1 * 6 = 343 bits. This value is significantly less than the 510 bits required without encoding.

In general, the more uneven the frequency distribution of characters and the larger the input file, the better the level of compression that can be obtained using the Huffman codes. This suggests that Huffman coding is not efficient if it is applied to a binary code file. Such a file usually contains a relatively equal distribution of characters. Thus, no significant compression can be obtained.

9.2.2 Huffman Algorithm

Define a tree node structure as follows:

```
typedef struct
{
  unsigned char ch;
  int bit;            /* 0 or 1.                       */
  int left, right;    /* Index pointers to children.   */
  int parent;         /* Index pointer to parent node. */
  } nodetype;
```

The Huffman tree is implemented as an array of nodetype. Each node in the tree is associated with an index location in this array. Each node has index pointers that point to a left and right child (-1 implies nil pointer or no child) and a parent node.

The algorithm for building a Huffman tree is given in pseudocode in Listing 9.1.

Listing 9.1 Huffman algorithm in pseudocode and C code

```
/*
  The array nodes stores the Huffman tree.
  The array leaves stores the leaf node index in the
  tree for character  i.
  The array roots stores the frequency of occurrence of the
  character with root node i.
*/

Compute the frequency of occurrence for each character and
store this is freq[ i ].

For each character in the input file, form a node in the
Huffman tree, form roots array and leaves array:
```
(continued)

```
              for ( i = 0; i < 256; i++ )
              {
                if ( freq[ i ] > 0 )
                {
                  nodes[ avail ].ch = ( unsigned char ) i;
                  nodes[ avail ].left = nodes[ avail ].right = nil;
                  nodes[ avail ].parent = -1;
                  leaves[ i ] = avail;
                  roots[ avail ] = freq[ i ];
                  avail++;
                }
              }

              // Construct Huffman tree
              do
              {
                /* Determine the index, min1, of the minimum value of
                   roots[].
                */
                min1 = 1000000;
                for ( i = 0; i < 512; i++ )
                {
                  if ( ( roots[ i ] <= min1 ) && ( roots[ i ] != 0 ) )
                  {
                    min1 = roots[ i ];
                    minindex1 = i;
                  }
                }

                roots[ minindex1 ] = 0;

                /* Determine the next minimum index, min2, in roots[]. */
                min2 = 1000000;
                minindex2 = minindex1;
                for ( i = 0; i < 512; i++ )
                {
                  if ( ( roots[ i ] <= min2 ) && ( roots[ i ] != 0 ) )
                  {
                    min2 = roots[ i ];
                    minindex2 = i;
                  }
                }

                if ( minindex1 != minindex2 )
                {
                  roots[ minindex2 ] = 0;
                  nodes[ avail ].left = minindex1;
                  tree[ avail ].left = minindex1;
                  tree[ avail ].ch = '$'; /* For printing purposes */
```

```
              nodes[ avail ].right = minindex2;
              tree[ avail ].right = minindex2;
              nodes[ minindex1 ].parent = avail;
              nodes[ minindex1 ].bit = 0;
              nodes[ minindex2 ].parent = avail;
              nodes[ minindex2 ].bit = 1;
              /* Create a new root */
              if ( avail == 512 )
              {
                printf( "\n\nRange error in avail" );
                return;
              }
              roots[ avail ] = min1 + min2;
              avail++;
        }
   }
   while ( minindex1 != minindex2 );
   tree_root = minindex1;
   nodes[ tree_root ].parent = -1;
```

Let us exercise the algorithm in Listing 9.1 by building a Huffman tree
from the following text file: AAABBC.

```
roots[ 0 ] = 3; roots[ 1 ] = 2; roots[ 2 ] = 1
leaves[ 65 ] = 0; leaves[ 66 ] = 1; leaves[ 67 ] = 2
avail = 3

min1 = 1; minindex1 = 2; roots[ 2 ] = 0;
min2 = 2; minindex2 = 1; roots[ 1 ] = 0;
nodes[ 3 ].left = 2
nodes[ 3 ].ch = '$'
nodes[ 3 ].right = 1
nodes[ 2 ].parent = 3
nodes[ 2 ].bit = 0
nodes[ 1 ].parent = 3
nodes[ 1 ].bit = 1
roots[ 3 ] = 3
avail = 4

min1 = 3; minindex1 = 3; roots[ 3 ] = 0
min2 = 3; minindex2 = 0; roots[ 0 ] = 0
nodes[ 4 ].left = 3
nodes[ 4 ].ch = '$'
nodes[ 4 ].right = 0
nodes[ 3 ].parent = 4
nodes[ 3 ].bit = 0
nodes[ 0 ].parent = 4
nodes[ 0 ].bit = 1                                    (continued)
```

```
roots[ 4 ] = 6
avail = 5

min1 = 6; minindex1 = 4; roots[ 4 ] = 0
min2 = 10000000; minindex2 = 4;

tree_root = 4
nodes[ 4 ].parent = -1
```

9.2.3   Construction of Output Bytes

After a Huffman tree is constructed, the input file must be encoded by
replacing each character by its bit code. A bit string is constructed until
eight bits are formed. The resulting character is then sent to the output
buffer, and a new bit string is initialized. A given eight bit string may be
formed from several different input characters or parts of characters.

In this implementation of file compression, the Huffman codes are not
stored but are rather computed for each character, on demand. This is
accomplished by starting at the leaf node of the tree corresponding to the
given character and traversing up the tree to the root node. The sequence
of bits that is encountered is recorded and then reversed. This yields the
correct Huffman code for the character.

Listing 9.2 contains two functions, output_bit_string, and write_bit.
The function output_bit_string traverses up the Huffman tree from a leaf
node (character node) to obtain the code sequence for the character (actually
the reverse of the code sequence). It then passes the bits to the function
write_bits.

Listing 9.2   Functions output_bit_string and write_bit

```
void output_bit_string( void )
{
  unsigned char ch;
  int node;
  int len;
  int i, j, k;
  int bits[ 40 ];

  rewind( in_file );
  do
  {
    total_read = fread( input_buffer, 1, 10000, in_file );
    for ( input_index = 0; input_index < total_read;  )
    {
      ch = input_buffer[ input_index ];
      node = leaves[ ch ];
      i = 0;
      do
```

```
        bits[ i++ ] = nodes[ node ].bit;
      while ( ( node = nodes[ node ].parent ) >= 0 );
      j = -i;
      for ( k = 0; k < i; k++ )
        write_bit( bits[ -j ] );
      if ( ch == 11 )
        input_index += 10;
      else
        input_index++;
    }
  }
  while ( total_read == 10000 );
  /* Write the last output byte */
  output_buffer[ out_index ] = byte;
}


void write_bit( int bit )
{
  int move = bit;

  if ( byte_index == 8 )
  {
    byte_index = 0;
    if ( out_index == 10000 )
    {
      fwrite( output_buffer, 1, 10000, e );
      bytes_written += 10000;
      out_index = 0;
    }
    output_buffer[ out_index++ ] = byte;
    byte = 0;
    if ( ( bytes_written + out_index ) % 2000 == 0 )
      printf( "%c%ld", carriage_return,
              bytes_written + out_index );
  }
  move <<= byte_index++;
  byte |= move;
}
```

9.2.4   *The Output File Header Block*

In addition to sending the encoded characters (Huffman codes) to the output
file, it is necessary to transmit the Huffman tree to the output file. Without
this tree, there is no way that the decompression program, darc.c, can
decode the archive file. It is also necessary to send the output file some

additional information such as the root node of the Huffman tree, the names of all the files that constitute the input, the size of these files, and some other data.

We focus here on the methods for accomplishing this. A data structure, headertype, is defined as follows:

```
typedef struct
{
  unsigned char filename[ FILE_NANE_SIZE ];
  long size;
} headertype;
```

A variable, header, is defined as:

```
headertype *header;
```

This variable is the address of an array of headertype structures. As all the input files are concatenated into a single big file, the header array is filled with the name and size of each input file. The single big file is used to obtain the histogram of character frequencies.

The code that writes header information to the output file is given in Listing 9.3.

The first datum written to the output file is the number of input files that are compressed.

Next the header array (array of structures) is written to the output file.

Next the integer array, data, is filled with the low word of the long integer bytes_read, the high word of bytes_read, the number of nodes in the Huffman tree and the index of the tree root.

Next the array that represents the Huffman tree is written to the output file.

Finally the encoded data is written to the output file.

Listing 9.3   Code that writes header information to the output file

```
out_file = fopen( outfile, "wb" );
fwrite( &number_files, sizeof( int ), 1, out_file );
fwrite( header, sizeof( struct headertype ), number_files,
        out_file );
data[ 0 ] = lowword( bytes_read );
data[ 1 ] = highword( bytes_read );
data[ 2 ] = 2 * count - 1; /* Nodes in Huffman tree */
data[ 3 ] = tree_root;
fwrite( data, sizeof( int ), 4, out_file );
fwrite( tree, sizeof( struct treenode ), 2 * count - 1,
        out_file );
/*
   Code for writing the encoded data to output file
   ...
*/
```

9.3 *Source Listing of arc.c*

The source listing for the file compression program, arc.c, is given in Listing 9.4.

Listing 9.4 Source listing for file compression program, arc.c

```
/*
Huffman algorithm file compression program.
Compile with the small memory model.

Usage:  arc (filename filename .. filename)
                     or
        arc /d (wildcard pattern)
File arc.c
*/

#include <stdio.h>
#include <io.h>
#include <string.h>
#include <alloc.h>
#include <stdlib.h>
#include <dos.h>

#define debug

#define carriage_return '\n'

#define nil ( -1 )
/* Used to terminate Huffman tree */

#define tab '\t'

#define ARRAY_SIZE 256
#define BUFFER_SIZE 10000
#define FILE_NAME_SIZE 14
#define MAX_FILES 200

/* Used to obtain the date, size and name of a file */
typedef struct filetype FILETYPE;

struct filetype
{
  char dos[ 24 ];
  unsigned date;
  long size;
  char file_name[ FILE_NAME_SIZE ];
};
```
(continued)

```
union REGS inreg, outreg;

struct SREGS sreg;

FILE *in_file,      /* File pointer for input file(s).    */
     *out_file,     /* File pointer for output file.      */
     *e,            /* File pointer to temporary file.    */
     *big;          /* File pointer to temporary file.    */

long freq[ ARRAY_SIZE ];  /* Freq of occurrence of
                              characters.                 */
int leaves[ ARRAY_SIZE ]; /* Tree indices of the leaf nodes
                              for each character.          */
long roots[ 512 ]; /* Initial index location of every
                      tree node.                          */

int tree_root;      /* The root node of the Huffman tree. */

long bytes_read = 0;
long bytes_written = 0;
int number_files;
int total_read;
int out_index = 0;
int input_index;
long *ptr;
unsigned char byte = 0;
int byte_index;

/* Input and output buffers.                              */
unsigned char input_buffer[ BUFFER_SIZE ],
              output_buffer[ BUFFER_SIZE ];

unsigned char filename[ FILE_NAME_SIZE ];
unsigned char outfile[ FILE_NAME_SIZE ];

int count = 0, /* The number of distinct character symbols
                  in input file.                          */
    avail = 0; /* The next available tree index for node. */

/* Used for date, size, and name of a file.               */
FILETYPE dta;

int error;
char pattern[ FILE_NAME_SIZE ];

/* Array of filenames to be compressed.                   */
char filenames[ MAX_FILES ][ FILE_NAME_SIZE ];
```

```c
/* Node of Huffman tree */
typedef struct nodetype
{
  unsigned char ch;
  int bit; /* 0 or 1 */
  int left, right;
  int parent;
};

/* Node of Huffman tree that is stored on file */
typedef struct treenode
{
  unsigned char ch;
  int left, right;
};

struct nodetype *nodes;

struct treenode *tree;

/* File header data structure */
typedef struct headertype
{
  unsigned char filename[ FILE_NAME_SIZE ];
  long size;
};

struct headertype *header;


main( int argc, char* argv[] )
{
  extern void clrscreen( void );
  extern void get_freq( void );
  extern void build_tree( void );
  extern void output_bit_string( void );
  extern int lowword( long lnum );
  extern int highword( long lnum );
  extern void get_files( void );
  extern void print_tree( int root, int pos );

  char *pos;
  int i;
  int data[ 4 ];
  int file_number;
  long size;
  int padlen;
  int j;
```

(continued)

```
clrscreen();
printf( "\n" );
printf( "                      File Compression Utility\n" );
number_files = argc - 1;
if ( number_files < 1 )
{
  /* Print the proper usage of program on the screen */
  printf( "\nUsage:\n\n  arc /d wildcard" );
  printf(
  " — Archive all files with wildcard pattern." );
  printf( "\n\n     OR\n\n" );
  printf( "  arc filename1 filename2 .. filenameN\n\n\n");
  exit( 1 );
}
printf(
"\nEnter the name of the compressed archive file: " );
scanf( "%s", outfile );
if (   ( argv[ 1 ][ 0 ] == '/' ) &&
       ( ( argv[ 1 ][ 1 ] == 'd' ) ||
         ( argv[ 1 ][ 1 ] == 'D' ) )   )
{
  if ( number_files > 1 )
    strcpy( pattern, argv[ 2 ] );
  else
    strcpy( pattern, "*.*" );
  get_files();
}
else
  for ( i = 0; i < number_files; i++ )
    strcpy( filenames[ i ], argv[ i + 1 ] );
/* Allocate space for header array */
header = ( struct headertype * ) malloc( number_files *
            sizeof( struct headertype ) );
if ( header == 0 )
  printf( "\n\aNo space for allocating header" );
for ( i = 0; i < number_files; i++ )
  strcpy( header[ i ].filename, filenames[ i ] );
printf(
  "\n\nCompressing the following files into %s :\n\n",
   outfile );
for ( i = 1; i <= number_files; i++ )
{
  printf( "%-19s", header[ i - 1 ].filename );
  if ( i % 4 == 0 )
    printf( "\n" );
}
printf( "\n\n                              Compressing ..." );
/* Concatenate all files into one big file */
big = fopen( "big", "wb" );
```

```
for ( file_number = 1; file_number <= number_files;
      file_number++ )
{
  in_file = fopen( filenames[ file_number - 1 ], "rb" );
  if ( in_file == 0 )
  {
   printf( "\a" );
   printf( "\n\n           %s does not exist.",
  filenames[ file_number - 1 ] );
    exit( 1 );
  }
  size = 0;
  do
  {
   total_read = fread( input_buffer, 1, BUFFER_SIZE,
                       in_file );
    size += total_read;
    fwrite( input_buffer, 1, total_read, big );
  }
  while ( total_read == BUFFER_SIZE );
  header[ file_number - 1 ].size = size;
  fclose( in_file );
}
e = fopen( "erase", "w+b" );
fclose( big );
in_file = fopen( "big", "r+b" );
get_freq();
/* Count the number of symbols in the file */
for ( i = 0; i < ARRAY_SIZE; i++ )
  if ( freq[ i ] > 0 )
    count++;
printf( "%c      ", carriage_return );
printf(
  "%c%ld\t—  The total number of input bytes",
  carriage_return, bytes_read );
printf( "\n0\t—  The number of output bytes%c",
        carriage_return );
/* Construct huffman tree */
build_tree();
/* Build output bit string */
output_bit_string();
bytes_written += out_index + 1;
printf( "%c%ld", carriage_return, bytes_written );
/*
  The structure of the output file is:
  (number files), (header),
  (bytes_read), (number of nodes in tree), (tree_root),
  (tree), output_buffer
```

(continued)

```
*/
out_file = fopen( outfile, "wb" );
fwrite( &number_files, 2, 1, out_file );
fwrite( header, sizeof( struct headertype ), number_files,
        out_file );
data[ 0 ] = lowword( bytes_read );
data[ 1 ] = highword( bytes_read );
data[ 2 ] = 2 * count - 1; /* Nodes in Huffman tree */
data[ 3 ] = tree_root;
fwrite( data, 2, 4, out_file );
fwrite( tree, sizeof( struct treenode ), 2 * count - 1,
        out_file );
if ( bytes_written >= BUFFER_SIZE )
{
  fwrite( output_buffer, 1, out_index + 1, e );
  rewind( e );
  do
  {
    total_read = fread( output_buffer, 1, BUFFER_SIZE,
                        e );
    if ( total_read > 0 )
      fwrite( output_buffer, 1, total_read, out_file );
  }
  while ( total_read == BUFFER_SIZE );
}
else
  fwrite( output_buffer, 1, out_index + 1, out_file );
fclose( out_file );
fclose( big );
fclose( e );
/* Remove the file 'erase' from disk */
inreg.x.ax = 0x4100;
strcpy( filename, "erase" );
ptr = ( long * ) filename;
sreg.ds = FP_SEG( ptr );
inreg.x.dx = FP_OFF( ptr );
intdosx( &inreg, &outreg, &sreg );

/* Remove the file 'big' from disk */
inreg.x.ax = 0x4100;
strcpy( filename, "big" );
ptr = ( long * ) filename;
sreg.ds = FP_SEG( ptr );
inreg.x.dx = FP_OFF( ptr );
intdosx( &inreg, &outreg, &sreg );
printf( "\n\n\n\n" );
#ifdef debug
  print_tree( tree_root, 70 );
#endif
}
```

```
/* Clear screen
**
** ARGUMENTS
**    none
**
** RETURNS
**    nothing
*/
void clrscreen( void )
/* See DOS reference manual. */
{
  /* Requires ANSI.SYS driver */
  unsigned int esc = 27;
  printf( "%c[2J", esc );
}


/* Returns the low-order word of long integer
**
** ARGUMENTS
**    lnum - long integer
**
** RETURNS
**    The low-order word of lnum
*/
int lowword( long lnum )
{
  return ( lnum & 0xFFFF );
}


/* Returns the high-order word of long integer
**
** ARGUMENTS
**    lnum - long integer
**
** RETURNS
**    The low-order word of lnum
*/
int highword( long lnum )
{
  return ( ( lnum >> 16 ) & 0xFFFF );
}


/* Add a bit to the variable byte.  If the byte_index is
** equal to 8, write the byte to the output file.
**
** ARGUMENTS
**    bit - The bit (0 or 1) to add to byte
```
(continued)

```
**
** RETURNS
**    nothing
*/
void write_bit( int bit )
{
  int move = bit;

  if ( byte_index == 8 )
  {
    byte_index = 0;
    if ( out_index == BUFFER_SIZE )
    {
     fwrite( output_buffer, 1, BUFFER_SIZE, e );
     bytes_written += BUFFER_SIZE;
     out_index = 0;
    }
    output_buffer[ out_index++ ] = byte;
    byte = 0;
    if ( ( bytes_written + out_index ) % 2000 == 0 )
      printf( "%c%ld", carriage_return,
              bytes_written + out_index );
  }
  move <<= byte_index++;
  byte |= move;
}


/* Read input file and output the appropriate sequence of
** bytes to the output file.
**
** ARGUMENTS
**    none
**
** RETURNS
**    nothing
*/
void output_bit_string( void )
{
  unsigned char ch;
  int node;
  int len;
  int i, j, k;
  int bits[ 40 ];

  rewind( in_file );
  do
  {
    total_read = fread( input_buffer, 1, BUFFER_SIZE,
                        in_file );
```

```
      for ( input_index = 0; input_index < total_read;  )
      {
        ch = input_buffer[ input_index ];
        node = leaves[ ch ];
        i= 0;
        do
          bits[ i++ ] = nodes[ node ].bit;
        while ( ( node = nodes[ node ].parent ) >= 0 );
        j = -i;
        for ( k = 0; k < i; k++ )
          write_bit( bits[ -j ] );
        if ( ch == tab )
          input_index += 10;
        else
          input_index++;
    }
  }
  while ( total_read == BUFFER_SIZE );
  /* Write the last output byte */
  output_buffer[ out_index ] = byte;
}


/* Construct Huffman tree from the frequency distribution
** of characters in the text.
**
** ARGUMENTS
**    none
**
** RETURNS
**    nothing
*/
void build_tree( void )
{
  int i;
  long min1, min2;
  long minindex1,
       minindex2;

  /* Allocate space for the node tree */
  nodes = ( struct nodetype * ) malloc( ( 2 * count - 1 ) *
            sizeof( struct nodetype ) );
  if ( nodes == 0 )
    printf( "\n\aNo space for allocating nodes" );
  tree = ( struct treenode * ) malloc( ( 2 * count - 1 ) *
            sizeof( struct treenode ) );
  if ( tree == 0 )
    printf( "\n\aNo space for allocating tree" );
  /* Form a node for each character in the frequency
     table.                                            */
```
(continued)

```
        for ( i = 0; i < ARRAY_SIZE; i++ )
          if ( freq[ i ] > 0 )
          {
            nodes[ avail ].ch = ( unsigned char ) i;
            tree[ avail ].ch = ( unsigned char ) i;
            nodes[ avail ].left = nodes[ avail ].right = nil;
            tree[ avail ].left = tree[ avail ].right = nil;
            nodes[ avail ].parent = -1;
            leaves[ i ] = avail;
            roots[ avail ] = freq[ i ];
            avail++;
          }
        /* Construct Huffman tree */
        do
        {
          min1 = 1000000;
          for ( i = 0; i < 512; i++ )
          {
            if ( ( roots[ i ] <= min1 ) && ( roots[ i ] != 0 ) )
            {
              min1 = roots[ i ];
              minindex1 = i;
            }
          }
          roots[ minindex1 ] = 0;
          min2 = 1000000;
          minindex2 = minindex1;
          for ( i = 0; i < 512; i++ )
          {
            if ( ( roots[ i ] <= min2 ) && ( roots[ i ] != 0 ) )
            {
              min2 = roots[ i ];
              minindex2 = i;
            }
          }
          if ( minindex1 != minindex2 )
          {
            roots[ minindex2 ] = 0;
            nodes[ avail ].left = minindex1;
            tree[ avail ].left = minindex1;
            tree[ avail ].ch = '$'; /* For printing purposes */
            nodes[ avail ].right = minindex2;
            tree[ avail ].right = minindex2;
            nodes[ minindex1 ].parent = avail;
            nodes[ minindex1 ].bit = 0;
            nodes[ minindex2 ].parent = avail;
            nodes[ minindex2 ].bit = 1;
            /* Create a new root */
            if ( avail == 512 )
```

```
        {
          printf( "\n\nRange error in avail" );
          return;
        }
        roots[ avail ] = min1 + min2;
        avail++;
      }
    }
    while ( minindex1 != minindex2 );
    tree_root = minindex1;
    nodes[ tree_root ].parent = -1;
}


/* Print the Huffman tree on the screen if debug
** is defined.
**
** ARGUMENTS
**      root - Root index of tree
**      pos  - Starting right column of tree on the screen
*/
#ifdef debug
void print_tree( int root, int pos )
{
  int i;

  if ( root != nil )
  {
    print_tree( tree[ root ].left, pos - 4 );
    for ( i = 1; i <= pos; i++ )
      printf( "%c", ' ' );
    printf( "%c", tree[ root ].ch );
    printf( "\n" );
    print_tree( tree[ root ].right, pos - 4 );
  }
}
#endif


/* Read the input files and get the frequency distribution
** of characters.
**
** ARGUMENTS
**      none
**
** RETURNS
**      nothing
*/
void get_freq( void )                                      (continued)
```

```
          {
            int i;
            unsigned char ch;
            int z;
            long offset;

            bytes_read = 0;
            do
            {
              total_read = fread( input_buffer, 1, BUFFER_SIZE,
                                     in_file );
              for ( i = 0; i < total_read; )
              {
                ch = input_buffer[ i ];
                if ( ch == 10 && i < 24990 ) /* line feed */
                {
                  freq[ 10 ]++;
                  /* Test to see whether next 10 characters are
                     blank. */
                  z = i++;
                  do
                    z++;
                  while ( z < i + 10 && input_buffer[ z ] == ' ' );
                  if ( z >= i + 10 )   /* 10 blanks found */
                  {
                    input_buffer[ i ] = tab;
                    offset = ( long ) ( bytes_read + i );
                    fseek( in_file, offset, SEEK_SET );
                    fwrite( &input_buffer[ i ], 1,  1, in_file );
                    freq[ tab ]++;
                    i += 10;
                  }
                }
                else
                  freq[ input_buffer[ i++ ] ]++;
              }
              bytes_read += total_read;
              fseek( in_file, bytes_read, SEEK_SET );
            }
            while ( total_read == BUFFER_SIZE );
          }


          /* Get the file names in the system of files to be
          ** compressed.
          **
          ** ARGUMENTS
          **    none
          **
```

```
**  RETURNS
**      nothing
*/
void get_files( void )
{
  int index;
  char str[ 50 ];
  char pat[ 90 ];

  number_files = 0;
  /* Set the data transfer area */
  ptr = ( long * ) &dta;
  sreg.ds = FP_SEG( ptr );
  inreg.x.dx = FP_OFF( ptr );
  inreg.x.ax = 0x1A00;
  intdosx( &inreg, &outreg, &sreg );
  /* Get the first file */
  inreg.x.ax = 0x4E00;
  inreg.x.cx = 16;
  ptr = ( long * ) pattern;
  sreg.ds = FP_SEG( ptr );
  inreg.x.dx = FP_OFF( ptr );
  intdosx( &inreg, &outreg, &sreg );
  error = outreg.x.ax;
  if (  ( ! error ) && ( dta.size != 0 )  )
    strcpy( filenames[ number_files++ ], dta.file_name );
  inreg.x.ax = 0x4F00;
  intdosx( &inreg, &outreg, &sreg );
  error = outreg.x.ax;
  while ( ! error )
  {
    if ( dta.size != 0 )
      strcpy( filenames[ number_files++ ], dta.file_name );
    intdosx( &inreg, &outreg, &sreg );
    error = outreg.x.ax;
  }
}
```

9.4 *File Decompression*

The program darc.c decompresses an encoded archive file and restores the original files. Its usage is

darc archive_file_name

The algorithm for file decompression is easier than the algorithm for file compression.

The Huffman tree is retrieved from the archive file. The root node is also obtained from this file. The sequence of encoded bits is read from the archive file. Starting at the root node of the Huffman tree, a traversal is performed based on the sequence of encoded 0's and 1's found in the archive file. When a leaf node is encountered, the character in that particular leaf node is sent to the output buffer. Another traversal of the tree is performed and another character is obtained and sent to the output buffer.

As an example, suppose the Huffman tree is given by the tree in Figure 9.1. Suppose the encoded bit sequence is 011101. The bit 0 takes us to the leaf node with character 'A'. The sequence 11 takes us to the leaf node with character 'B'. Finally, the sequence 101 takes us to the leaf node with character 'C'. The decoded message is therefore "ABC".

Listing 9.5 contains the source code for the program darc.c, the file decompression program. Because of the similarity that this code has to the arc.c program in Listing 9.4, there is no discussion of this code presented.

Listing 9.5 Source code for the file decompression program darc.c

```
/*
File decompression program.
Compile with the small memory model.

Usage:  darc (filename)
File arc.c
*/

#include <stdio.h>
#include <string.h>
#include <alloc.h>
#include <dos.h>
#include "fileio.h"

#define array_size 25000
#define FILE_NAME_SIZE 14

#define tab 11

const int nil = -1;

int f, g; /* File handles */

unsigned char input_buffer[ array_size ],
              original[ array_size ];

typedef struct treenode
{
  unsigned char ch;
  int left, right;
};
```

```
struct treenode *tree;

typedef struct headertype
{
  unsigned char filename[ FILE_NAME_SIZE ];
  long size;
};

struct headertype *header;


main( int argc, char* argv[] )
{
  extern void clrscreen( void );

  unsigned data[ 4 ];
  int tree_root;     /* Index to the root of Huffman tree. */
  int number_nodes;  /* Number of nodes in nodes.          */
  long num_char;
  int number_files;
  int file_number;
  char filename[ FILE_NAME_SIZE ];
  unsigned char ch;
  int index = 0;     /* Index in compressed buffer. */
  unsigned org_index = 0;
  char path_name[ 50 ],
       name[ 60 ];
  int to_read;
  long count = 0,
       total_count = 0,
       compare = 2000;
  long size;
  int total_read;
  int j;
  int z;
  int padlen;
  int path_flag;
  int newfile;

  register int node, bit, byte_index = 0;

  /*
     The structure of the input file is:
     (number_files ), (header),
     (bytes_read), (number of nodes in tree), (tree_root),
     (tree), input_buffer
  */
  clrscreen();
  printf( "\n" );                              (continued)
```

```
printf(
"                                    Decompression Utility\n" );
if ( argc == 2 )
{
  f = lookupfile( argv[ 1 ], &newfile );
  if ( f == 0 )
  {
    printf( "\a" );
    printf(
    "\n\n                    File %s not found.", argv[ 1 ] );
    exit( 1 );
  }
  printf( "\nEnter path for extracted files " );
  printf( "(CR for current path): " );
  gets( path_name );
  if ( path_name[ 0 ] != '\0' )
    path_flag = 1;
  else
    path_flag = 0;
  readfile( f, 2, &number_files );
  header = ( struct headertype * ) malloc( number_files *
              sizeof( struct headertype ) );
  if ( header == 0 )
  {
   printf( "\n\aNo space for allocating header" );
   exit( 1 );
  }
  readfile( f, sizeof( struct headertype ) * number_files,
              header );
  printf(
  "\n\nDecompressing archive file %s to form files:\n\n",
   argv[ 1 ] );
  for ( file_number = 1;
        file_number <= number_files;
        file_number++ )
  {
   printf( "%-19s", header[ file_number - 1 ].filename );
   if ( file_number % 4 == 0 )
      printf( "\n" );
  }
  printf( "\n\n" );
  readfile( f, 8, data );
  num_char = 65536L * data[ 1 ] + data[ 0 ];
  number_nodes = data[ 2 ];
  tree_root = data[ 3 ];
  tree = ( struct treenode * ) malloc( number_nodes *
            sizeof( struct treenode ) );
  if ( tree == 0 )
    printf( "\n\aNo space for allocating tree" );
```

```c
readfile( f, sizeof( struct treenode ) * number_nodes,
          tree );
readfile( f, array_size, input_buffer );
ch = input_buffer[ index++ ];
printf( "%ld\t-  Total number of bytes to output\n",
        num_char );
printf( "\t-  Bytes output" );
file_number = 1;
do
{
  size = header[ file_number - 1 ].size;
  if ( path_flag )
  {
    name[ 0 ] = '\0';
    strcat( name, path_name );
    if ( strchr( name, '\\' ) != 0 )
      strcat( name, "\\" );
    strcat( name, header[ file_number - 1 ].filename );
    g = lookupfile( name, &newfile );
  }
  else
    g = lookupfile( header[ file_number - 1 ].filename,
        &newfile );
  do
  {
    node = tree_root;
    do
    {
      if ( byte_index == 8 )
      {
        if ( index == array_size )
        {
          readfile( f, array_size, input_buffer );
          index = 0;
        }
        ch = input_buffer[ index++ ];
        byte_index = 0;
      }
      bit = ( ch >> byte_index++ ) & 1;
      if ( bit )
        node = tree[ node ].right;
      else
        node = tree[ node ].left;
    }
    while ( tree[ node ].left != nil );
    if ( org_index == array_size )
    {
      writefile( g, array_size, original );
      org_index = 0;
    }
```

(continued)

```
                if ( tree[ node ].ch == tab )
                {
                  /* Blow 10 spaces into output file */
                  for ( z = 1; z <= 10; z++ )
                  {
                    if ( org_index == array_size )
                    {
                      writefile( g, array_size, original );
                      org_index = 0;
                    }
                    original[ org_index++ ] = ' ';
                  }
                  count += 10;
                  total_count += 10;
                }
                else
                {
                  original[ org_index++ ] = tree[ node ].ch;
                  count++;
                  total_count++;
                }
                if ( total_count >= compare )
                {
                  compare += 2000;
                  printf( "%c%ld", 13, total_count );
                }
              }
              while ( count < size );
              writefile( g, org_index, original );
              closefile( g );
              file_number++;
              count = 0;
              org_index = 0;
            }
            while ( file_number <= number_files );
            printf( "%c%ld", 13, num_char );
          }
}


/* Clear screen
**
** ARGUMENTS
**    none
**
** RETURNS
*/
void clrscreen( void )
/* See DOS reference manual, page 2-12. */
```

```
{
  unsigned int esc = 27;
  printf( "%c[2J", esc );
}


/* Hot key input from keyboard
**
** ARGUMENTS
**    ch - Character returned
**
** RETURNS
**    nothing
*/
void get_key( unsigned char *ch )
{
  union REGS regs;

  regs.h.ah = 0x8;
  intdos( &regs, &regs );
  *ch = regs.h.al;
}
```

9.5   *Test of Compression and Decompression Program*

As a test of the file compression program, the first nine draft chapters of this book were compressed into an archive file, book.arc. The total number of bytes for the nine chapters before compression was 380,433. After compression, the archive file contained 227,202 bytes. The archive file was 60% of the size of the original file.

After producing the archive file, book.arc, the original nine chapters were erased from the subdirectory. The darc.c program was run, and all nine files were recovered intact.

Another practical application of this program occurred in the fall of 1987 when this author was requested to condense the three disks that were prepared for the book *MODULA-2 Software Components*, Richard Sincovec and Richard Wiener, John Wiley and Sons, 1987. After completing this software, written for that occasion, the three disks were compressed down to one disk with very few bytes to spare! File compression can indeed be practical.

10

A Rollbook Data-Base System

This chapter presents a data-base application that demonstrates the use of important file input/output functions from the Turbo C library and the use of the generic sort function presented in Chapter 4. Three different types of sorting operations are performed within the application. With minor modifications, this rollbook program could be transformed to a more general purpose data base or text manipulation program. As it currently stands, it is a useful rollbook program.

10.1 A Description of the Utility

The rollbook data-base program, roll.c, to be described in this chapter, converts a loosely formatted text file (ASCII file) of general comments, names, grades (scores), column headings, and a grading formula into one of two possible nicely formatted output files. The first possible output file consists of an alphabetized list of student names and their scores, in formatted columns, with averages and medians listed for each exam (column of data). Each column of data has a column heading. The second possible output file consists of the names and weighted averages for each student presented in rank order of weighted averages, from highest to lowest.

The program, roll.c, is a text formatter with limited data processing capability. There is no interactive user input. Two or three command line arguments and an ASCII text file serve as the input to the program. An ASCII text file is the program output. This text file can later be used as input.

In addition to the functions provided by this program, many rollbook programs allow a user to insert, delete, or modify names and scores interactively. It is believed by this author that a full-feature text editor or word processing program provides a much more powerful mechanism for editing an existing data-base of names and grades. Why should a rollbook program have to provide limited editing capabilities and attempt to compete with a full-feature text editor? Furthermore, portability considerations suggest that it is most desirable to use ASCII files as input and output. Such files can be processed in any operating system using any C compiler. The binary data files that are so often associated with rollbook programs or data-base programs in general are machine and operating system specific.

To provide a quick preview of how the program works, Listing 10.1 shows an input rollbook file, in typical ragged format. Listings 10.2 and 10.3 show the two possible output rollbook files produced by the program.

Listing 10.1 Input file for rollbook program

```
Rollbook For CS 100   Fall 1987   December 10, 1987
───────────────────────────────────────────────────

Lastname Z received extra credit.

Grading: 30s1 + 40s2 + 10s3 + 10s4 + 10s5

Name Exam1
Exam2
Hmk1 Hmk2 Hmk3


Lastname Z: 96
38 80 100 100
Lastname Y: 89 67 100 100 100
Lastname X: 86 90 100 90 100
Lastname W:
76
65
80
90
94
Lastname V: 90 80 90 100 100
Lastname U: 59 80 100 100 90
Lastname T: 44 79 100 90  100
Lastname S: 68 99 12 10 x
Lastname R: 100 100 100 100 99
Lastname Q:88 86 91 94 58
Lastname P: x  x  18 100 10
Lastname O: 90 80 77 65 42
Lastname N: 20 60 80 90 100
Lastname M: 10 x  x  x  x
Lastname L: 100 100 100 100 100
```

```
Lastname K: 75   78 94 92 10
Lastname J: 44 100 25 77 68
Lastname I: 47 12  13  55  10
Lastname H: 100 100 0 50  50
Lastname G: 75 80 80 90 50
Lastname F: 88 75 72 90 100
Lastname E: 40 x 15 x x
Lastname D: 0 40 35 66 77
Lastname C: 100 68 90 95 100
Lastname B: 82 78 76 75 72
Lastname A: 79 82 84 83 95
```

Listing 10.2 First output file from rollbook program

```
Rollbook For CS 100  Fall 1987  December 10, 1987
```

Lastname Z received extra credit.

Grading: 30s1 + 40s2 + 10s3 + 10s4 + 10s5

Name	Exam1	Exam2	Hmk1	Hmk2	Hmk3
Lastname A:	79	82	84	83	95
Lastname B:	82	78	76	75	72
Lastname C:	100	68	90	95	100
Lastname D:	0	40	35	66	77
Lastname E:	40	x	15	x	x
Lastname F:	88	75	72	90	100
Lastname G:	75	80	80	90	50
Lastname H:	100	100	0	50	50
Lastname I:	47	12	13	55	10
Lastname J:	44	100	25	77	68
Lastname K:	75	78	94	92	10
Lastname L:	100	100	100	100	100
Lastname M:	10	x	x	x	x
Lastname N:	20	60	80	90	100
Lastname O:	90	80	77	65	42
Lastname P:	x	x	18	100	10
Lastname Q:	88	86	91	94	58
Lastname R:	100	100	100	100	99
Lastname S:	68	99	12	10	x
Lastname T:	44	79	100	90	100
Lastname U:	59	80	100	100	90
Lastname V:	90	80	90	100	100
Lastname W:	76	65	80	90	94
Lastname X:	86	90	100	90	100
Lastname Y:	89	67	100	100	100
Lastname Z:	96	38	80	100	100

Average:	69.8	75.5	68.5	83.4	75.0
Median:	79.0	80.0	80.0	90.0	94.0

Listing 10.3 Second output file for rollbook program

Rollbook For CS 100 Fall 1987 December 10, 1987
_____

Lastname Z received extra credit.

Grading: 30s1 + 40s2 + 10s3 + 10s4 + 10s5

Name	Weighted Average

_____

Name	Weighted Average
Lastname L:	100.0
Lastname R:	99.9
Lastname X:	90.8
Lastname V:	88.0
Lastname C:	85.7
Lastname Q:	85.1
Lastname Y:	83.5
Lastname A:	82.7
Lastname F:	82.6
Lastname H:	80.0
Lastname U:	78.7
Lastname B:	78.1
Lastname O:	77.4
Lastname G:	76.5
Lastname W:	75.2
Lastname T:	73.8
Lastname K:	73.3
Lastname Z:	72.0
Lastname J:	70.2
Lastname N:	57.0
Lastname D:	33.8
Lastname I:	26.7
Lastname S:	x
Lastname P:	x
Lastname M:	x
Lastname E:	x

The roll.c program is used as follows:

```
roll input_file output_file [rank]
```

If the optional "rank" command line string is not present, the program produces a formatted output of names, scores, averages, and medians (for example, Listing 10.2). If the optional "rank" string is present, the program produces a formatted output of names and weighted averages in rank order from highest to lowest (for example, Listing 10.3).

The program aborts and emits an error message if the user attempts to assign the same name to the output file as the input file.

An input file contains four sections.

The first section of the input file consists of any number of lines of comments. This section is terminated by one or more blank lines. At least one line of comments is required. This might consist of the name of the course, the current date, and any other appropriate header information that the user wishes to include. Any number of additional comments can be added as long as there are no intervening blank lines. The first section is terminated by one or more blank lines.

The second section of the input file is a single line that begins with the required word, "Grading:". This is followed by a grading formula of the form:

`[*] (num1) s (num2)  +  [*] (num3) s (num4)  +  ....`

Example 1:

`Grading: 20s1 + 30s2 + 10s3 + 40s4.`

This implies that score 1 counts 20%, score 2 counts 30%, score 3 counts 10%, and score 4 counts 40%.

Example 2:

`Grading: *50s1 + *30s2 + *20s3`

The asterisk in front of a number establishes a "best" weighting. Specifically, for example 2, the grading formula reads: "Take the best score of scores 1, 2, and 3, and count it 50%, the second best score of the three and count it 30%, and the lowest score of the three and count it 20%. An equivalent formula would be:

`Grading: *20s1 + *50s2 + *30s3`

Example 3:

`Grading: *30s1 + 20s2 + *40s3 + 10s4`

This formula weights the second score 20%, the fourth score 10%, and takes the best of scores 1 and 3 and counts it 40%, and the second best of scores 1 and 3 and counts it 30%.

Example 4:

Suppose we have given five exams, and we wish to drop the lowest grade. We can accomplish this as follows:

`Grading: *25s1 + *25s2 + *25s3 + *25s4 + *0s5`

The score coefficients must add up to 100, otherwise an error message is emitted, and the program is aborted. If there are any other errors in the grading formula, an error message is emitted, and the program is aborted.

The third section of the input file consists of any number of lines of column labels. These labels are each constrained to be seven characters or less. This section is terminated by one or more blank lines. A typical second section might be

```
Name Exam1 Exam2 Exam3
Hmk1 Hmk2 Hmk3
```

One or more spaces are used as separators between column labels.

The fourth and final section of the input file consists of the raw data of names and scores. A colon must follow each name, otherwise an error message is emitted, and the program aborted. The scores can then be distributed over any number of lines. A placeholder, 'x', must be used for any missing data (a student absence from the exam). This section is terminated by the end of file or by one or more blank lines. A typical section might look like this:

```
Name 2: 60 70 x 80
90 x 100
Name 1: 30 40 50 60 x x 70
Name 3: x x
        75 76
        10 15
```

There are two types of output files. The first type presents an alphabetized list of students with their scores in columns of width 8. For each column of scores, the average and median score are listed under the given column. Missing grades are not counted in computing averages and medians. The output is formatted so that it may be used as future input.

The second type of output file presents a rank order list of students and their weighted averages computed according to the grading formula that is input. If a student has one or more missing grades, the average is given as 'x'. It is up to the user to determine how to perform the averaging for such a student.

An additional sample input file and the two possible output files are presented below in Listings 10.4, 10.5, and 10.6.

Listing 10.4 Sample input file for rollbook program

```
CS 123 Fall 1987    Date: December 9, 1987

Grading: 50s1 *30s2 15s3 *5s4

Name   Exam1   Exam2 Exam3   Exam4

Name 3: 0   100 0   50
Name 2: x     x   100 x
Name 1: 100 40 60 80
```

Listing 10.5 Output file 1 from rollbook program

```
CS 123 Fall 1987   Date: December 9, 1987

Grading: 50s1 *30s2 15s3 *5s4
```

NameExam1	Exam2	Exam3	Exam4	
Name 1:	100	40	60	80
Name 2:	x	x	100	x
Name 3:	0	100	0	50
Average:	50.0	70.0	53.3	65.0
Median:	50.0	70.0	60.0	65.0

Listing 10.6 Output file 2 from rollbook program

```
Sample Output File 2
```

```
CS 123 Fall 1987   Date: December 9, 1987

Grading: 50s1 *30s2 15s3 *5s4
```

Name	Weighted Average
Name 1:	85.0
Name 3:	32.5
Name 2:	x

A general description of an input file is the following:

Section 1: Any number of lines of text (comments) with no intervening blank lines.

Section 2: A single line of a grading formula.

Section 3: Any number of lines of column headings with one or more spaces as separators between headings and no intervening blank lines.

Section 4: Any number of lines of raw names and scores. Each name must be terminated with a colon. One or more spaces are used a separators between scores. The 'x' character is used as a placeholder when no grade is present for a given exam.

10.2 Technical Background and Algorithms for Rollbook Program

There are no formal algorithms used in developing the code for the rollbook program. The program relies heavily on the Turbo C functions fprint, fgets, and fputs and on the generic sort function presented in Chapter 4.

10.3 A Presentation and Discussion of the Code for the Rollbook Program

Rather than present all of the source code in one listing in this section, each major segment of code is presented and discussed separately.

10.3.1 The Rollbook Program through function main

Listing 10.7 presents the code of the rollbook program through the main program function.

The data structure, RECORD, that stores the rollbook data is defined in Listing 10.7.

The data-base of names and scores, data_base[number_records], is also defined here.

The prototypes for many functions defined either below function main or in separate files are given at the beginning of this function.

Function main works generally as follows:

1. The input and output files are determined from the command line arguments.
2. The optional command line string "rank" determines whether the global variable rank is set to 1 or if it remains at its initial value of 0.
3. If the command line arguments do not match the correct program usage, an appropriate error message is emitted.
4. A title is put on the screen.
5. The input and output files are opened, if they exist.
6. The first section of the input file, the header material, is transferred from the input file to the output file. Function transfer_header is used for this purpose.
7. The grading formula is scanned, and the grading coefficients are obtained. Function scan_grading_formula is used for this purpose.
8. The third section of the input file, the column headings, are transferred from the input file to the output file. The headings are

formatted during this process. Function formatted_column_titles is used for this purpose.

9. The data-base is initialized. Function initialize_data_base is used for this purpose.

10. The fourth section of the input file is scanned, and the data-base of names and scores is loaded.

11. The output file of formatted names, grades, average grades per exam, and median grade per exam is produced if the value of rank is 0.

12. The output file of ranked weighted averages is produced if the value of rank is 1.

Listing 10.7 Rollbook program function main

```
/*
   Roll book data base system.
   Compile with small model.
*/

#include <stdio.h>
#include <string.h>
#include <stdlib.h>
#include <ctype.h>
#include <mem.h>
#include "util.h"
#include "sort.h"

#define number_records 300
#define number_scores 50
#define line_length 255

typedef struct record RECORD;

struct record
{
   char name[ 24 ];
   /* Scores initialized to -1.  Not present during exam
      gets a score of -2.
   */
   int score[ number_scores ];
   float average;
};

/* Data-base of names and scores. */
RECORD data_base[ number_records ];

/* Used to store grading coefficients. */
int weights[ number_scores ];
```

```c
/* Used to store "best" weighting coefficients. */
int best[ number_scores ];

/* Used to sort "best" weighted scores. */
int temp[ number_scores ];

/* Used to sort "best" weighted grading coefficients. */
int btemp[ number_scores ];

int number_exams;        /* The number of exams given. */
int number_students;     /* The number of students.    */
FILE *in_file;           /* Input file.                */
FILE *out_file;          /* Output files.              */
char input_file[ 60 ],   /* Input file name.           */
     output_file[ 60 ];  /* Output file name.          */
char word[ 60 ];         /* Word of text.              */
char *line;              /* Line of text.              */
int spacing;             /* Spacing parameter.         */
int index,
    word_index,
    num_words;
int rank = 0;            /* rank = 0 -> raw scores
                            rank = 1 -> rank order scores
                         */
int row, col;


main( int argc, char *argv[] )
{
  extern void title( void );
  extern void usage( void );
  extern int blank( char *line );
  extern void open_files( void );
  extern void transfer_header( void );
  extern void formatted_column_titles( void );
  extern void scan_grading_formula( void );
  extern void initialize_data_base( void );
  extern void load_data_base( void );
  extern void output_data_base( void );
  extern void output_ranked_data( void );

  clrscreen();

  /* Retrieve and test command line arguments. */
  if ( argc < 3 || argc > 4 )
  {
    usage();
    exit( 1 );
  }
```

```
    else
    {
      strcpy( input_file, argv[ 1 ] );
      strcpy( output_file, argv[ 2 ] );
      if ( strcmp( input_file, output_file ) == 0 )
      {
        printf( "\a" );
        gotoxy( 0, 10 );
        centermessage(
        "Input file name the same as output file name." );
        printf( "\n" );
        exit( 1 );
      }
      if ( argc == 4 && strcmp( argv[ 3 ], "rank" ) == 0 )
        rank = 1;
    }

    title();

    /* Open input and output files. */
    open_files();

    /* Allocate storage for a line. */
    if ( !( line = ( char * ) malloc( line_length ) ) )
    {
      printf( "\a" );
      printf( "\n\nStorage allocation error.\n" );
      exit( 1 );
    }

    /* Transfer header material to output file. */
    transfer_header();

    /* Scan grading formula. */
    scan_grading_formula();

    /* Output formatted column titles. */
    formatted_column_titles();

    /* Initialize data base. */
    initialize_data_base();

    /* Load data base. */
    load_data_base();

    if ( !rank )
      output_data_base();
    else
      output_ranked_data();
```

(continued)

```
        gotoxy( 0, 11 );
        printf( "                              Number students : %d\n",
                number_students );
        printf( "                              Number scores   : %d\n",
                number_exams );
        printf( "\n\n\n\n\n\n\n" );
}
```

10.3.2 Functions title, usage, blank, and open_files

Listing 10.8 contains the code for functions title, usage, blank, and open_files.
The extern declaration for these functions are given in function main.

The function blank checks a given line to see whether any printable
characters are present on the line. If any are present, the function returns
the value 1, otherwise it returns the value 0.

Listing 10.8 Functions title, usage, blank, and open_files

```
/* Puts program title on the screen
**
** ARGUMENTS
**    none
**
** RETURNS
**    nothing
*/
void title( void )
{
   char str[ 80 ];
   gotoxy( 0, 4 );
   centermessage(
   "Roll Book Program    Version 1.0    Copyright (C) 1987" );
   printf( "\n" );
   centermessage(
   "_____" );
   gotoxy( 0, 7 );
   printf( "%24s", " " );
   printf( "Transforming input file : " );
   printf( "%s\n", input_file );
   printf( "%24s", " " );
   printf( "To output file: " );
   printf( output_file );
}


/* Puts usage on the screen
**
```

```
**  ARGUMENTS
**     none
**
**  RETURNS
**     nothing
*/
void usage( void )
{
  printf( "\a" );
  gotoxy( 0, 10 );
  centermessage(
  "Usage:  roll input_file output_file [ rank ]" );
  printf( "\n\n\n\n\n\n\n\n" );
}


/* Tests for a blank line
**
**  ARGUMENTS
**     line - String of characters
**
**  RETURNS
**     0 - Line is not blank
**     1 - Line is blank
*/
int blank( char *line )
{
  int i;

  for ( i = 0; i < strlen( line ); i++ )
    if ( ( line[ i ] >= ' ' && line[ i ] <= '^' ) ||
         ( line[ i ] >= 'a' && line[ i ] <= '~' ) )
      return 0;
  return 1;
}


/* Opens the input file and the output file
**
**  ARGUMENTS
**     none
**
**  RETURNS
**     nothing
*/
void open_files( void )
{
```

(continued)

```
      /* Open input and output files */
      in_file = fopen( input_file, "rt" );
      if ( in_file == 0 )
      {
        printf( "\a" );
        gotoxy( 0, 10 );
        centermessage( "Input file does not exist" );
        printf( "\n" );
        exit( 1 );
      }
      out_file = fopen( output_file, "wt" );
      if ( out_file == 0 )
      {
printf( "\a" );
        gotoxy( 0, 10 );
        centermessage( "Output file cannot be opened" );
        printf( "\n" );
        exit( 1 );
      }
}
```

10.3.3   Function transfer_header

Listing 10.9 presents contains the code for function transfer_header. The
extern declaration for this function is given in function main.

The code in Listing 10.9 inputs and outputs lines until the first blank
line is encountered. The Turbo C library functions, fgets and fputs, are
featured in this function.

Listing 10.9   Function transfer_header

```
/* Scans the first section of the input file and transfers
** this section to the output file
**
** ARGUMENTS
**    none
**
** RETURNS
**    nothing
*/
void transfer_header( void )
{
   /* Scan for the first non-blank line. */
   fgets( line, line_length, in_file );
   while ( blank( line ) )
     fgets( line, line_length, in_file );

   /* Output lines until first blank line is reached. */
   while ( !blank( line ) )
   {
```

```
      fputs( line, out_file );
      fgets( line, line_length, in_file );
   }
   fputc( '\n', out_file );

   /* Scan for the first non-blank line. */
   fgets( line, line_length, in_file );
   while ( blank( line ) )
      fgets( line, line_length, in_file );
}
```

10.3.4   Function scan_grading_formula

Listing 10.10 contains the code for function scan_grading_formula.

First the code scans for the word "Grading:". Then the standard function isdigit from the Turbo C library is used to scan for digits and nondigits in the line. The grading coefficients are stored in the array weights. The standard function atoi from the Turbo C library is used to convert a string of numerals to an integer value.

Listing 10.10 Function scan_grading_formula

```
/* Scans the second section of the input file and transfers
** this section to the output file
**
** ARGUMENTS
**    none
**
** RETURNS
**    nothing
*/
void scan_grading_formula( void )
{
   char subscript[ 8 ];
   int bst = 0;
   int sum;
   int i;

   /* Scan for the word Grading: */
   index = 0;
   while ( index < line_length && line[ index ] != 'G' )
      index++;
   if ( index < 246 )
   {
      memmove( word, &line[ index ], 8 );
      word[ 9 ] = '\0';
   }
```

(continued)

```
          if ( index >= 246 || strcmp( word, "Grading:" ) != 0 )
          {
            gotoxy( 30,10 );
            printf( "\aGrading formula not present\n" );
            exit( 1 );
          }
          /* Advance the index past "Grading:" */
          index += 8;

          do
          {
            /* Scan for a digit or an asterisk. */
            while ( !isdigit( line[ index ] ) &&
                    line[ index ] != '\n' &&
                    line[ index ] != '*' )
              index++;
            if ( line[ index ] == '\n' )
              break;

            if ( line[ index ] == '*' &&
                 !isdigit( line[ index +1 ] ) )
            {
              gotoxy( 30, 10 );
              printf( "\aError in grading formula\n" );
              exit( 1 );
            }

            if ( line[ index ] == '*' )
            {
              bst = 1;
              index++;
            }

            word_index = 0;
            /* Scan for an 's' and build word. */
            while ( isdigit( line[ index ] ) )
              word[ word_index++ ] = line[ index++ ];
            word[ word_index ] = '\0';
            if ( line[ index ] != 's' )
            {
              gotoxy( 30, 10 );
              printf( "\aError in grading formula\n" );
              exit( 1 );
            }

            index++;

            /* Test the next digit. */
            if ( !isdigit( line[ index ] ) )
```

```
    {
      gotoxy( 30, 10 );
      printf( "\aError in grading formula\n" );
      exit( 1 );
    }

    /* Scan until digits end and build subscript. */
    word_index = 0;
    while ( isdigit( line[ index ] ) )
      subscript[ word_index++ ] = line[ index++ ];
    subscript[ word_index ] = '\0';
    weights[ atoi( subscript ) - 1 ] = atoi( word );
    if ( bst )
    {
      best[ atoi( subscript ) - 1 ] = atoi( word );
      bst = 0;
    }
  }
  while ( line[ index ] != 'n' );

  fprintf( out_file, "%s\n", line );

  sum = 0;
  for ( i = 0; i < number_scores; i++ )
    sum += weights[ i ];
  if ( sum != 100 )
  {
    gotoxy( 30, 10 );
    printf(
    "\aGrading formula error: Weights do not add to 100\n" );
    exit( 1 );
  }

  /* Scan for the first non-blank line. */
  fgets( line, line_length, in_file );
  while ( blank( line ) )
    fgets( line, line_length, in_file );
}
```

10.3.5 Function formatted_column_titles

Listing 10.11 contains the code for function formatted_column_titles.

The standard function isalum from the Turbo C libraries is used to detect alphabetic characters or numerals. If a column heading is larger than seven characters, it is truncated to seven characters.

Listing 10.11   Function formatted_column_titles

```c
/* Scans the third section of the input file and transfers
** this section to the output file
**
** ARGUMENTS
**    none
**
** RETURNS
**    nothing
*/
void formatted_column_titles( void )
{
  index = 0;
  while ( !blank( line ) )
  {
    do
    {
      /* Scan for first character */
      while ( !isalnum( line[ index ] ) &&
              line[ index ] != '\n' )
        index++;
      if ( line[ index ] == '\n' )
        break;

      /* Scan for first blank and build word */
      word_index = 0;
      while( isalnum( line[ index ] ) )
        word[ word_index++ ] = line[ index++ ];
      word[ word_index ] = '\0';
      if ( spacing != 0 )
        num_words++;

      if ( spacing == 0 )
      {
        if ( strlen( word ) > 23 )
          word[ 23 ] = '\0';
      }
      else
      {
        if ( strlen( word ) > 7 )
          word[ 7 ] = '\0';
      }
      spacing = ( spacing == 0 ) ? 24 : 8;
      if ( !rank )
        fprintf( out_file, "%-*s", spacing, word );
    }
    while ( num_words < 7 && line[ index ] != '\n' );
    if ( line[ index ] == '\n' )
    {
```

```
      fgets( line, line_length, in_file );
        index = 0;
    }
    if ( num_words == 7 )
    {
      if ( !rank )
        fprintf( out_file, "\n%-*s", 24, " " );
      num_words = 0;
    }
  }

  /* Scan for the first non-blank line. */
  fgets( line, line_length, in_file );
  while ( blank( line ) )
    fgets( line, line_length, in_file );
}
```

10.3.6   Functions initialize_data_base and load_data_base

Listing 10.12 contains the code for the functions initialize_data_base and load_data_base.

The functions isdigit and atoi, mentioned above, are used to detect and convert numerals. The information gleaned from the input file is loaded into the array of structures, data_base.

Listing 10.12   Functions initialize_data_base and load_data_base

```
/* Initialize the data base
**
** ARGUMENTS
**    none
**
** RETURNS
**    nothing
*/
void initialize_data_base( void )
{
  int i, j;

  for ( i = 0; i < number_records; i++ )
    for ( j = 0; j < number_scores; j++ )
      data_base[ i ].score[ j ] = -1;
}
```

(continued)

```c
/* Scan the fourth section of the input file and loads the
** data base
**
** ARGUMENTS
**    none
**
** RETURNS
**    nothing
*/
void load_data_base( void )
{
  char *ptr;
  int z;

  index = 0;
  row = 0;
  while ( !blank( line ) )
  {
    /* Scan for first character */
    while ( !isalnum( line[ index ] ) &&
            line[ index ] != '\n' )
      index++;

    /* Scan for first colon and build word */
    word_index = 0;
    while( word_index < 24 && line[ index ] != ':' )
    {
      word[ word_index++ ] = line[ index ];
      index++;
    }

    if ( word_index >= 24 )
    {
      printf( "\a" );
      gotoxy( 0, 10 );
      centermessage( "Colon missing from name." );
      printf( "\n" );
      exit( 1 );
    }

    word[ word_index++ ] = ':';
    word[ word_index ] = '\0';
    if ( strlen( word ) > 23 )
    {
      word[ 22 ] = ':';
      word[ 23 ] = '\0';
    }
    strcpy( data_base[ row ].name, word );
```

```
back: do
{
  /* Scan for first numeral. */
  while ( !isdigit( line[ index ] ) &&
          line[ index ] != '\n' &&
          line[ index ] != 'x' )
    index++;

  if ( line[ index ] == 'x' )
  {
    data_base[ row ].score[ col++ ] = -2;
    index++;
    continue;
  }

  /* Scan for first non-digit and build word. */
  word_index = 0;
  while ( isdigit( line[ index ] ) )
    word[ word_index++ ] = line[ index++ ];
  word[ word_index ] = '\0';
  if ( strlen( word ) > 0 )
  {
    data_base[ row ].score[ col++ ] = atoi( word );
  }
}
while ( line[ index ] != '\n' );
ptr = fgets( line, line_length, in_file );
if ( ptr == NULL )
{
  row++;
  if ( row > number_students )
    number_students = row;
  if ( col > number_exams )
    number_exams = col;
  break;
}
if ( !blank( line ) && strchr( line, ':' ) == 0 )
{
  /* Check first character on line and insure
     that it is a digit. */
  z = 0;
  while ( !isalnum( line[ z ] ) )
    z++;
  if ( isdigit( line[ z ] ) )
  {
    index = 0;
    goto back;
  }
```

(continued)

```
      else
      {
        printf( "\a" );
        gotoxy( 0, 10 );
        centermessage( "Colon missing from name.\n" );
        printf( "\n" );
        exit( 1 );
      }
    }
    row++;
    if ( col > number_exams )
      number_exams = col;
    if ( row > number_students )
      number_students = row;
    col = 0;
    index = 0;
  }
}
```

10.3.7   Functions compare_by_name, compare_by_average, and compare_integer

Listing 10.13 contains the code for the functions compare_by_name, compare_by_average, and compare_integer. These functions are used as parameters in the generic sort function.

Listing 10.13 Functions compare_by_name, compare_by_average and compare_integer

```
/* Compare RECORDS by name
**
** ARGUMENTS
**    rec1, rec2 - Records to compare
**
** RETURNS
**    -1 : rec1 "smaller" than rec2
**     0 : rec1 "equal" to rec2
**     1 : rec1 "larger" than rec2
*/
int compare_by_name( void *rec1, void *rec2 )
{
  RECORD *r1 = ( RECORD * ) rec1,
         *r2 = ( RECORD * ) rec2;

  return ( strcmp( r1 -> name, r2 -> name ) );
}
```

```c
/* Compare RECORDS by average
**
** ARGUMENTS
**    rec1, rec2 - Records to compare
**
** RETURNS
**    -1 : rec1 "smaller" than rec2
**     0 : rec1 "equal" to rec2
**     1 : rec1 "larger" than rec2
*/
int compare_by_average( void *rec1, void *rec2 )
{
  RECORD *r1 = ( RECORD * ) rec1,
         *r2 = ( RECORD * ) rec2;

  if ( r1 -> average > r2 -> average )
    return -1;
  else if ( r1 -> average == r2 -> average )
    return 0;
  else
    return 1;
}


/* Compare integers
**
** ARGUMENTS
**    rec1, rec2 - Records to compare
**
** RETURNS
**    -1 : rec1 "smaller" than rec2
**     0 : rec1 "equal" to rec2
**     1 : rec1 "larger" than rec2
*/
int compare_integer( void *rec1, void *rec2 )
{
  int *i1 = rec1,
      *i2 = rec2;

  if ( *i1 > *i2 )
    return -1;
  else if ( *i1 == *i2 )
    return 0;
  else
    return 1;
}
```

10.3.8 Function output_data_base

Listing 10.14 contains the code for function output_data_base. The average and median score for each column of data are computed from the array of records, data_base.

Listing 10.14 Function output_data_base

```
/* Output names and grades of data base.  Compute average
** and median for each exam.
**
** ARGUMENTS
**    none
**
** RETURNS
**    nothing
*/
void output_data_base( void )
{
  int i, j;
  float sum;
  int count;
  int num_items;
  float median;
  int index;

  fprintf( out_file, "\n" );
  sort( ( char * ) data_base,
        number_students,
        sizeof( RECORD ),
        compare_by_name );
  for ( i = 0; i < number_students; i++ )
  {
    fprintf( out_file, "\n%-*s", 24, data_base[ i ].name );
    for ( j = 0; j < number_exams; j++ )
    {
      if ( j == 7 )
        fprintf( out_file, "\n%-*s", 24, " " );
      if ( data_base[ i ].score[ j ] == -2 )
        fprintf( out_file, "%-*c", 8, 'x' );
      else
        fprintf( out_file, "%-*d", 8,
                 data_base[ i ].score[ j ] );
    }
  }

  /* Compute averages for each exam. */
  fprintf( out_file, "\n\n%-*s", 24, "Average:" );
```

```
    num_items = 0;
    for ( i = 0; i < number_exams; i++ )
    {
      sum = 0.0;
      count = 0;
      for ( j = 0; j < number_students; j++ )
      {
        if ( data_base[ j ].score[ i ] >= 0 )
        {
          sum += data_base[ j ].score[ i ];
          count++;
        }
      }
      if ( count > 0 )
        fprintf( out_file, "%-*.1f", 8, sum / count );
      else
        fprintf( out_file, "%-*.c", 8, 'x' );
      num_items++;
      if ( num_items == 7 )
      {
        fprintf( out_file, "\n%-*s", 24, " " );
        num_items = 0;
      }
    }

    /* Compute medians for each exam. */
    fprintf( out_file, "\n\n%-*s", 24, "Median:" );
    num_items = 0;
    for ( j = 0; j < number_exams; j++ )
    {
      count = 0;
      for ( i = 0; i < number_students; i++ )
      {
        if ( data_base[ i ].score[ j ] >= 0 )
        {
          temp[ count++ ] = data_base[ i ].score[ j ];
        }
      }
      sort( ( char * ) temp, count, sizeof( int ),
            compare_integer );
      median = ( float ) temp[ index = ( count - 1 ) / 2 ];
      if ( ( count % 2 ) == 0 )
        median = ( median + temp[ index + 1 ] ) / 2.0;
      if ( count > 0 )
        fprintf( out_file, "%-*.1f", 8, median );
      else
        fprintf( out_file, "%-*.c", 8, 'x' );
      num_items++;
      if ( num_items == 7 )                          (continued)
```

```
    {
        fprintf( out_file, "\n%-*s", 24,    " " );
        num_items = 0;
    }
    }
}
```

10.3.9 Function output_ranked_data

Listing 10.15 contains the code for function output_ranked_data. The
generic function sort is used to sort the arrays of integers temp and btemp,
as well as to sort the array data_base based on the average for each student
record.

Two temporary storage structures, temp and btemp, are used to
compute "best" weighted averages. The array, temp, is used to hold the data
that were tagged with an asterisk indicating "best" weighting. The array
btemp is used to hold the weighting coefficients for the fields tagged as
"best." These two arrays are sorted using the generic sorting function, sort.
After sorting these two arrays, the sum of products is taken to obtain the
"best" weighted average.

Listing 10.15 Function output_ranked_data

```
/* Output the names and weighted averages of students in
** rank order from largest to smallest
**
** ARGUMENTS
**    none
**
** RETURNS
**    nothing
*/
void output_ranked_data( void )
{
    int i, j;
    float sum;
    int count;
    int number_best;

    fprintf( out_file, "%-*s", 24, "Name" );
    fprintf( out_file, "%-30s\n", "Weighted Average" );
    fprintf( out_file,
    "_____ \n\n" );
    /* Compute weighted average for each student. */
    for ( i = 0; i < number_students; i++ )
    {
```

```
  sum = 0.0;
  count = 0;
  for ( j = 0; j < number_exams; j++ )
  {
    if ( data_base[ i ].score[ j ] >= 0 && !best[ j ] )
    {
      sum += data_base[ i ].score[ j ] * weights[ j ];
      count++;
    }
  }

  number_best = 0;
  /* Fill temp array with scores where best is marked. */
  for ( j = 0; j < number_exams; j++ )
  {
    if ( best[ j ] != 0 )
    {
      if ( data_base[ i ].score[ j ] >= 0 )
        temp[ number_best ] = data_base[ i ].score[ j ];
      else
      {
        number_best = 0;
        break;
      }
    }
  }
  if ( number_best )
  {
    sort( ( char * ) temp, number_best, sizeof( int ),
          compare_integer );
    sort( ( char * ) btemp, number_best, sizeof( int ),
          compare_integer );
    for ( j = 0; j < number_best; j++ )
    {
      sum += temp[ j ] * btemp[ j ];
      count++;
    }
  }

  if ( count == number_exams )
    data_base[ i ].average = sum / 100.0;
  else
    data_base[ i ].average = -2;
}

sort( ( char * ) data_base,
      number_students,
      sizeof( RECORD ),
      compare_by_average );                              (continued)
```

```
        for ( i = 0; i < number_students; i++ )
        {
          fprintf( out_file, "%-*s", 24, data_base[ i ].name );
          if ( data_base[ i ].average != -2.0 )
            fprintf( out_file, "%-*.1f\n", 8,
                     data_base[ i ].average );
          else
            fprintf( out_file, "%-*c\n", 8, 'x' );
        }
      }
```

11

Screen Dump Utility

This chapter presents a short but practical screen dump utility that enables a screen of text to be dumped to a user- named file. This file can be edited, combined with other screen dump files, and sent to a printer.

The use of the MS-DOS | more pipe enables a user to display output that would scroll data across the screen, one screen at a time. The user can write each screen to a sequence of files, then later combine the files into one file.

11.1　A Description of the Utility

The user invokes the program screen.c by typing the name of the program, screen. No command line parameters are required. A prompt asks the user to enter the output file name. The default name is "screen.dmp." This default can be activated by responding with the "Enter" key. Otherwise, a legal DOS file name must be entered.

11.2　Technical Background and Algorithms for Screen Program

The program screen.c requires no formal algorithms. It requires the use of the Turbo C library function peekb to transfer characters from selected memory locations in the video adaptor card to an internal data structure, buffer.

11.3 A Presentation and Discussion of the Code for the Screen Dump Program

The source code for the program screen.c is given in Listing 11.1.

A structure ADDRESS is defined to hold the segment and offset of a given memory address.

A global variable, video, is used to determine whether the starting address of the memory-mapped screen is 0xb000 or 0xb800, corresponding to a monochrome adaptor card or a CGA adaptor card. The reader may wish to modify this code to include EGA or VGA adaptor cards. The type of card is determined by the following line of code:

```
video = ( peekb( 0, 0x449 ) == 7 );
```

If the value 7 is present at memory location 0x449, the card is a monochrome adaptor card, otherwise it is a CGA card.

The program begins by determining the type of card that is present.

Next, function save_top_five is invoked. This function stores the top five lines of the screen into a two-dimensional array, top. These lines must be saved because, later, the title and a prompt are written on the top five lines of the screen. Once the prompt is no longer needed, the five saved lines are redisplayed on the screen. This array is filled as follows:

```
adr.seg = ( video ) ? 0xb000 : 0xb800;
for ( i = 0; i < 5; i++ )
{
  for ( j = 0; j < 80; j++ )
  {
    adr.off = i * 160 + j * 2;
    top[ i ][ j ] = peekb( adr.seg, adr.off );
  }
  top[ i ][ 80 ] = '\0';
}
```

Only even offset values are used because they hold the ASCII value of the character at the given screen location. The odd offset values hold the attribute of the character for a given screen location.

Next, the title and prompt are written to the screen. The user must either hit the "Enter" key or enter a new file name. The appropriate text file is opened for writing only.

Next, the original top five lines of the screen are replaced on the screen in preparation for saving the screen. Each row of the screen is copied to the array buffer and then written to the output file as follows:

```
for ( i = 1; i <= 2000; )
{
```

```
   buffer[ index++ ] = peekb( adr.seg, adr.off );
   adr.off += 2;
   if ( i % 80 == 0 )
   {
     /* Scan backwards and remove blanks */
     index--;
     while ( buffer[ index ] == ' ' )
       index--;
     index++;
     buffer[ index++ ] = '\n';
     write( f, buffer, index );
     index = 0;
   }
   i++;
}
```

All trailing blanks are stripped from each row of the screen before writing
the data to the output file. This shortens the size of the output file.

Listing 11.1 Source code for the program screen.c

```
/*
   Screen dump utility
   Compile in the small memory model and link to util.obj.
*/

#include <stdio.h>
#include <fcntl.h>
#include <sys\stat.h>
#include <dos.h>
#include "util.h"

typedef struct address ADDRESS;

struct address
{
  unsigned off;
  unsigned seg;
};

/* 1 for monochrome adaptor, 0 for CGA adaptor */
int video;

char buffer[ 81 ];

char top[ 5 ][ 81 ];


main()
{
```

(continued)

```
            int f;
            int i;
            int index;
            ADDRESS adr;
            char dump_file[ 30 ];

            extern void save_top_five( void );
            extern void replace_top_five( void );
            extern void dump_border( void );

            video = ( peekb( 0, 0x449 ) == 7 );
            save_top_five();
            dump_border();
            gets( dump_file );
            if ( dump_file[ 0 ] != '\0' )
              f = open( dump_file, O_WRONLY | O_CREAT | O_TEXT,
                        S_IWRITE );
            else
              f = open( "screen.dmp", O_WRONLY | O_CREAT | O_TEXT,
                        S_IWRITE );
            if ( f == -1 )
              printf( "\n\nOpen failed on output file." );

            adr.seg = ( video ) ? 0xb000 : 0xb800;
            adr.off = 0x0;
            index = 0;
            replace_top_five();
            for ( i = 1; i <= 2000; )
            {
              buffer[ index++ ] = peekb( adr.seg, adr.off );
              adr.off += 2;
              if ( i % 80 == 0 )
              {
                /* Scan backwards and remove blanks */
                index--;
                while ( buffer[ index ] == ' ' )
                  index--;
                index++;
                buffer[ index++ ] = '\n';
                write( f, buffer, index );
                index = 0;
              }
              i++;
            }
            close( f );
        }
```

```c
/* Save the top five lines of the screen
**
** ARGUMENTS
**    none
**
** RETURNS
**    nothing
*/
void save_top_five( void )
{
  int i, j;
  ADDRESS adr;

  adr.seg = ( video ) ? 0xb000 : 0xb800;
  for ( i = 0; i < 5; i++ )
  {
    for ( j = 0; j < 80; j++ )
    {
      adr.off = i * 160 + j * 2;
      top[ i ][ j ] = peekb( adr.seg, adr.off );
    }
    top[ i ][ 80 ] = '\0';
  }
}


/* Replace the top five lines of the screen
**
** ARGUMENTS
**    none
**
** RETURNS
**    nothing
*/
void replace_top_five( void )
{
  int i;

  gotoxy( 0, 0 );
  for ( i = 0; i < 5; i++ )
    printf( "%s", top[ i ] );
}


/* Put title on screen
**
** ARGUMENTS
**    none
**
```

(continued)

```
** RETURNS
**    nothing
*/
void dump_border( void )
{
  char str[ 81 ];
  char str2[ 81 ];
  int i;

  gotoxy( 0, 0 );
  printf( "%c", 218 );   /* ⌐ */
  for ( i = 0; i <= 77; i++ )
    str[ i ] = 196;      /* - */
  str[ 78 ] = '\0';
  printf( "%s%c", str, 191 );      /* ⌐ */
  gotoxy( 3, 0 );
  printf( "E. & R. Wiener" );
  gotoxy( 32, 0 );
  printf( "HIT-AND-RUN DUMP" );
  gotoxy( 69, 0 );
  printf( "(C) 1987" );
  gotoxy( 0, 1 );
  printf( "%c", 198 );   /* ⊨ */
  for ( i = 0; i <= 77; i++ )
    str2[ i ] = 205;     /* = */
  str2[ 78 ] = '\0';
  printf( "%s%c", str2, 181 );      /* ⊣ */
  gotoxy( 0, 2 );
  for ( i = 0; i <= 79; i++ )
    str2[ i ] = ' ';
  str2[ 80 ] = '\0';
  printf( "%s", str2 );
  gotoxy( 0, 2 );
  printf( "%c%22s", 179,
             "Name of file to dump to : SCREEN.DMP" );
  gotoxy( 79, 2 );
  printf( "%c", 179 );/* | */
  gotoxy( 0, 3 );
  printf( "%c", 192 ); /* ∟ */
  printf( "%s%c", str, 217 );      /* ⌐ */
  gotoxy( 0, 4 );
  printf( "%s", str2 );
  gotoxy( 27, 2 );
}
```

12

A Disk Update Utility

This chapter presents a practical utility for updating disks or subdirectories of a hard disk. Many important disk directory handling functions from the Turbo C library are used in implementing the program. In addition, dynamic list and tree structures are used extensively.

12.1 A Description of the Utility

The program update.c allows a user to compare two subdirectories on the same or different disks henceforth referred to as the source and target, and select for copying (update) two classes of files given as follows:

1. Files that are common to both the source and target that are newer on the source. This is a default option.

2. Files that are on the source but not on the target. The user must select this option.

The program update.c is typically used when a software system is being developed on the source disk or subdirectory, usually a subdirectory of a hard disk, and backups are periodically being made on a floppy disk, the target. The update utility allows the user to copy only those files that have been created more recently than corresponding files on the target or files that do not exist on the target. In addition to copying such files, the utility allows the user to examine and compare various attributes of the source and target files. Some users may find the utility useful for this purpose only.

All files are initially selected for copying. The user can deselect or reselect any subset of the files on the source for copying to the target.

The program either issues a prompt or allows the user to enter the target path on the command line.

The use of the program is illustrated below by actually showing the running of the program.

This author has been making backup copies of the text of this book as chapters are written and completed. In the past few days a few changes have been made to Chapters 2, 4, and 10. In addition, new text in this chapter has been added.

The program is invoked by typing update. Figure 12.1 shows the screen display (without the reverse video of course) after the program is invoked. The user is prompted for the name of the target pathname. In this case the response is "a:\cbook". Next the user is asked whether files that are on the source but not the target should be copied to the target. In this case the response is 'n'. Therefore only files that are common to the source and the target and are newer on the source are listed in both columns. If the answer had been 'y', then additional files would be listed in the left column but not in the right column.

The next screen display is shown in Figure 12.2. The Chap10 in the left column is in reverse video. The user may select or deselect files for copying by hitting the space bar on the file name displayed in reverse video. The up or down arrow keys can be used to reverse video any of the file names in the left column. The page up or page down keys can be used in the event that all the files do not fit onto the screen window at once.

If the user does not wish to copy any source files to the target, he or she may hit the escape key. If the "Enter" key is hit, all the selected files are copied from the source to the target.

```
HIT-AND-RUN SOFTWARE:                                           Version  1.00
   Richard Wiener              U P D A T E                     Copyright (C)
   Erik Wiener                                                 July, 1987
 ┌─────────────────────────────────────────────────────────────────────────┐
 │                                                                           │
 │                                                                           │
 │    Enter target pathname (CR to exit): a:\cbook                           │
 │                                                                           │
 │    Copy files on source that are not on target (Y/N)? n                   │
 │                                                                           │
 │                                                                           │
 │                                                                           │
 │                                                                           │
 ├───────────────────────────────────────────────────────────────────────────┤
 │                                                                           │
 │                                                                           │
 └─────────────────────────────────────────────────────────────────────────┘
```

Figure 12.1   User interface in update program

```
HIT-AND-RUN SOFTWARE:                                              Version  1.00
   Richard Wiener                 U P D A T E                     Copyright (C)
   Erik Wiener                                                    July, 1987
┌───────────────────────────────────────────────────────────────────────────┐
│   State of current file: SELECTED                                           │
│ ══════════════════════SOURCE══════════════════════   ═══════TARGET═══════   │
│   C:\TURBOBK\CHAPTERS                              │  a:\CBOOK               │
│                                                    │                        │
│   CHAP10        39303   12-17-87   10:15   CHAP10     39303   12-16-87  19:00│
│   CHAP12         1710   12-17-87   10:15   CHAP12       393   12-16-87  22:59│
│   CHAP2         52352   12-17-87   10:15   CHAP2      52352   10-20-87   9:20│
│   CHAP4         64024   12-17-87   10:15   CHAP4      64024   11-11-87  20:50│
│                                                    │                        │
│                                                    │                        │
│                                                    │                        │
│                                                    │                        │
├───────────────────────────────────────────────────────────────────────────┤
│                  Highlighted Files Selected For Copying                      │
│  PGDN/PGUP: Next/previous page  ARROWS: Next/previous file  SPACEBAR: Select │
│                        <CR> Update      <ESC> Exit                           │
└───────────────────────────────────────────────────────────────────────────┘
```

Figure 12.2   Screen display in update program

This was done. The screen display shown in Figure 12.3 results from this action. As each file is copied, its name is listed on the screen. If an entire window is filled, the currently displayed files are erased, and the list is continued from the top of the screen.

```
HIT-AND-RUN SOFTWARE:                                              Version  1.00
   Richard Wiener                 U P D A T E                     Copyright (C)
   Erik Wiener                                                    July, 1987
┌───────────────────────────────────────────────────────────────────────────┐
│                                                                             │
│     Copying from C:\TURBOBK\CHAPTERS to a:\CBOOK ...                         │
│                                                                             │
│     CHAP10                                                                  │
│     CHAP12                                                                  │
│     CHAP2                                                                   │
│     CHAP4                                                                   │
│                                                                             │
│                                                                             │
│                                                                             │
│                                                                             │
├───────────────────────────────────────────────────────────────────────────┤
│                                                                             │
│                                                                             │
└───────────────────────────────────────────────────────────────────────────┘
```

Figure 12.3   Final screen display in update program

12.2 Technical Background and Algorithm for the Update Program

Several dynamic data structures are constructed to determine the files that need to be copied from the source to the target, namely: a source tree, a target tree, a source list, and a target list.

The data structures for these are given as follows:

```
#define FILEINFO struct ffblk
typedef struct list LIST;

extern FILEINFO; /* From dir.h */

struct list
{
  FILEINFO fileinfo;
  int selected;
  LIST *next;
  LIST *prev;
};

typedef struct tree TREE;

struct tree
{
  FILEINFO fileinfo;
  int in_target;
  TREE *left;
  TREE *right;
};
```

The ffblck is defined in the Turbo C header file, dir.h, and is given as follows:

```
struct ffblk
{
  char ff_reserved[ 21 ];
  char ff_attrib;
  unsigned ff_ftime;
  unsigned ff_fdate;
  long ff_fsize;
  char ff_name[ 13 ];
};
```

The list structure is a doubly linked list with two information fields, fileinfo of type ffblk, and a boolean field, selected, that determines whether the given node is selected for copying.

The tree structure contains two information fields, fileinfo of type ffblk, and a boolean field, in_target. If this flag is 1 (true), the source file is present in the target. If this flag is 0 (false), the source file is not present in the target.

Finally, the ffblk structure, given in dir.h, contains the attribute of the file, its time of creation, its date of creation, its size, and its name.

The algorithm, in pseudocode, for determining the files to be copied is given in Listing 12.1.

Listing 12.1 Algorithm for determining the files to copy in the update program

1. Build a target tree from all the files in the target path. Set the in_target flag to 0 for each node in the tree.
2. Build a source tree from all the files in the source that are present in the target and newer than the target files, and all the files in the source that are not present in the target. Assign the flag in_target = 1 to all the files in the source that are newer than the target, and the flag in_target = 0 to all the files that are in the source but not in the target. Assign the flag in_target = 1 to all the files in the target tree that are in the source.
3. Build an alphabetized source list from the source tree consisting first of all files in the source tree with in_target flags of 1. Then the files in the source tree with an in_target flags of 0 are added to the source list.
4. The source tree is deallocated.
5. Build an alphabetized target list from the target tree consisting of only the files with in_target flags of 1.
6. The target tree is deallocated.
7. Display both lists and allow the user to deselect or reselect files.
8. Copy the files from the source list that have been selected to the target. If the user has elected to copy files from the source that are not in the target, these are copied if they remain selected.

12.3   *Discussion and Listing of Code*

The software system is organized into three major modules. These are described below.

```
update.c   Main driver program
struct.h   Header file for the dynamic structures and their operations
struct.c   Definitions for the operations on the dynamic structures
display.h  Header file for the select and display operations
display.c  Definitions for the select and display operations
```

In addition, there is an header file kb.h that contains useful keyboard definitions.

Listing 12.2 presents the main driver program module update.c. The main program function, follows the pseudocode algorithm perfectly. The functions build_source_tree and build_target_tree are written at a high level of abstraction. Functions such as insert_node, and is_present_and_newer are invoked. These functions are defined in module struct.c. In addition, the important Turbo C functions findfirst and findnext are used in build_source_tree and build_target_tree.

The function findfirst takes a DOS pathname string as its first parameter. The second parameter is the address of a ffblk structure. The third parameter is the file attribute. Here, the attribute 0 means read all files execpt directories, hidden, system, and label. See the Turbo C reference manual for more details. The function findnext takes a single parameter, the address of a ffblk structure.

Listing 12.2 Main driver program module, update.c

```
/* Disk update program.
   Compile in the small memory model and link with
   struct.obj, display.obj, and util.obj.
*/

#include <stdio.h>
#include <stdlib.h>
#include <string.h>
#include <dir.h>
#include <dos.h>
#include "util.h"
#include "struct.h"
#include "display.h"

int create_files;
/* 1 if user chooses to copy file from source that do
   not exist on target, otherwise 0.
*/

static LIST *source_list, *target_list;

static TREE *source_tree, *target_tree;

char current_directory[ 80 ];

char target_path[ 80 ];

char source_path[ 80 ];

int source_disk, target_disk;
```

```c
/* Return the target drive number
**
** ARGUMENTS
**    none
**
** RETURNS
**    1 -> Drive A
**    2 -> Drive B
**    3 -> Drive C
**    ...
*/
int target_drive( void )
{
  char *ch;

  ch = strchr( target_path, ':' );
  if ( ch )
  {
    return ( *( ch - 1 ) - 'a' + 1 );
  }
  else
    return 0;
}



/* Build a binary tree containing all the fileinfo
** structures on the target subdirectory.  The
** in_target flag of all nodes are set to 0.
**
** ARGUMENTS
**    none
**
** RETURNS
**    nothing
*/
void build_target_tree( void )
{
  int done;
  FILEINFO fileinfo;
  char *pathname = ( char * ) malloc( 80 );
  char *ch;

  strcpy( pathname, target_path );
  if ( pathname[ strlen( pathname ) - 1 ] != '\\' )
    strcat( pathname, "\\" );
  strcat( pathname, "*.*" );
  done = findfirst( pathname, &fileinfo, 0 );
  while ( !done )
  {
```

(continued)

```c
      insert_node( &target_tree, &fileinfo, 0 );
      done = findnext( &fileinfo );
  }
}


/* Build a binary tree with fileinfo structures containing:
** 1. All files that are common to both the source and
**    target subdirectories with the newer file on the
**    source subdirectory.  Such files get the flag
**    in_target set to 1.
** 2. All files that are on the source subdirectory but not
**    on the target subdirectory.  Such files get the flag
**    in_target set to 0.
**
** ARGUMENTS
**    none
**
** RETURNS
**    nothing
*/
void build_source_tree( void )
{
  int done;
  FILEINFO fileinfo;

  done = findfirst( "*.*", &fileinfo, 0 );
  while ( !done )
  {
    if ( is_present_and_newer( target_tree, &fileinfo ) )
    {
      insert_node( &source_tree, &fileinfo, 1 );
      /* Change the in_target attribute from 0 to 1 */
      change_in_target( target_tree, fileinfo.ff_name );
    }
    else if ( create_files &&
              !is_present( target_tree, &fileinfo ) )
      insert_node( &source_tree, &fileinfo, 0 );
    done = findnext( &fileinfo );
  }
}


/* Computes the difference in size (bytes) between
** the source file and target file.
**
** ARGUMENTS
**    filesize - size, in bytes, of source file
**    filename - name of source and target files
```

```
**
** RETURNS
**    source file size - target file size
*/
long copy_bytes( long filesize, char *filename )
{
  LIST *lst;
  long bytes = filesize;

  if ( bytes )
  {
    lst = target_list -> next;
    while ( lst )
    {
      if ( strcmp( lst -> fileinfo.ff_name,
          filename ) == 0 )
        break;
      lst = lst -> next;
    }
    if ( lst )
      bytes -= lst -> fileinfo.ff_fsize;
  }
  return bytes;
}


/* Copies selected source files to target subdirectory.
**
** ARGUMENTS
**    none
**
** RETURNS
**    nothing
*/
void copy_files( void )
{
  LIST *lst;
  char command_string[ 80 ];
  struct dfree f;
  long free_bytes;

  title();
  gotoxy( 5, 6 );
  printf( "Copying from %s to %s ...", source_path,
          target_path );
  lst = source_list -> next;
  while ( lst )
  {
```

(continued)

```
         if ( lst -> selected )
         {
           show_copy_files( lst -> fileinfo.ff_name );
           getdfree( target_drive(), &f );
           free_bytes = ( long )
             f.df_avail * f.df_bsec * f.df_sclus;
           if ( copy_bytes( lst -> fileinfo.ff_fsize,
                lst -> fileinfo.ff_name ) - free_bytes < 0 )
           {
             strcpy( command_string, "copy " );
             strcat( command_string, lst -> fileinfo.ff_name );
             strcat( command_string, " " );
             strcat( command_string, target_path );
             strcat( command_string, " > nul" );
             system( command_string );
           }
           else
             error( "ERROR: Insufficient disk space." );
         }
         lst = lst -> next;
      }
   }


   main( int argc, char *argv[] )
   {
     title();
     user_input( argc, argv );
     build_target_tree();

     /* current_directory set in function user_input */
     chdir( current_directory );

     build_source_tree();
     define( &source_list );
     define( &target_list );
     build_list( source_tree, source_list, 1 );
     build_list( source_tree, source_list, 0 );
     destroy( source_tree );
     build_list( target_tree, target_list, 1 );
     destroy( target_tree );
     if ( select( source_list, target_list ) )
       copy_files();
     restore_cursor();
     gotoxy( 0, 23 );
   }
```

Listing 12.3 presents the prototypes for the dynamic structures module.

Listing 12.3 Prototypes for the dynamic structures module, struct.h

```
#include <dir.h>

#define FILEINFO struct ffblk
typedef struct list LIST;

extern FILEINFO;

struct list
{
  FILEINFO fileinfo;
  int selected;
  LIST *next;
  LIST *prev;
};

void define( LIST **lst );

int append( LIST *lst, FILEINFO *info );
/* Returns 1 if normal, otherwise 0 */

typedef struct tree TREE;

struct tree
{
  FILEINFO fileinfo;
  int in_target;
  TREE *left;
  TREE *right;
};

void destroy( TREE *root );

void delete_node( TREE **root, FILEINFO *item );

void insert_node( TREE **root, FILEINFO *item, int in_tar );

void change_in_target( TREE *root, char *name );

int is_present( TREE *root, FILEINFO *item );

int is_present_and_newer( TREE *tree, FILEINFO *item );

void build_list( TREE *tree, LIST *lst, int in_tar );
```

Listing 12.4 presents the definitions for the dynamic structures module. Because the implementation of trees and lists have been discussed earlier in the book, there is no further discussion of these functions here.

The code is commented in appropriate places to provide assistance in understanding its functionality.

Listing 12.4   Definitions for the dynamic structures module, struct.c

```c
#include "struct.h"
#include <string.h>
#include <alloc.h>
#include "display.h"

/* Define a list
**
** ARGUMENTS
**    lst - List that is defined
**
** RETURNS
**    nothing
*/
void define( LIST **lst )
{
  LIST *root;

  root = ( LIST * ) malloc( sizeof( LIST ) );
  if ( root == 0 )
  {
    printf( "\nHeap overflow error in defining a list." );
    exit( 1 );
  }
  root -> next = root -> prev = 0;
  root -> fileinfo.ff_name[ 0 ] = '\0';
  root -> selected = 0;
  *lst = root;
}


/* Append a new node to list
**
** ARGUMENTS
**    lst  - List to append node to
**    info - Pointer to fileinfo block
**
** RETURNS
**    1 - Normal return
**    0 - Heap overflow error
*/
int append( LIST *lst, FILEINFO *info )
{
  LIST *new_node;
  LIST *previous, *current;
```

```c
  if ( ( new_node = ( LIST * )
    malloc( sizeof( LIST ) ) ) != 0 )
  {
    new_node -> fileinfo = *info;
    new_node -> selected = 1;
    current = lst;
    while ( current != 0 )
    {
      previous = current;
      current = current -> next;
    }
    previous -> next = new_node;
    new_node -> prev = previous;
    new_node -> next = 0;
    return 1;
  }
  else
  {
    error( "ERROR: Heap overflow error in building list." );
    return 0;
  }
}


/* Create a node
**
** ARGUMENTS
**    item - Pointer to fileinfo block
**
** RETURNS
**    Pointer to a tree node
*/
static TREE* create_node( FILEINFO *item )
{
  TREE *node;

  if ( ( node = ( TREE * )
    malloc( sizeof( TREE ) ) ) != 0 )
  {
    node -> fileinfo = *item;
    return node;
  }
  else
    error( "ERROR: Heap overflow error in building list." );
  return 0;
}
```

(continued)

```
/* Deallocate the storage for an entire tree
**
** ARGUMENTS
**    root - Pointer to the root node of tree
**
** RETURNS
**    nothing
*/
void destroy( TREE *root )
{
  if ( root )
  {
    destroy( root -> left );
    destroy( root -> right );
    free( root );
  }
}


/* Delete a node from tree with given fileinfo block
**
** ARGUMENTS
**    root - Pointer to a pointer to the root node of tree
**    item - Pointer to the fileinfo block to be deleted
**
** RETURNS
**    nothing
*/
void delete_node( TREE **root, FILEINFO *item )
{

  TREE *previous = 0,
       *present = *root,
       *replace,
       *s,
       *parent;
  int found = 0;

  while ( present && !found )
  {
    if ( strcmp( item -> ff_name,
         present -> fileinfo.ff_name ) == 0 )
      found = 1;
    else
    {
      previous = present;
      if ( strcmp( item -> ff_name,
                   present -> fileinfo.ff_name ) < 0 )
        present = present -> left;
```

```
        else
          present = present -> right;
      }
    }
    if ( found )
    {
      if ( present -> left == 0 )
        replace = present -> right;
      else
        if ( present -> right == 0 )
          replace = present -> left;
        else
        {
          parent = present;
          replace = present -> right;
          s = replace -> left;
          while ( s != 0 )
          {
            parent = replace;
            replace = s;
            s = replace -> left;
          }
          if ( parent != present )
          {
            parent -> left = replace -> right;
            replace -> right = present -> right;
          }
          replace -> left = present -> left;
        }
      if ( previous == 0 )
        *root = replace;
      else
        if ( present == previous -> left )
          previous -> left = replace;
        else
          previous -> right = replace;
      free( present );
    }
}


/* Insert a node into tree with given fileinfo block
**
** ARGUMENTS
**    root   - Pointer to a pointer to the root node of tree
**    item   - Pointer to the fileinfo block to be deleted
**    in_tar - 1 : File in both source and target
**                 subdirectory with source file newer than
**                 target file                            (continued)
```

```
**
** RETURNS
**    nothing
*/
void insert_node( TREE **root,  FILEINFO *item, int in_tar )
{
  TREE *parent = 0,
       *current = *root;
  TREE *new_node;
  int found = 0;

  while ( current && !found )
  {
    if ( strcmp( item -> ff_name,
         current -> fileinfo.ff_name ) == 0 )
      found = 1;
    else
    {
      parent = current;
      if ( strcmp( item -> ff_name,
           current -> fileinfo.ff_name ) < 0 )
        current = current -> left;
      else
        current = current -> right;
    }
  }
  if ( found == 0 )
  {
    if ( parent == 0 )
    /* First node in the tree */
    {
      *root = create_node( item );
      ( *root ) -> left = ( *root ) -> right = 0;
      ( *root ) -> in_target = in_tar;
    }
    else
    {
      new_node = create_node( item );
      new_node -> left = new_node -> right = 0;
      new_node -> in_target = in_tar;
      if ( strcmp( item -> ff_name,
           parent -> fileinfo.ff_name ) < 0 )
        parent -> left = new_node;
      else
        parent -> right = new_node;
    }
  }
}
```

```
/* Change in_tar flag in tree with given file name
**
** ARGUMENTS
**    root - Pointer to the root node of tree
**    name - File name to change the in_tar flag
**
** RETURNS
**    nothing
*/
void change_in_target( TREE *root, char *name )
{
  TREE *current = root;
  int found = 0;

  while ( current && !found )
  {
    if ( strcmp( name, current -> fileinfo.ff_name ) == 0 )
    {
      current -> in_target = 1;
      break;
    }
    else
    {
      if ( strcmp( name, current -> fileinfo.ff_name ) < 0 )
        current = current -> left;
      else
        current = current -> right;
    }
  }
}


/* Determines whether item is present
**
** ARGUMENTS
**    root - Pointer to the root node of the tree
**    item - Pointer to the fileinfo block
**
** RETURNS
**    1 - item is present
**    0 - item is not present
*/
int is_present( TREE *root, FILEINFO *item )
{
  TREE *current = root;
  int found = 0;

  while ( current && !found )
  {
```

(continued)

```
        if ( strcmp( item -> ff_name,
              current -> fileinfo.ff_name ) == 0 )
          found = 1;
        else
        {
          if ( strcmp( item -> ff_name,
                current -> fileinfo.ff_name ) < 0 )
            current = current -> left;
          else
            current = current -> right;
        }
      }
    return found;
    }


/* Determines whether item in source subdirectory is
** more recent that the corresponding file in the target
** subdirectory.
**
** ARGUMENTS
**    root - Pointer to the root node of the tree
**    item - Pointer to a fileinfo block
**
** RETURNS
**    1 - item in source is newer than item in target
**    0 - item in source is not newer than item in target
*/
int is_present_and_newer( TREE *root, FILEINFO *item )
{
  TREE *current = root;
  int found = 0;

  while ( current && !found )
  {
    if ( ( strcmp( item -> ff_name,
      current -> fileinfo.ff_name ) == 0 ) &&
      ( item -> ff_fdate > current -> fileinfo.ff_fdate ||
      ( item -> ff_fdate == current -> fileinfo.ff_fdate ) &&
      ( item -> ff_ftime > current -> fileinfo.ff_ftime ) ) )
        found = 1;
    else
    {
      if ( strcmp( item -> ff_name,
            current -> fileinfo.ff_name ) < 0 )
        current = current -> left;
      else
        current = current -> right;
    }
```

```
    }
    return found;
}


/* Construct a list of fileinfo blocks for nodes in tree
** with the given in_tar flag.
**
** ARGUMENTS
**    tree   - Pointer to the root node of the tree
**    lst    - Pointer to the header node of the list
**    in_tar - Value of the flag
**
** RETURNS
**    nothing
*/
void build_list( TREE *tree, LIST *lst, int in_tar )
{
  if ( tree )
  {
    build_list( tree -> left, lst, in_tar );
    if ( in_tar == tree -> in_target )
      append( lst, &tree -> fileinfo );
    build_list( tree -> right, lst, in_tar );
  }
}
```

Listing 12.5 presents the header file, kb.h, that contains useful constant definitions.

Listing 12.5   Header file kb.h

```
/* File kb.h */

#define F1 128
#define F2 129
#define F3 130
#define F4 131
#define F5 132
#define F6 133
#define F7 134
#define F8 135
#define F9 136
#define F10 137

#define ctla 138
#define ctlb 139
#define ctlc 140
#define ctld 141
```

(continued)

```
#define ctle 142
#define ctlf 143
#define ctlg 144
#define ctlj 145
#define ctlk 146
#define ctll 147
#define ctln 148
#define ctlo 149
#define ctlp 150
#define ctlq 151
#define ctlr 152
#define ctls 153
#define ctlt 154
#define ctlu 155
#define ctlv 156
#define ctlw 157
#define ctlx 158
#define ctly 159
#define ctlz 160

#define altt 178
#define alts 179
#define altf 181

#define ua 161
#define da 162
#define ra 163
#define la 164
#define pu 165
#define pd 166
#define hm 167
#define en 168
#define ctlhm 172
#define ctlen 173
#define ctlpgup 174
#define ctlpgdn 175
#define ctlla 176
#define ctlra 177

#define del 169
#define stab 170
#define ret 171
#define bs 8
#define tab 9

#define lf 10
#define cr 13
#define eof 26
#define esc 27
#define bkch 32
```

Listing 12.6 presents the prototypes for the display module, display.h.

Listing 12.6 Prototypes for the display module, display.h

```
int select( LIST *source, LIST *target );

void title();

void user_input( int argc, char *argv[] );
/* Captures command line information and prompts user
   about copying files from source that are not on target.
   The global variable, create_files, is set by this
   function.
*/

void show_copy_files( char *name );

void error( char *str );
```

Finally, Listing 12.7 presents the definitions for the display module, display.c. The functions contained in this listing perform all the screen displays. It is left as an exercise for the reader to study and understand this code.

Listing 12.7 Definitions for the display module, display.c

```
#include "util.h"
#include "struct.h"
#include "kb.h"

/* From update.c file */
extern char target_path[ 80 ];
extern char current_directory[ 80];
extern char source_path[ 80 ];
extern int create_files;


/* Puts program title on the screen
**
** ARGUMENTS
**    none
**
** RETURNS
**    nothing
*/
void title()
{
   int i;
```

(continued)

```c
      clrscreen();
      writestring_attr( "HIT-AND-RUN SOFTWARE:", reverse );
      writestring_attr(
      "                                                        ",
      reverse );
      writestring_attr( "Version  1.00 ", reverse );
      gotoxy( 0, 1 );
      writestring_attr(
      "  Richard Wiener                          U P D A T E           "
      "                  "          Copyright (C)  ",
      reverse );
      gotoxy( 0, 2 );
      writestring_attr(
      "  Erik Wiener                                            "
      "                         July, 1987            ",
                         reverse );
      gotoxy( 0, 3 );
      writestring_attr(
      "┌──────────────────────────────────────────────────┐"
      "══════════════════════════════════════╗", normal );
      for ( i = 4; i <= 22; i++ )
      {
        gotoxy( 0, i );
        writestring_attr( "‖", normal );
        gotoxy( 79, i );
        writestring_attr( "‖", normal );
      }
      gotoxy( 0, 19 );
      writestring_attr(
      "╠──────────────────────────────────────────────────"
      "═══════════════════════════════════════╣", normal );
      gotoxy( 0, 23 );
      writestring_attr(
      "└──────────────────────────────────────────────────"
      "═══════════════════════════════════════┘", normal );
}


/* Display files in two columns
**
** ARGUMENTS
**    source     - The list of source files to be displayed
**    target     - The list of target files to be displayed
**    page       - The screen window page currently displayed
**    top_source - Pointer to pointer to node at the top of
**                 a window page for source column
**    top_target - Pointer to pointer to node at the top of
**                 a window page for target column
**
```

```
**  RETURNS
**      nothing
*/
void list_files( LIST *source, LIST *target, int *page,
                 LIST **top_source, LIST **top_target )
{
  LIST *curr_source = source -> next;
  LIST *curr_target = target -> next;
  int no_target = 0;
  int i;
  int date;
  int time;
  char out[ 10 ];

  if ( !curr_target )
    no_target = 1;
  for ( i = 1; i <= ( *page - 1 ) * 10 &&
        curr_source -> next; i++ )
  {
    curr_source = curr_source -> next;
    if ( curr_target -> next )
      curr_target = curr_target -> next;
  }
  if ( *page == i / 10 + 1 && ( !curr_target -> next &&
      !( curr_target -> prev == target && *page == 1 ) ) )
    no_target = 1;
  if ( *page == i / 10 + 1 && ( curr_source -> next ||
      i % 10 == 1 ) )
  /* Is possible to display the given page */
  {
    *top_source = curr_source;
    *top_target = curr_target;
  }
  else
  {
    curr_source = *top_source;
    curr_target = *top_target;
    if ( i % 10 == 0 )
      i--;
    *page = i / 10 + 1;
    return;
  }
  for ( i = 8; i <= 17; i++ )
  {
    gotoxy( 3, i );
    writestring_attr(
    "          ", normal );
    gotoxy( 41, i );
    writestring_attr(
```

(continued)

```c
                "        ", normal );
    if ( curr_source )
    {
      gotoxy( 3, i );
      if ( curr_source -> selected )
        writestring_attr( curr_source -> fileinfo.ff_name,
                          highlight );
      else
        writestring_attr( curr_source -> fileinfo.ff_name,
                          normal );
      gotoxy( 17, i );
      sprintf( out, "%ld",
               curr_source -> fileinfo.ff_fsize );
      writestring_attr( out, normal );
      gotoxy( 24, i );
      date = curr_source -> fileinfo.ff_fdate;
      sprintf( out, "%2d-%02d-%2d", ( date & 480 ) >> 5,
               date & 31,
               ( ( date & 15872 ) >> 9 ) + 80 );
      writestring_attr( out, normal );
      gotoxy( 34, i );
      time = curr_source -> fileinfo.ff_ftime;
      sprintf( out, "%2d:%02d", time >> 11 & 31,
               time >> 5 & 63 );
      writestring_attr( out, normal );
      if ( !no_target )
      {
        gotoxy( 42, i );
        writestring_attr( curr_target -> fileinfo.ff_name,
                          normal );
        gotoxy( 56, i );
        sprintf( out, "%ld",
                 curr_target -> fileinfo.ff_fsize );
        writestring_attr( out, normal );
        gotoxy( 63, i );
        date = curr_target -> fileinfo.ff_fdate;
        sprintf( out, "%2d-%02d-%2d", ( date & 480 ) >> 5,
                 date & 31,
                 ( ( date & 15872 ) >> 9 ) + 80 );
        writestring_attr( out, normal );
        gotoxy( 73, i );
        time = curr_target -> fileinfo.ff_ftime;
        sprintf( out, "%2d:%02d", time >> 11 & 31,
                 time >> 5 & 63 );
        writestring_attr( out, normal );
      }
      curr_source = curr_source -> next;
      if ( curr_target -> next )
        curr_target = curr_target -> next;
```

```
            else
                no_target = 1;
        }
    }
    gotoxy( 10, 18 );
    if ( curr_source )
        writestring_attr( "– MORE –", normal );
    else
        writestring_attr( "", normal );

}


/* Remove reverse video from file name
**
** ARGUMENTS
**      oldfile - The row on the screen of the previously
**                selected file that needs to be unreversed
**      top     - Pointer to the node in the source list that
**                is currently on top of the screen
**
** RETURNS
**      nothing
*/
void unreverse_name( int oldfile, LIST *top )
{
    int i;
    LIST *curr = top;

    for ( i = 1; i < oldfile; i++ )
        curr = curr -> next;
    gotoxy( 3, oldfile + 7 );
    if ( curr -> selected )
        writestring_attr( curr -> fileinfo.ff_name, highlight );
    else
        writestring_attr( curr -> fileinfo.ff_name, normal );
}


/* Reverse video file name
**
** ARGUMENTS
**      file - The row on the screen of the selected
**             file that needs to be reversed
**      top  - Pointer to the node in the source list that
**             is currently on top of the screen
**
** RETURNS
**      nothing                                    (continued)
```

```
*/
void reverse_name( int file, LIST *top )
{
  int i;
  LIST *curr = top;

  for ( i = 1; i < file; i++ )
    curr = curr -> next;
  gotoxy( 3, file + 7 );
  writestring_attr( curr -> fileinfo.ff_name, reverse );
  gotoxy( 26, 4 );
  if ( curr -> selected )
    writestring_attr( "SELECTED  ", normal );
  else
    writestring_attr( "UNSELECTED", normal );
}


/* Select files from source
**
** ARGUMENTS
**    source - Source list
**    target - Target list
**
** RETURNS
**    1 -> normal selection
**    0 -> no files are selected
*/
int select( LIST *source, LIST *target )
{
  int page = 1;
  int file = 1;
  int success;
  int oldfile = 1;
  unsigned char ch;
  LIST *top_source;
  LIST *top_target;
  LIST *current;
  int i;

  if ( !source -> next )
  {
    /* Source list empty */
    gotoxy( 28, 10 );
    printf( "\aTarget Drive Is Updated" );
    gotoxy( 26, 11 );
    printf( "No Files Need To Be Copied" );
    return 0;
  }
```

```
remove_cursor();
gotoxy( 22, 20 );
writestring_attr(
"Highlighted Files Selected For Copying", normal );
gotoxy( 2, 21 );
writestring_attr(
"PGDN/PGUP: Next/previous page  ARROWS: Next/previous file"
"  SPACEBAR: Select", normal );
gotoxy( 27, 22 );
writestring_attr( "<CR> Update        <ESC> Exit", normal );
gotoxy( 3, 4 );
writestring_attr( "State of current file: SELECTED",
                  normal );
getcwd( source_path, 80 );
source_path[ 35 ] = '\0';
gotoxy( 3, 6 );
writestring_attr( source_path, normal );
gotoxy( 42, 6 );
writestring_attr( target_path, normal );
gotoxy( 1, 5 );
for ( i = 1; i <= 78; i++ )
  writestring_attr( "=", normal );
gotoxy( 1, 7 );
for ( i = 1; i <= 78; i++ )
  writestring_attr( "-", normal );
gotoxy( 17, 5 );
writestring_attr( "SOURCE", normal );
gotoxy( 57, 5 );
writestring_attr( "TARGET", normal );
for ( i = 6; i <= 18; i++ )
{
  gotoxy( 40, i );
  writestring_attr( " | ", normal );
}
gotoxy( 40, 5 );
writestring_attr( " ⊤", normal );
gotoxy( 0, 7 );
writestring_attr( " ⊩", normal );
gotoxy( 79, 7 );
writestring_attr( " ⊣|", normal );
gotoxy( 0, 5 );
writestring_attr( " ⊫", normal );
gotoxy( 79, 5 );
writestring_attr( " ⊣|", normal );
gotoxy( 40, 7 );
writestring_attr( " +", normal );
gotoxy( 40, 19 );
writestring_attr( " ⊥", normal );
top_source = source;                              (continued)
```

```
            top_target = target;
            current = source -> next;
            list_files( source, target, &page, &top_source,
                        &top_target );
            success = 1;
            do
            {
              if ( success )
              {
                unreverse_name( oldfile, top_source );
                reverse_name( file, top_source );
                oldfile = file;
              }
              success = 1;
              do
              {
                get_key( &ch, 0 );
              }
              while ( ch != pu && ch != pd && ch != ua && ch != da &&
                      ch != la && ch != ra && ch != cr && ch != esc &&
                      ch != ' ' );
              if ( ch == pu )
              {
                if ( page > 1 )
                {
                  int oldpage = --page;

                  list_files( source, target, &page, &top_source,
                              &top_target );
                  if ( page == oldpage )
                  {
                    oldfile = file = 1;
                    current = top_source;
                  }
                  else
                    success = 0;
                }
                else
                  success = 0;
              }
              else if ( ch == pd )
              {
                int oldpage = ++page;

                list_files( source, target, &page, &top_source,
                            &top_target );
                if ( page == oldpage )
                {
```

```
        oldfile = file = 1;
        current = top_source;
      }
      else
        success = 0;
    }
    else if ( ch == da || ch == ra )
    {
      if ( current -> next )
      {
        file++;
        if ( file == 11 )
        {
          int oldpage = ++page;

          list_files( source, target, &page, &top_source,
                      &top_target );
          if ( page == oldpage )
          {
            oldfile = file = 1;
            current = top_source;
          }
          else
            success = 0;
        }
        else
          current = current -> next;
      }
      else
        success = 0;
    }
    else if ( ( ch == ua || ch == la ) && current -> prev )
    {
      int i;

      file--;
      if ( file == 0 )
      {
        if ( page > 1 )
        {
          int oldpage = --page;

          list_files( source, target, &page, &top_source,
                      &top_target );
          if ( page == oldpage )
          {
            oldfile = file = 1;
            current = top_source;
```

(continued)

```
              for ( i = 1; i < 10 && current -> next; i++ )
                current = current -> next;
              file = i;
            }
            else
              success = 0;
          }
          else
          {
            file = 1;
            success = 0;
          }
        }
        else
          current = current -> prev;
      }
      else if ( ch == ' ' )
      {
        current -> selected = !current -> selected;
        gotoxy( 26, 4 );
        if ( current -> selected )
          writestring_attr( "Selected  ", normal );
        else
          writestring_attr( "Unselected", normal );
      }
    }
    while ( ch != cr && ch != esc );
    restore_cursor();
    return ch == cr;
}


/* Process command line arguments
**
** ARGUMENTS
**    argc - The number of command line strings
**    argv - The command line strings
**
** RETURNS
**    nothing
*/
void user_input( int argc, char *argv[] )
{
    extern void error( char *str );
    extern int target_drive();

    char curr_dir[ 80 ];
    char ch;
    char *chptr;
```

```c
if ( argc >= 2 )
{
  strcpy( target_path, argv[ 1 ] );
  gotoxy( 5, 8 );
  printf( "Enter target pathname: %s", target_path );
}
else
{
  gotoxy( 5, 8 );
  printf( "Enter target pathname (CR to exit): " );
  gets( target_path );
  if ( target_path[ 0 ] == 0 )
  {
    gotoxy( 0, 23 );
    exit( 1 );
  }
}
getcurdir( target_drive(), curr_dir );
chptr = ( char * ) strchr( target_path, ':' );
if ( chptr != 0 )
{
  current_directory[ 0 ] = *( chptr - 1 );
  current_directory[ 1 ] = ':';
  current_directory[ 2 ] = '\\';
  current_directory[ 3 ] = '\0';
  strcat( current_directory, curr_dir );
}
else
{
  current_directory[ 0 ] = '\\';
  current_directory[ 1 ] = '\0';
  strcat( current_directory, curr_dir );
}
if ( target_path[ strlen( target_path ) - 1 ] == ':' )
  strcpy( target_path, current_directory );
else if ( target_path[ 1 ] == ':' )
{
  if ( target_path[ 2 ] != '\\' )
  {
    strcpy( curr_dir, current_directory );
    strcat( curr_dir, "\\" );
    strcat( curr_dir, &target_path[ 2 ] );
    strcpy( target_path, curr_dir );
  }
}
else if ( target_path[ 0 ] != '\\' )
{
  strcpy( curr_dir, current_directory );
  strcat( curr_dir, "\\" );                              (continued)
```

```c
      strcat( curr_dir, target_path );
      strcpy( target_path, curr_dir );
   }
   if ( chdir( target_path ) == -1 )
      error( "ERROR: Target path name does not exist." );
   gotoxy( 5, 11 );
   printf(
   "Copy files on source that are not on target (Y/N)? " );
   do
   {
      get_key( &ch, 0 );
      ch = toupper( ch );
   }
   while ( ch != 'Y' && ch != 'N' );
   create_files = ch == 'Y';
   remove_cursor();
   gotoxy( 5, 8 );
   printf( "                                    "
           "                        " );
   gotoxy( 5, 11 );
   printf( "                                       "
           "                   " );
}


/* Show the files that are copied
**
** ARGUMENTS
**    name - Name of file that is copied
**
** RETURNS
**    nothing
*/
void show_copy_files( char *name )
{
   static int number = 0;
   int i;

   remove_cursor();
   number++;
   if ( number == 11 )
   {
      for ( i = 8; i <= 17; i++ )
      {
         gotoxy( 5, i );
         writestring_attr( "                             "
                           "                            ",
                           normal );
```

```
      }
      number = 1;
    }
  gotoxy( 5, 7 + number );
  writestring_attr( name, normal );
}


/* Emit error message
**
** ARGUMENTS
**    str - Errormessage
**
** RETURNS
**    nothing
*/
void error( char *str )
{
  gotoxy( 5, 21 );
  printf( "\a%s", str );
  gotoxy( 0, 23 );
  restore_cursor();
  exit( 1 );
}
```

Appendix

fileio.h and fileio.c

```
/*
    Prototypes for a customized file input/output library.
    File fileio.h
*/

/* Open a file for read and write access.
** The file must already exist.
**
** ARGUMENTS
**    filename - The path name of the file to be opened
**
** RETURNS
**    1 - File successfully opened
**    0 - File unsuccessfully opened;
**
**  RETURNS
**     The file handle
*/
extern int openfile( char* filename );
/* Delete a file
**
** ARGUMENTS
**    filename - The path name of the file to be deleted
**
** RETURNS
**    nothing
*/
extern void delete_file( char *filename );
```

```c
/* Create a new file or open an existing file.
** If file does not exist, it is created,
** if file exists it is opened.
**
** ARGUMENTS
**   filename - The path name of the file to be created or
**              opened.
**   newfile  - Returns 1 if the file is created, otherwise
**              returns 0.
**
** RETURNS
**   The file handle of the opened or created file
*/
extern int lookupfile( char* filename, int *newfile );
/* Write a block of data to an opened file
**
** ARGUMENTS
**   filehandle   - The file handle
**   bytestowrite - The number of bytes to write
**   fromlocation - The memory address of the source
**
** RETURNS
**   The number of bytes actually written to disk
*/
extern unsigned writefile( int filehandle, unsigned bytestowrite,
                 void *fromlocation );

/* Read a block of data from an opened file
**
** ARGUMENTS
**   filehandle  - The file handle
**   bytestoread - The number of bytes to read
**   tolocation  - The memory address to write to
**
** RETURNS
**   The number of bytes actually read from disk
*/
extern unsigned readfile( int filehandle, unsigned bytestoread,
                 void *tolocation );

/* Close a file
**
** ARGUMENTS
**   filehandle - The file handle
**
** RETURNS
**   nothing
*/
extern void closefile( int filehandle );
```

```
/* Definitions for a customized file input/output library.
   File fileio.c
*/

#include <dos.h>

union REGS inreg, outreg;

struct SREGS segreg;

static int error;

/* Global error flag shared by several functions */


/* Open a file for read and write access.
** The file must already exist.
**
** ARGUMENTS
**    filename - The path name of the file to be opened
**
** RETURNS
**    1 - File successfully opened
**    0 - File unsuccessfully opened
*/
int openfile( char* filename )
{
  inreg.x.ax = 0x3D02; /* Read and write access */
  #if defined( _COMPACT_ ) || defined( _LARGE_ ) || \
      defined( _HUGE_ )
  inreg.x.dx = FP_OFF( ( long ) filename );
  segreg.ds = FP_SEG( ( long ) filename );
  intdosx( &inreg, &outreg, &segreg );
  #else
  inreg.x.dx = ( int ) filename;
  intdos( &inreg, &outreg );
  #endif
  error = outreg.x.cflag;
  return outreg.x.ax;
}
/* Delete a file
**
** ARGUMENTS
**    filename - The path name of the file to be deleted
**
** RETURNS
**    nothing
*/
void delete_file( char *filename )
```

```c
{
 inreg.x.ax = 0x4100;
 #if defined( _COMPACT_ ) || defined( _LARGE_ ) || \
     defined( _HUGE_ )
 inreg.x.dx = FP_OFF( ( long ) filename );
 segreg.ds = FP_SEG( ( long ) filename );
 intdosx( &inreg, &outreg, &segreg );
 #else
 inreg.x.dx = ( int ) filename;
 intdos( &inreg, &outreg );
 #endif
}

/* Create a new file or open an existing file.
** If file does not exist, it is created,
** if file exists it is opened.
**
** ARGUMENTS
**   filename - The path name of the file to be created or
**              opened.
**   newfile  - Returns 1 if the file is created, otherwise
**              returns 0.
**
** RETURNS
**   The file handle of the opened or created file
*/
int lookupfile( char* filename, int *newfile )
{
 int result;

 result = openfile( filename );
 if ( result == 2 )
  {

   inreg.x.ax = 0x3C00;
   inreg.x.cx = 0;
   #if defined( _COMPACT_ ) || defined( _LARGE_ ) || \
       defined( _HUGE_ )
   inreg.x.dx = FP_OFF( ( long ) filename );
   segreg.ds = FP_SEG( ( long ) filename );
   intdosx( &inreg, &outreg, &segreg );
   #else
   inreg.x.dx = ( int ) filename;
   intdos( &inreg, &outreg );
   #endif
   *newfile = 1;
   return outreg.x.ax;
  }
 else
```

```
  {
    *newfile = 0;
    if ( error )
     {
       *newfile = 1;
       error = 0;
     }
    return result;
  }
}


/* Write a block of data to an opened file
**
** ARGUMENTS
**   filehandle   - The file handle
**   bytestowrite - The number of bytes to write
**   fromlocation - The memory address of the source
**
** RETURNS
**   The number of bytes actually written to disk
*/
unsigned writefile( int filehandle, unsigned bytestowrite,
                    void *fromlocation )
{
  inreg.x.ax = 0x4000;
  inreg.x.bx = filehandle;
  inreg.x.cx = bytestowrite;
  #if defined( _COMPACT_ ) || defined( _LARGE_ ) || \
      defined( _HUGE_ )
  inreg.x.dx = FP_OFF( fromlocation );
  segreg.ds = FP_SEG( fromlocation );
  intdosx( &inreg, &outreg, &segreg );
  #else
  inreg.x.dx = ( int ) fromlocation;
  intdos( &inreg, &outreg );
  #endif
  return outreg.x.ax;
}


/* Read a block of data from an opened file
**
** ARGUMENTS
**   filehandle  - The file handle
**   bytestoread - The number of bytes to read
**   tolocation  - The memory address to write to
**
** RETURNS
**   The number of bytes actually read from disk
*/
```

```c
unsigned readfile( int filehandle, unsigned bytestoread,
                   void *tolocation )
{
  inreg.x.ax = 0x3F00;
  inreg.x.bx = filehandle;
  inreg.x.cx = bytestoread;
  #if defined( _COMPACT_ ) || defined( _LARGE_ ) || \
      defined( _HUGE_ )
  inreg.x.dx = FP_OFF( tolocation );
  segreg.ds + FP_SEG( tolocation );
  intdosx( &inreg, &outreg, &segreg );
  #else
  inreg.x.dx = ( int ) tolocation;
  intdos( &inreg, &outreg );
  #endif
  return outreg.x.ax;
}
/* Close a file
**
** ARGUMENTS
**    filehandle - The file handle
**
** RETURNS
**    nothing
*/
void closefile( int filehandle )
{
  inreg.x.ax = 0x3E00;
  inreg.x.bx = filehandle;
  intdos( &inreg, &outreg );
}
```

INDEX